THE LANGUAGE OF ADAM
ON THE LIMITS AND SYSTEMS OF DISCOURSE

The Language of Adam

ON THE LIMITS AND SYSTEMS OF DISCOURSE

Russell Fraser

COLUMBIA UNIVERSITY PRESS · NEW YORK · 1977

Library of Congress Cataloging in Publication Data

Fraser, Russell A
The language of Adam.

Bibliography: p.
Includes index.
1. Languages—Philosophy.   2. Language, Universal.
3. Literature.
I. Title.
P106.F7   401   77-3528
ISBN 0-231-04256-6

Columbia University Press
New York   Guildford, Surrey
Copyright © 1977 Columbia University Press
Printed in the United States of America

FOR Walt Litz, who was with me in the ships at Mylae, and for Marian, the substance of our show

CONTENTS

PREFACE

THE language of Adam expresses in a metaphor our enduring desire to overcome linguistic barriers and so to make a more nearly homogeneous society. The modern age, beginning in the Renaissance, attempts to translate the metaphor to fact. I have sought to describe the attempt, to locate it in its historical and psychological context, and to suggest how it bears on the world we inhabit today. Here my text is Churchill's: "Let us remember only so much of the past as will make us creative for the future." The quest for the *lingua adamica* is worth remembering as, like the metaphor of the dark ages and the age of gold or that of the war against poetry, it offers a point of vantage. From this point, we are able to look into our origins. The yield, prospectively, is the augmenting of self knowledge.

In the Garden of Eden, Adam spoke a language in which one word conveyed the root meaning of one thing without the possibility of confusion. His language was semiotic. It ignored or rather penetrated the surfaces of things, because the surface is multiform and therefore confusing. It moved directly, and like an arrow, to inner natures, illuminating them instantly and once and for all. This plenary instrument of communication was necessarily transparent, for colors and substances occlude. It was everywhere comprehensible, not pestered, like our own partial instrument of speaking and writing, with ambiguity or distracting connotations. The essential alphabet bequeathed to Adam by the deity remained our inheritance until the fall of the Tower of Babel. So runs the received version of the myth. After the fall came the differentiating or confusion of tongues.

Man in the modern age is defined by his abhorrence of confusion. He is the connoisseur of form and aims to set things straight. Characteristically, he is impatient of conventional discourse because of its imprecision, a condition of its involvement with the phenomenal world. Just as characteristically, he hopes and expects to forge a better instrument, perfectly denotative and free of the contamination he associates with particulars. He thinks that particularity diminishes the infinite to the finite, so enshadows a cantle of the truth. The linguistic reformers of the Renaissance and later, as they cherish the truth, construed narrowly or monistically, are fiercely jealous of whatever obscures it. They want to banish "the shadow cast by language upon truth" (Auden's phrase), that the lineaments of truth may be revealed in their original comeliness and clearness. They are profoundly optimistic. Pilate's question seems to them not thorny but frivolous. What is truth? In answering the question, they distinguish between knowledge and belief. Priority goes to the former. But the knowledge they value chiefly is not that of the vulgar empiric, rather that of the perspicuous seer to whom Nature is a spume that plays upon a ghostly paradigm. The knowledge or final truth on whose traces they direct the reason is identified with eternal abstractions.

The scientific cosmos, as elaborated in the seventeenth century, is made up of abstract forms. "That which is bounded by two points is a line"—I am quoting Philo Judaeus, a proleptic writer of the early Christian centuries—"and that which has two dimensions or intervals is a superficies." The integrity of matter is denied. The scientific distrust of matter (the secondary or superficial truth) tallies with the distrust the new linguist evinces for the lower-case or peculiar exemplification. The history of linguistic reform in the Renaissance is a footnote to the history of Renaissance science. The attempt to get rid of language as we understand it is to be read in terms of the grander attempt of the classical scientist to impose order on the physical world by divesting it of physicality. Johnson says, in his preface to the English Dictionary: "Language is only the instrument of science, and words are but the signs of ideas: I wish, however, that the instrument might be less apt to decay, and that signs might be permanent, like the things they denote." These permanent things are not material but conceptual. Comenius, the chief propagandist in the seventeenth century of a catholic or pansophical language, possesses as his birthright a "pattern of universal knowledge." He is guided from within, so indifferent to sensory perception. On the other hand his contemporary, the poet Lovelace, exclaims: "Give me a nakedness with her clothes on." He does not presume to say what is doing in the heavens without inspecting the ground at his feet. Between these jars—let us say, employing familiar terms, of structuralism and positivism—lies the subject of this book.

My conclusion, discovered in the course of writing, is that the distinction between the One and its many exemplifications does not enforce, as the structuralists suppose, a distinction between essence and existence, where the latter is defined as a transient state. Rather, each exists—literal and actual existence being the only reality—though the One is identical with His existence, while His creatures or emanations only participate in it. Since my business is not theology, I am not much engrossed by the concessive clause. So I should revise and say: the One and the many, if they live at all, live in time and space, and are the same.

The scientist and new linguist hypothesize, below the world of phenomenal fact, a substrate or primary world. They conceive the latter as accessible to reason, the function of which is to subdue eccentricity by achieving or asserting the hegemony of law. "What else are all things but exercises for the reason? Persevere until thou shalt have made all things thine own." The saying of the Stoic philosopher is often reiterated in the seventeenth century and communicates often an insistent need to categorize, which means to control. The concrete exemplar is refractory, so its existence is called in question. There are no individual beings or entities, the attesting of our senses notwithstanding. Dante at the end of the Middle Ages—where my story begins—thinks that "the blessed state rests in the act of seeing, not in that of love, which follows after." First of all, we must see. As the modern age dishonors the injunction, it sponsors an impalpable world that only in our time has begun to come apart. The evoking of this world by the scientist and his mystical or visionary colleagues turns on their common hatred of the word made flesh.

Hatred of the word and the carnal thing it presents is conspicuous in the seventeenth century. But St. Anselm in the eleventh century wants us to abandon this temporal Jerusalem whose treasures "are to be seized on with hands steeped in blood, and set out on the road to the heavenly Jerusalem" where treasures await "which only those who despise these earthly ones can receive." He is anticipating, even in the language he uses, the strictures of the Jacobean clergyman Joseph Hall. Evidently, nothing is new. Ralegh says: "as the sap and juice wherein the life of plants is preserved doth ever more ascend or descend, so is it with the life of man" and the history he composes. The terms are different but the metaphor is essentially that of the double helix, as formulated by Sir Thomas Browne. And now and then in history, a major shift in emphasis is perceptible. In this sense it is surely right to describe the seventeenth century as a time of endings and beginnings. When Donne in a satiric vision takes us to Hell, he observes that "the gates are seldom opened, nor scarce oftener than once in an age." Destiny favors him, so that he arrives at the propitious moment. "I was present then, and saw all the pretenders, and all that affected an entrance, and Lucifer himself, who then came out into the outward chamber to hear them plead their own causes." In the seventeenth century there occurs an opening of the gates, whence the great protagonists emerge whose pleading is decisive for the centuries to come.

My account of these protagonists is tendentious. I think the reading and writing of history is partly a heuristic exercise, "for in history you have a record of the infinite variety of human experience plainly set out for all to see; and in that record you can find for yourself and your country both examples and warnings; fine things to take as models, base things, rotten through and through, to avoid." Maybe, in this quotation from Livy, the plainness of the record is oversaid and the didacticism overemphatic. But as one takes the present to heart, he will not look on the past with a languid or indifferent eye. "What's past is prologue."

With this book I complete a trilogy which might be called generically, The Modern World Begins. What I have made depends substantially on scholarship but in the last resort is personal statement and will stand or fall as it engenders emotional assent. A different view of things is potential in the facts I have mustered. This is my view.

I have tried to be sparing of footnotes and have modernized spelling and punctuation throughout, seeing no use in putting needless obstacles in the reader's way. My research has been conducted chiefly in the British Museum, to a lesser extent in the John Crerar Library (Chicago), the Biblioteca Apostolica (Vatican), and the libraries of the British Council and the American Academy, Rome. I am grateful to the Guggenheim Foundation, which awarded me a fellowship in 1973–74, and to the Rackham School of the University of Michigan. The criticism and advice of my friends Robert Hollander, S. F. Johnson, and Robert Stilwell has been important to me. Here and there I have levied on essays of mine which appeared initially in the *Kenyon Review,* the *Michigan Quarterly Review,* and *Comparative Drama.*

Alcuin of York, in his treatise *On Grammar* composed for the instruction of Charlemagne, associates the liberal arts with the seven pillars that support the House of Wisdom. So I am pleased that this book makes seven chapters. The title of the penultimate chapter, "A Rage for Order," is meant for a tribute to my friend Austin Warren. The last chapter, though an integer like the others, functions also as an epilogue to the whole.

Russell Fraser

THE LANGUAGE OF ADAM
ON THE LIMITS AND SYSTEMS OF DISCOURSE

Beauty is momentary in the mind—
The fitful tracing of a portal;
But in the flesh it is immortal.
                              Wallace Stevens

   There's something new come into my thought
That must, and shall, be sung high and aloof,
Safe from the wolves' black jaw and the dull asses' hoof.
                              Ben Jonson

Lieto leggerò i neri
segni dei rami sul bianco
come un essenziale alfabeto.
                              Eugenio Montale

CHAPTER ONE

The Legacy of Nimrod

THE myth of the Tower of Babel, like that of the transgression in the Garden, is an attempt to come to terms with the origin of evil. It is more poignant, perhaps it is more pessimistic than the Biblical account of man's first disobedience. That is because its issue is not knowledge, however hard won, but the confounding of knowledge. The fall of the Tower is an irreversible fall. In the rubble, the homogeneous society for which we are still yearning is buried. Responsibility rests with the Old One. Is He jealous or beneficent? Genesis reports the event but does not gloss it. "And the whole earth was of one language and of one speech." This harmony in the beginning is fractured by the very human undertaking of the men of Shinar, who offer at the heavens to make themselves a name lest their annals be scattered upon the earth. The hopeful labor in which they are involved is the subject of a miniature illustrating a manuscript of the fifteenth century. Little men, whose slightness accentuates their pathos, are toiling up a winding stair. They are carrying stones and wielding picks, they are dropping plumb lines to make the structure true. Speech is gratuitous as understanding is perfect. Above their heads the sphere of fire is waiting. "And the Lord said, Behold, the people is all one and they have all one language. . . . Go to, let us go down and there confound their language that they may not understand one another's speech." The discord which is history follows.

The razing of the Tower is the emblem of despair. It suggests for the long future the isolation of man in historical time. "Now the world is as a flood of waters," writes St. Augustine in the *City of God*. He is lamenting but accepting the difference of language that divides man from man. For all other ills "undue grace" is availing. But the alienation of human beings, who cannot speak their minds or open their hearts, has no remedy, "so that a man had rather be with his own dog than with another man of a strange language." [1] The perpetual imprisonment to which we are condemned, "in the sea of life enisled," is understood as normative until the Renaissance. In the seventeenth century this understanding, also the psychology that informs it, begins to be queried. Men like Bacon and Hobbes, Bishops Wilkins and Sprat, on the Continent Descartes and Leibniz, John Amos Comenius see a way to annul the confusion of tongues and restore the primitive concord. The goal to which they are tending is the enfranchisement of man. Put more boldly, it is a reversal of the primal fall. John Wilkins, the humanitarian cleric and promoter of new science, finds his life's work in redressing the "two general curses inflicted on mankind." To deal with the imposition of hard labor is the business of technology. "All those common arts and professions about which the world is busied" in Wilkins' time will enable mankind "to abate the sweat of their brows in the earning of their bread." The second general curse is the legacy of Nimrod and perhaps not so easily cleared. Nimrod, as Dante remembers, destroys the common language in building the Tower of Babel. Through his "wicked counsel One tongue no longer prevails in the world" (*Inferno* XXXI). The ancient disaster continues to reverberate "not only in the confusion of writing but also of speech." Where is the remedy? Wilkins, who offers to supply it, is only the spokesman for his age. The offer is still on the table. What is wanted is a "universal character to express things and notions," a character or common writing sufficiently transferrable that men of different nations "might with the same ease both write and read it." [2]

In attempting to reconstitute the language of Adam, a catholic instrument of speech and writing powerful against the barriers of

1. Bk. XIX, Ch. vii; XIV, i.
2. *Mercury*, 1694, Ch. XVIII, pp. 143–46; XIII, pp. 105–10.

nationality and race, the linguistic reformers of the seventeenth century begin with a critique of that provincial and postlapsarian language which is their common inheritance. The poet Abraham Cowley versifies this critique in his "Ode to the Royal Society." Sir Francis Bacon is saluted as he brings us "from Words which are but pictures of the thought . . . to Things, the mind's right object." There it is in a phrase, the opposition between words and things which the seventeenth century will make decisive for the darkening of knowledge. In the affrighted past, says Cowley, before the scarecrow deity was broken, "like foolish birds to painted grapes we flew." Bacon, by utilizing "the plain magic of true reason's light"—the conjunction is unconsciously telling—marks out for our use the real tree which lives and bears. Plucking the grapes, he expresses their yield in the right "mechanic" way,

> Till all their juice did in one vessel join,
> Ferment into a nourishment divine,
> The thirsty soul's refreshing wine.

Cowley is a jingle-man—"join" makes a banal triplet with "divine" and "wine"—partly because his thinking is banal. Bishop Sprat, the historian of the Royal Society, as he has tasted this heavenly nectar, is content to trust the inclination of the age in which he writes. It is far readier to promote mechanic studies involved with natural things "than any other time that has gone before us." [3] The antecedent time, all history to the present, loses its way as it puts a premium on exility. Get free of the convolutions of language, Wilkins is saying, and "that great part of our time which is now required to the learning of words might then be employed in the study of things." This employment is scanted as we are captive to the past. In our tender years—John Webster, an Army chaplain who would like to lay hands on them, is pontificating here—we do not so much "receive the impression of the knowing of matter and things as of words." That is why Bacon, who believes that "the first distemper of learning [is] when men study words and not matter,"

---

3. *History of the Royal Society,* 1667, p. 5.

censures the learning of the Schoolmen. In a striking phrase he describes it as productive mostly of "vermicular questions": wriggly and ductile but lacking in pith. The Schools are hateful to him—also Aristotle, to whose authority they appeal—as their attention is given to "the quirks of words" rather than "the subtleties of things." [4] That is the major count against them and more rhetorical than just.

This hostile critique takes strength from the anti-Ciceronianism of poets like Sir Philip Sidney, as set forth in these "echo verses" from the *Arcadia:*

> But when I first did fall, what brought most fall
> to my heart?   Art.
> Art? what can be that art which thou dost mean
> by my speech?   Speech.
> What be the fruits of speaking art? What grows
> by the words?   Words.

Language is solipsistic. To speak at all, Borges will say in his story called "Babel," is to fall into tautology. Bacon, though he verges on this radical discountenancing of language, is at bottom optimistic. His skepticism is forensic. He is not a philosopher but a practical critic. Here is a resumé of his brisk but facile thinking, as set forth in the *Advancement of Learning.* So long as the mind works on itself, like the spider, it has no end but produces only cobwebs of learning, "admirable indeed for the fineness of the thread but of no substance or profit." Scholastic philosophy, literary discourse submit "the shows of things to the desires of the mind." The appropriate opposition is to reason, which buckles the mind to the nature of things. The word monger, says Sprat, who is mostly Bacon's glossarian to the next age, is used to declaim in the shade of a school. When he comes to plead his cause in the open air, he wants the judges to move their seat under the roof because the light offends him. The point is that the light is enabling.

This whimsical sally makes us think of Plato on the Idols of the

---

4. *Mercury,* Ch. XIII; Webster, *Academiarum Examen,* 1653, Ch. III, p. 22; *Advancement of Learning,* 1605, Bks. I and II (*Works,* III, 284–86, 343–44).

Cave. What governs in the resemblance is a common belief in the divisibility of truth. Common, as often, means vulgar. The Royal Society is founded on this belief. Its principal endeavor is "to separate the knowledge of nature from the colors of rhetoric, the devices of fancy, or the delightful deceit of fables." The rhetorician or fabulist, as he is unwilling to discriminate, figures as Narcissus, like the poet Robert Frost:

> Others taunt me with having knelt at well-curbs
> Always wrong to the light, so never seeing
> Deeper down in the well than where the water
> Gives me back in a shining surface picture
> Me myself in the summer heaven godlike.

Even science exemplifies this circular preoccupation. The design of the Royal Society is menaced by redundance and superfluity of speech. Sprat, who abhors superfluity—in his bones he is an esthetician—decides that "eloquence ought to be banished out of all civil societies." [5] Eloquence is form, where form means superficies.

The fateful distinction between form and substance, or truth at the bottom of the well, explains the prodigious activity of Erasmus, whether as polemicist (*Ciceronianus*) or encapsulator (*Adagia*) or purifying scholar (the edition of St. Cyprian). Erasmus begins with the proposition that all knowledge falls into one of two divisions: the knowledge of "truths" and the knowledge of "words." In philosophy, this division is the source of much acidulous comment in the sixteenth and seventeenth centuries. The dominant or Aristotelian philosophy, according to John Webster, as it is merely verbal or speculative, fails "to lead men practically to dive into the internal center of nature's abstruse and occult operations." It confines itself to "the accidental, external, and recollacious qualities of things." The curious word means "empirically gathered." That is surprising and will require comment. Webster's prose sets the teeth on edge and is not to be taken in large doses. He is illustrating for us, before the term is coined, the fallacy of imitative form. The same division he enforces holds in politics. "Our business," says Crom-

5. *History*, pp. 62, 111, 339.

well, "is to speak things." But Scripture is separable also. A polemical clergyman who is advancing as he thinks the interest of reason in religion strips from the "richer quarry of things" the "stately dress of words." Stately is starchy, for which see below. Dress is adventitious, like form. Bishop Wilkins, in a manual on preaching, desires his pupils to put away the dress—it is only "a starched speech full of puerileworded rhetoric"—and to cleave to the thing itself by employing "the most easy perspicuous phrase that may be." It is his particular half truth that "when the notion itself is good, the best way to set it off is the most obvious plain expression." Bacon's dubious judgment is ratified: if we were to boil down the corpus of English sermons, "leaving out the largeness of exhortations and applications," we would hold as a precipitate the best work in divinity written since the time of the Apostles. But this candid distillation is "darkened with the affection of Scholastical harshness or rhetorical flourishes." [6] The rhetorician deceives others, also himself.

Unexpectedly, the scientist is like the preacher and the politician. Galileo and his friends of the Accademia dei Lincei—founded in the early years of the seventeenth century and still fighting the good fight today—though they are principally devoted to the study of nature, entertain an auxiliary purpose not to neglect "the ornaments of elegant literature and philology, which like graceful garments adorn the whole body of science." Trouble ensues, however, as the shell is regarded "more than the kernel, and the shadow more than the substance." Elegant literature, etc., is the shadow. In consequence of this myopic regarding, all human arts are sick. That is the diagnosis of the German physician Henry Cornelius Agrippa. But Agrippa, as he is prescriptive, is hopeful. "Diseased bodies, having some infirmity, are not to be abandoned but to be recured, preserved, and cherished." So with the sciences, now "to be purged from their chaff and brought to their former perfection." When was that perfection? Perhaps when the Tower of Babel was standing. In fact "the absolute perfection of the true philosophy" is just around the corner. We have learned to be

6. Wilkins, *Ecclesiastes*, 1646, pp. 72, 12, 44; the nonconformist divine Robert Ferguson, *The Interest of Reason in Religion*, 1675, p. 160; Webster, *Academiarum*, p. 67.

sparing of this kind of talk. In the seventeenth century, it is conventional. Sprat can hardly contain himself, "so near is mankind to its happiness." His high purpose—he is speaking for his colleagues of the Royal Society—is "to restore the truths that have lain neglected, to push on those which are already known to more various uses, and to make the way more passable to what remains unrevealed." I am moving back and forth in time, here and elsewhere, to emphasize the sameness in psychology of these scientific theorizers over a period of roughly two hundred years. Like the structuralist philosophers who are the villains of the piece, I suppose an organic continuum, associating my protagonists, rather than a merely linear series. Already the sixteenth-century humanist Juan Vives, musing on the corruption of the arts and the desuetude of contemporary science, announces his intention "to free the sciences from impious doubts." Vives wants to know "what employment of thought could be more useful than that of bringing men out of darkness into light." [7]

There are intimations here of an anterior lapsing from grace. Joseph Glanvill, a brilliant if sometimes muddled polemical writer of the later seventeenth century, is sure that in the beginning, "Adam needed no spectacles" nor Galileo's telescope. Since man is subject to "decay and ruins by the fall," it is logical to conclude of science "that it may be trussed up in the same room with the *Iliads*." Science is flummery, like everything else. Glanvill is an interesting writer partly as he is so mercurial. Though he finds all knowledge "at best a most confused adumbration," he celebrates new science. He is also a skeptic who mocks its pretensions. "How our bodies are formed is inexplicable." The "art of the soul" lies equally outside his intellectual ken. "Aristotle" incurs his contempt, as when he observes that all the certainty of these pretenders to the ancient philosophy who are the "voluminous Schoolmen" might be bound in the compass of a penny. But "Plato" does not fare any better. If like children those who strive to apprehend the essence will "run behind the glass to see its naked face, their

7. Vives in preface to *De Disciplinis*, 1531; Sprat, *History*, p. 61; Agrippa, *Of the Vanitie . . . of Artes and Sciences*, tr. 1569, preface (presumably by James Sanford); *Academiarum*, pp. 88–89; *Prescriptiones*, pub. 1624.

expectation will meet with nothing but vacuity and emptiness."
They find their model in Ixion and like him they embrace a cloud.
On this cloud a monster is begotten. Glanvill's strident skepticism
is heuristic and histrionic. He wants first of all to explode all private prepossessions that the absolute truth—codified, I think, in
new science—may be admitted. His patron in skepticism and
eventual dogmatism is Descartes, ultimately Nicholas of Cusa. Like
Cusa, the knowledge he teaches is ignorance.[8] By his total Pyrrhonism he undercuts the Cartesian way to truth and so prefigures
the voluntaristic universe of the later twentieth century.

Agrippa, writing early in the sixteenth century, also depre-
ciates the possibility of knowing absolutely. Truth is not to be perceived with the speculations of science or reason "but with faith
only." But Agrippa is also a Baconian before his time. He is hostile
to the arts and sciences not as they are progressive but as they are
reactionary, which means as they fail to explore "the inward bowels
of things." His program is "to search out the verity of the matter
and not the garnishing of speech." [9] Agrippa himself is partly unconscious of the tendency of his thought. But in this poisonous and
semi-hysterical railer, one sees in embryonic form the rationale of
the succeeding age.

Humility and aspiration are antipodal constants, notwithstanding they are reconcilable in the same time, even in the same
human being. What are we but so many exemplars of the *discordia
concors?* The Puritan ecclesiastic is bitten by ancient ideas of concupiscence. Still he is optimistic of the ascent to perfection. As he
affirms his belief in the clarity of truth, he belongs to the party of
progress. "For those many grounds of truth do yield from them
such a clear light that they do not only appear in their own brightness but also discover the blackness of error." He is concerned,
however, to insist on depravity, which stifles the possibility of attaining to truth. "Whatsoever is in man, within and without, from
the top to the toe, is by nature nothing else but a lump and mass of
all uncleanness." This wavering between antithetical positions is

8. *Vanity of Dogmatizing*, 1661, pp. 5, 10, 14, 66, 41, 26, 18.

9. *Vanitie of Artes*, B4, Blv.

conspicuous in Bishop Wilkins, who announces in the old dyspeptic way that "no man can add one cubit to his stature nor raise himself as he pleases and be the master of his own fortunes." But Wilkins in his character of the scientific projector is sufficiently eupeptic. Most of those who speak for the true philosophy are more consistent. As they believe with Glanvill, after Bacon, that antiquity is "the world's nonage," they will believe in subsequent progress. Nonage is what comes first. If the method of new science were followed attentively, says the experimental philosopher Robert Hooke, there is nothing within the power of human wit or, "which is far more effectual, of human industry, which we might not compass." The classical scientist continues to honor the dispiriting idea of the Fall. We are subject to error both from that "corruption innate and born" with us and from our "breeding and converse with men." But Hooke is not dispirited. He has discovered how to effect the "universal cure of the mind." Let talk be superseded by labor and "all the fine dreams of opinions" will give place to solid works.[10] The prose runs easily and hurries us with it. We should decline to be hurried. They are all rhetoricians, these writers of the seventeenth century, not least when they asperse rhetoric.

It is worth asking: what have we to do with labor which thought does not inform? If thinking is only contention—Hooke makes the equivalence, Sprat also—how do we achieve the fruitful knowledge on which our salvation depends? Are we persuaded that labor is really the vade mecum? The logic of the argument suggests a different conclusion. These important questions are muffled by suavity of style. Looking hard at the argument, this is what it tells us. We are to be thoughtful in moderation (pious in moderation, honest in moderation). We do not prosecute salvation but find it in our way. As our first parents fell by tasting of the tree of knowledge, so we, their posterity, may rise. By the sin of Adam, Adam's descendants are saved. It is, however, inapposite, at least a breach

---

10. Hooke, preface to *Micrographia*, 1665; *Vanity of Dogmatizing*, p. 141; Wilkins, *A Discourse concerning . . . Providence*, 1649, p. 103. The Puritan ecclesiastic is the anonymous author of *The Summe of Sacred Divinitie*, c. 1630, assigned (erroneously) to the publisher John Downhame.

in decorum, to invoke the idea of sin. Nor is the tasting of the forbidden fruit, as we follow the analogy, a laborious exercise. This seems too good to be true.

But if labor is not imposed on us—whether it is penitential, whether it is the means to an end—how are we saved? Faith is our salvation, also the pathway to knowledge. Descartes can follow the path as its signposts "are given by intuition." But the metaphor is not exact. We see a man walking the road. That is what Descartes does not do. The guidons he requires are presented to him already by "the undoubting conception of an unclouded and attentive mind." From this mind which is its own place and which antedates experience, he derives the axioms of mathematics. He guesses that "a triangle is bounded by three lines only, a sphere by a single superficies, and so on." He has no alternative, neither do we. "Any man who rightly observes the limitations of the senses and what precisely it is that can penetrate through this medium to our faculty of thinking must needs admit that no ideas of things, in the shape in which we envisage them by thought, are presented to us by the senses." Nothing comes through to us from the world "out there."

But Descartes escapes from solipsism as, like a warlock, he summons up innate ideas. When, says Sprat, he "retired to search into truth, he at once rejected all the impressions which he had before received from what he had heard and read, and wholly gave himself over to a reflection on the naked ideas of his own mind." [11] It is Adam in the Garden, giving names at God's behest to all the creatures, except that the enabling presence of God is no longer required. We have, Laplace will say, no need of that "hypothesis."

Descartes is only the choice and greatest exemplar of the asseverating man. Locke, who distrusts the imprecision endemic in language, has no remedy to offer but prayerful application. Leibniz, as he elevates faith above works, attempts to find a precise expression independent of language or labor. Symbolic logic and logistic, the history of which begins with him, is the issue of this attempt. Its provenance, as he defines it, is suggestive. The starting

11. *History*, pp. 96–97; Descartes, "Reply to Objections, v," in *Meditations*, 1644; *Notes Directed Against a Certain Program*, 1647, pp. 442–43.

point is not the logic-chopping of the Schools but the enthusiastic writings of Bishop Wilkins, the unsupported ipse dixit of half-forgotten cranks like George Dalgarno and Athanasius Kircher, also the Great Art of Ramón Lull. Glanvill, who asseverates, is no bad representative of the scientific or progressive intelligence. He has little room for "that discouraging maxim, *Nil dictum quod non dictum prius.*" He will not tie up his belief to the wisdom of Solomon: after all there has been something new under the sun. In the triumph of new science he has seen "what antiquity never saw, no, not in a dream." This is exciting and both true and false. The element of falseness is suggested by the subject and tenor of the next chapter in Glanvill's treatise, which opens at once. It is "A story of a Scholar that turned Gypsy." Sprat is not partial to gypsies or stories either. Unlike Matthew Arnold, he disbelieves in other "days when wits were fresh and clear." Progress runs in a straight line. We have not been expelled from the Garden but are still to attain it. Now since the return of King Charles, "the blindness of the former ages and the miseries of this last are vanished away." Now men are satiated with religious disputes. Now their eyes are open and their hands prepared to labor. "Now there is a universal desire and appetite after knowledge, after the peaceable, the fruitful, the nourishing knowledge, and not after that of ancient sects which only yielded hard indigestible arguments or sharp contentions instead of food: which, when the minds of men required bread, gave them only a stone." [12] This stone is like the counterfeit of Zeus with which Rhea beguiles the savage god. As it is rejected, the overthrow of Cronus, who figures the old order, begins.

The impatient hungering after a more substantial diet is intimately involved with the nature of language. The scientist, as he believes that the older mode of discourse lacks nutriment—gnawing on flint, says Wilkins—desires to repair or supplant it. Really what he wants is to make language superfluous: to replace the "glorious pomp of words" with "the silent, effectual, and unanswerable arguments of real productions." In the seventeenth century this desire begins to quicken in the schools. When the academician

---

12. *History*, pp. 152–53; *Vanity of Dogmatizing*, pp. 187–89.

Seth Ward turns to consider the critique of education formulated by John Webster, it is essentially his point that the schools have repudiated their long allegiance to Aristotle, also their hostility to linguistic reform. The regenerate Schoolman is like the scientific projector. Each rejects "amplifications, digressions, and swellings." Each envisages "a society that prefers work before words." The business community is partial to this new society, a good omen, says Robert Hooke, "that their attempts will bring philosophy from words to action." [13] I think what they see in the mind's eye is Coketown of the pistons and black canals.

The Industrial Age still awaits its incarnation. In the meantime progress falters. Bacon equates the "idols of the market-place" with the assigning of names to non-existent things like fortune or chance, which permit that "a good man's fortune may grow out at heels." Because language is equivocal, disputes "often terminate in controversies about words and names." Glanvill also can attest that the word is "diversly apprehended by contenders and so made the subject of controversies." Webster adduces the writings of the Stagyrite, whose doctrine is "so uncertain and obscure that to fish out his meaning there is need of a Delian urinator." Bacon declines to countenance the need. He sees or thinks he sees that science to the present is useless "for the discovery of effects," as the present system of logic is useless "for the discovery of the sciences." Each is infected by conventional discourse. And therefore, in the *Advancement of Learning* and again in *De Augmentis*, he calls for the elaborating of a system of characters, kindred as he imagines to Chinese ideograms, and able to "express neither letters nor words in gross but things or notions." In this he anticipates the central purpose of the Royal Society: "the intention is not the artifice of words but a bare knowledge of things." [14]

The intention is not new in the seventeenth century, only it is enormously heightened. Already "Cato" is supposed to enjoin it: "Rem tene, verba sequentur." (This Cato is not the Roman stoic

13. Preface to *Micrographia;* Ward, *Vindiciae Academiarum,* 1654, H3v, A2v-4; Sprat, *History,* pp. 62, 17–18, 113, 434; Wilkins, *Ecclesiastes,* p. 49.

14. Sprat, *History,* p. 40; *Novum Organum,* 1620, Aphorisms I, xi, xxxix–lxviii; Webster, *Academiarum,* p. 62; *Vanity of Dogmatizing,* pp. 160–61.

but the ubiquitous sage of the Renaissance *florilegia*.) Wilkins, establishing the provenance of his once-famous *Essay on a Real Character and a Philosophical Language* (1668), alleges as progenitors not only Bacon and his graphic Chinese but certain speculations of Galen. Sir Thomas Urquhart, the translator of Rabelais and the contriver of a universal language, is only approving the ancient adage, "Philosophia sunt res, non verba." The Royal Society finds the motto it is looking for in Horace (though not without twisting the sense): "Nullius in verba." Cicero vaporizes. That is what Erasmus and Gabriel Harvey suppose, so they condemn him. The wrongheaded condemning of Cicero is among the important stories of the Renaissance, important as it is emblematic. The scientific intelligence chooses not to "regard the credit of names but things" and so discovers Cicero among the misleaders. But a poet like Sidney is just as severe. Ciceronianism is the chief abuse of Oxford, "where those who follow words neglect the things themselves." Cambridge is more progressive but differs from Oxford only in degree. The Royal Society is instituted to keep the sister universities up to the mark. Its job is to return language, in Sprat's celebrated prescription, "to the primitive purity and shortness when men delivered so many things almost in an equal number of words." [15] The conventional criticism of Cicero is certainly unjust. As that is so, it tells us something. Cicero is a circumstantial writer, not vaporous, and for that reason he is put down as against Demosthenes. And Sidney, to recur to him, how gravid is he as a poet? In his criticism Sidney is faithful to Peter Ramus. In his poetry he is anti-Ramistic. Verbal latencies are to the fore. If we feel that he is mostly more artificial or literary (no bad thing) than gravid, what is the occasion of his quarrel with Cicero? with language?

As the seventeenth century opens, the forging of an exact correspondence between names and things becomes a matter of impatient concern. Donne is amused at those "curious and entangled wits" who vex themselves to know whether in the world there are more of one than the other. The schoolmaster Henry Edmundson

15. *History*, pp. 62, 105, 113; Sidney to his brother Robert, 1580 (letter XLII in Feuillerat); *De Oratore*, II, 63; Urquhart, *Logopandecteison*, 1653, B4.

is sufficiently curious. His "Natural Language of Languages" is founded professedly on the resemblance "of words with the things which by the sound they are made to signify." The parallels in sound and sense Edmundson adduces are perhaps not so congruent, unless to himself. To his ear, the English word "popgun" proclaims its affinity to *Scloppus* or *Sloppus*. Urquhart bases the universal language on phonograms as he has discovered in them a just proportion "betwixt things and words." All modern and ancient languages except his own fail to exhibit this proportion. Many common things cannot "without circumlocution" be expressed by conventional discourse. So he contrives "a mark whereby words of the same faculty, art, trade, or science should be diagnosed from those of another by the very sound of the word at the first hearing." *Neaudethaumata*, he avers, or *Chrestasebeia*, or even *Cleronomaporia*. The intention is that "things semblable in nature should be signified by words of a like pronounciation." [16]

This language or anti-language of "inarticulate sounds" suggests to Wilkins a method of discourse "equally speakable by all people and nations." As niceties are abraded, it should be possible to employ only "tunes and musical notes"—stirring tunes, I think, and a limited register—"contrived for the expression, not of words and letters but of things and notions." (How often Bacon's phrasing recurs in the literature of linguistic reform and new science.) Good hope suggests further that the "utterance of these musical tunes may serve for the universal language, and the writing of them for the universal character." The philosophical position is important. Wilkins gives it in a sentence. "As all nations do agree in the same conceit of things, so likewise in the same conceit of harmonies." [17] Invariance is the key.

Among the great names of the seventeenth century is the Czech theologian and philosopher of education, John Amos Comenius. In the judgment of this cloudy divinator, "we are all nought but sounding brass and tinkling cymbals so long as words

16. *Logopandecteison*, A3, B-lv; Edmundson, *Lingua Linguarum*, 1655 (quoting edn. of 1658, A2r); Donne, *Essays in Divinity*, pub. 1651 (p. 23 in Simpson edn.).

17. *Mercury*, pp. 108–09, 143–46.

not things (the husks of words, I say, not the kernels of meanings) be in our mouths." Setting forth rules for the *lingua universalis*, Comenius is adamant that "the framers of the new language shall rather follow the guidance of things themselves, since everything in our new language must be adapted to the exact and perfect representation of things." There is about Comenius the whiff of Madame Blavatsky and damp auditories in Bloomsbury where disciples of Rudolf Steiner foregather. Reading him, one is transported to the workshop of Jonathan Swift. All the background for the crazed projectors of *Gulliver's Travels* is there. The madness of Comenius is a function of his considerable humanity. A noble and risible pathos surrounds him. He spurns the delimiting earth with his foot and soars above it. What he is after is "the reform of the whole world." To effect this reform he stipulates four requirements: "Universal Books, Universal Schools, a Universal College, a Universal Language." Comenius is sure that if the *lingua universalis* which existed "in the state of man's innocence" and which survives in attenuated form in the symbolic characters of the East could be retrieved and brought into practice, it would afford "a perfectly open way for teaching all necessary things to all men." Hence his passionate undertaking to formulate an entirely new language as an infallible corrective to confusion of thought. But this "universal antidote" can operate only "if it contains neither more nor fewer names than there are things." Comenius sees the difficulty which attends on the realizing of this perfect equation. Assurance is, however, his hallmark, also a fierce alacrity. Let us hasten the advent of the common language, he cries, that "there may be one Lord and his name one, and all the land be turned into a plain." [18] I know of no more precise a statement of the aims and psychology of the modern world, to the present. The summons is to homogeneity. Really what it signifies is the reconstituting of the Tower of Babel, the redressing of the Fall.

It is easy to go wrong here, in construing the opposition of words to things. If we understand the terminology of the scientist

---

18. *Continuatio*, 1669, tr. R. Young, p. 31; *The Way of Light*, 1668, Chs. xv, xix; Zechariah 14:9–10.

and the linguistic reformer in its ordinary acceptance, we will associate words to the synthesizer, a discredited figure, and things to
the modern or analytic man who gets high marks for his devotion
to physical fact. That is the customary construction. It does not
bear scrutiny. Comenius, distinguishing between the husks of
words and the kernels of meanings, supplies the clue to a more
nearly accurate reading. Stated succinctly: "Nothing in words"
means Nothing in the surface of things. "I do not question you
about the name," says Galileo to a simple-minded antagonist, "but
about the essence of the thing." What is this essence? It is the ideal
form, what medieval philosophers call "reality." The definition is
aloof from common sense and on it depends the universe in which
we are living today. William of Ockham, the spectre who haunts
modern philosophy, disputes the definition. Physical fact is evidently sacrosanct. Ockham in his skepticism is "descriptive." The
terminists of the fourteenth century and after, who reverence the
Invincible Doctor as the fount of their school, are, however, aggressively "philosophical." Essentiality informs their interest in
mathematics and natural science. They are announcing from afar
the scientific renascence of the seventeenth century, to which a
provisional or nominalist psychology would appear to be implacably
opposed.

But the new philosophy of Bacon and Sprat, like the explor-
atory essays of the *via moderna*, depends on the securing of priority to the world of ideal forms. What Bacon means by induction is
the rejecting of particulars and the intuiting of a capital-letter
"Form affirmative, solid, and true and well defined." Induction is
regressive. Bacon is not a thoroughgoing empiric and Sprat only by
turns. The depreciating of words does not entail for either a venerating of brute fact. The opposite is true. The things Bacon covets
and wants language to express are not phenomenal. They are conceptual. The scientific investigator is wrong "to confine his aim to
the investigation and working out of some one discovery and no
more, such as the nature of the magnet, the ebb and flow of the
sea, the system of the heavens, and things of this kind." The off-
handedness is staggering. To the maker of the new organon it is
folly "to investigate the nature of anything in the thing itself"—

which is not to be confused with the *ding an sich*—"seeing that the same nature which appears in some things to be latent and hidden is in others manifest and palpable." Induction "which proceeds by simple enumeration" is "childish." [19] I think we take the point of William Harvey's acerbic remark that Bacon wrote science like a Lord Chancellor.

The method which Bacon and his predecessors of the modern way desire to put in practice is deductive and anti-material and it begins to assert its old appeal over the minds of men just in that period when the reality of things receives, in the *Summa* of Aquinas, a little later in the *Divine Comedy,* its most memorable affirmation. Aquinas, the lawgiver to that mundane city which is the greatest achievement of the High Middle Ages, comes close to identifying the sign with the thing it signifies. Truth is the conformity between intellect and thing. The word points to the concept but through the concept it points also to the thing. Ockham separates the concept and the thing. Possibly the former is equivocal. Truth or falsity is predicable of a statement only in personal supposition. Moral or ontological truth is not at issue. What is at issue—as the symbolic logician will put it, many centuries later—is the "satisfiability" of propositions. Hamlet says satirically: "there is nothing either good or bad but thinking makes it so." Nominalism rejects the possibility of *a priori* knowledge. The role of sensory perception is indispensable. It is all we have. But as Ockham undermines this role by questioning the validity of the vector or sign, he sweeps the way for Galileo and Descartes. If the word stands for nothing ontological, our language—to employ the terminology of Gödel's Proof—is at best and inevitably metamathematical. "Although we speak of the thing, yet we speak of it by the intermediacy of propositions and terms." To carry the skeptical view of perception one step further: perhaps we are not speaking of the thing at all. As early as the first half of the sixteenth century, in the theocratic stronghold of Calvin's Geneva, the heretical but impeccably logical theologian Sebastian Castello is willing to assert that

---

19. *Novum Organum,* Aphorisms I, lxxxviii, II, xv, xvi; Galileo, *Dialog on the Two World Systems,* 1632.

to tell the truth is to say what one believes to be true. Who, after Ockham, is going to contradict him?

The contribution of Ockham's disciples, the harbingers of the modern age, is to suggest between the sign and the signified thing a relation not depending on physical correspondence but esthetic coherence. The world of these disciples, as the razor is applied with sufficient lack of ruth, is that of the *hortus inclusus*. It is the world of Euclid or Riemann whose antithetical constructions are verifiable as they are consistent, but not empirically, only internally. Mathematics exhibits this internal consistency. It is an appropriate study to the terminists of the waning Middle Ages. With the cultivating of mathematics, nominalism returns or approximates to a realist position—and ushers in sequentially the new science of the Renaissance. Names, says Henry Edmundson, quoting again from his "Language of Languages," are merely "Signa Rerum." What we perceive does not always agree with what is. As the proposition is received, the abstract constructions of classical science are hypostasized as alternative versions of the mundane world. Knowledge of the thing which the sign represents is reserved to "the inventions of the intellect" (Einstein). To a creative view of knowledge the terminist is driven, with this view the scientific conceptualizer begins. Plato and his followers, against whom Ockham sets his face, are readmitted as by the back door. This surprising *volte face* is implicit in Ockham's Franciscan (Augustinian) bias. The will is superior to the intellect. Voluntarism carries it away. Total skepticism reverts to dogmatic assertion.

The intuitive act is supposed to culminate in demonstration, which popular iconography identifies as the whole business of science. The scientific quantifier is recognized as he wears a white coat, maybe a white goatee emblematic of sagacity. As he fulfills his appointed role, he engages in titration or calibration. Like Leeuwenhoek he bends over the microscope, or like the Tuscan artist he consults his optic glass. He is the culture hero to the modern age. Imagination, the high priori road, is assigned to the maker of artistic fictions. In his most successful avatar, the scientist is, however, averse to the labor of quantification. Algebra is the hebetude of the abstracting intelligence. Quoting Oppenheimer, in conversation: "The one thing the scientist does not want to do is count." Like Democritus the Abderite, he puts out his eyes so as not to be hindered in prosecuting the abstract theory by which he lives. Thales of Miletus, the ancient astronomer and geometrician, hardly lives in his senses at all. Contemplating the stars, Thales fails to notice the ditch at his feet. He tumbles in the ditch. The absentmindedness which betrays him is comic, it is also the sign of his imaginative habit. The kind of temperament I take him as presenting will always exalt the deductive method above induction, not least as it makes induction an article of faith. Urquhart loses the books and papers on which his new language depends in the rout of the loyalist army, "after the fatal blow given at Worcester" (September 3, 1651). He has no recourse but to appeal from the world of factual data to his own inner promptings and conclusions. In this he resembles the mathematician, for example William Oughtred (1574–1660), the inventor of the rectilinear slide rule. Oughtred is a clergyman and too preoccupied by day with his ministerial labors to engage in speculative activity. At night his thrifty wife denies him the use of a candle. Like Descartes, he is blessed, however, with the proleptic faculty. What he sees and hears is imparted from within.

To the Cartesian maxims for the conduct of inquiry as set forth in the *Discourse on Method*, the Jansenist logicians of Port-Royal appeal in justifying their attack on the logic of Aristotle. The old-fashioned logic is moribund because it is antiexperimental. That is how they describe it but that is not what they mean. Really what they mean is the opposite of what they say, a familiar failing and not necessarily willful. The first of the Cartesian maxims seems to require that assaying or induction come first. It is "never to accept anything for truth which I did not clearly know to be such." But knowledge of truth is a function of the "innate cognoscitive power" of the mind. Ockham, the dogged champion of the physical world, falls like a woodcock in his own springe. The Pyrrhonism to which his logic inexorably conducts attracts Descartes only as an enabling preface to the establishing of ultimate certitude. But Descartes has got to outflank the conclusion that we cannot realize knowledge of ourselves. The expedient he proposes is irrational, for Ockham has demonstrated that reason in last things is unavailing. The irrational hypothesizing of ideal truth is, however, the foundation of scientific or philosophical grammar. If the foundation is made of papier-maché, that is worth knowing.

To discover the truth about language, the grammarians of Port-Royal begin by asserting an abstract paradigm equated with "the natural manner in which we express our thoughts." Though the definitions of nouns are whimsical, "the definitions of things do not depend on us but on what is involved in the true idea of the thing." In working up their conclusions, the creators of the *Grammaire générale* are not tied to matter of fact. Arnauld goes his way, says Sainte-Beuve, "independently of particular languages to which he afterwards applies his general principles." Adopting in the Grammar the point of view Descartes adopts in his philosophy and physics, "Il crée la grammaire." I think this creation is arbitrary fabrication. The Port-Royalists think it is the enunciating of a pattern which presents itself to the intellect from the beginning. Sainte-Beuve again: "The incontestable clarity of the formula, *I think, therefore I am*, which supposes a distinct conception of *thinking* and *being*, suffices, according to Port-Royal, to prove that all ideas come not from the senses, that there are other ideas than those which attach themselves to particular images." [20] The resuscitating of these other ideas, which have "no affinity with movements and no relation to them," is one way to measure or describe the superseding of the past by the present. In the seventeenth century the old Aristotelian word *subjective* ceases to mean "existing in itself" and takes on its modern sense of existing only "in human consciousness." But this mental existence, as the physical world disintegrates, presents itself to us as more nearly true. It is in any case more seductive than existence in physical fact.

The data the empiricist gathers, or the oldfashioned linguist or logician, is only an overlay. Against it is the "truth itself, naked and delightful." The quotation is from a preface to the first English translation of the *Port-Royal Logic* (1685). New logic and grammar

20. Sainte-Beuve, *Port-Royal*, IV, pp. 66–76; *Port-Royal Logic*, tr. T. S. Baynes, Pt. II, Ch. xvi.

are able to dispense with a carefully reticulated structure of evidence. Bernard Lamy, a rhetorician and clerical follower of Descartes, has little to say of "the order of words and the rules we must observe in the arrangement of discourse." What this writer calls "la lumière naturelle" illustrates the necessary procedures so vividly that no comment is required. Bishop Wilkins distinguishes customary constructions from those which manifest the "natural sense and order of the words." He is unwilling to discuss the latter. Wilkins is not in his proclivities a merely descriptive grammarian. It is only that, like the Port-Royalists, he supposes the clear presence of the Urform—the province of philosophical grammar—to make discussion gratuitous. This cursory man, who invokes the real character against the particularities of ordinary discourse and serves as first co-secretary of the Royal Society, is the brother-in-law of Oliver Cromwell, who prefers "real" security to dependence on political "forms." Wilkins is born in the house of his mother's father, the hysterical and once-celebrated clergyman John Dod. Reverend Dod, like his grandchild, is blessed with the gift of tongues. A gentlewoman, only hearing him, falls into a frenzy so extreme as to beseech her husband—successfully, says Jonson to Drummond—"that for the procreation of an angel or saint he might lie with her." That is the right lineage for Bishop Wilkins.

Bacon makes no claim to the pentecostal faculty. Truth is not abruptly tumescent but "rising by a gradual and unbroken ascent" from the senses and particulars. But it is not the process that absorbs him, rather the arriving "at the most general axiom last of all." The "men of experiment," a term of opprobrium, forbear to take the ultimate step. As their interest is exhausted in the senses and particulars, they resemble the ants who "only collect and use." Against this mindless activity Bacon poses the labor of the synthetic intelligence as figured in the bee, which "gathers its own material from the flowers of the garden and of the field but transforms and digests it by a power of its own." The transforming power remains contingent on the gathering of material. Bacon has, at least formally, little patience with the mere reasoners who "make cobwebs out of their own substance." But already the work of the synthesizer is understood to represent the farthest reach of human enterprise. "Where then is truth?" asks the interlocutor or straight man in a dialog by Giordano Bruno. He is answered: "In the sensible object as in a mirror, in the reason through inference and discussion, in the intellect through premise or conclusion, in the mind in absolute living form." [21] But the reason, like the intellect, is myopic. And the mirror is concave. Sensible objects resemble the truth only analogically. We see as in a fun fair.

The later seventeenth century disallows even a contingent empiricism. As for metaphors, says the historian of science, we can do without them. "Poterimus vivere sine illis." Spinoza distinguishes three grades of cognitive activity. The lowest is sense perception. It is open to error, so its testimony is rejected. But even the reasonable apprehension of things, although superior as it affirms their subjection to universal law, is overgone by the intuitive knowledge which apprehends the universe as a coherent design. Liebniz sees the world under this triune aspect. The animated units of which reality is composed ascend in value from inert matter through the merely conscious souls of the animal kingdom to the selfconscious spirits or rational souls which dwell in the highest plane of being. In his polemical treatise on church government, Milton describes the transcendent knowledge of God as "the only high valuable wisdom." In feeble comparison to it is "that knowledge that rests in the contemplation of natural causes and dimensions, which must needs be a lower wisdom as the object is low." Comenius, though he thinks it desirable to investigate the School of Nature, posits as more worthy of interest a Metaphysical School in which God's image is "impressed upon our mind." A century later Jonathan Edwards, who shows us how Calvinism and Platonism are opposite faces of a single coin, discerns in the "inferior, secondary beauty" of the natural world no more than a pale reflex of "the highest and primary beauty" in which the "agreement and consent of spiritual beings" is entire.[22]

It is all atrocious nonsense, this hypothetical ascending from

21. De l'infinito, universo e mondi, 1584; Novum Organum, Aphorisms I, lxxxviii.

22. Edwards, The Nature of True Virtue, 1755, Ch. III; The Way of Light, pp. 13–14; The Reason of Church Government Urged Against Prelaty, 1641, Bk. II; Sprat, History, p. 327.

less to more, and not to boggle at it is to forfeit our humanbeing-
ness, also our lien or handhold on divinity. There is no place here
for the infant Jesus who seems, as Italian painters of the Trecento
imagine him, to be only God in posse. Certainly there is no place
for the human mother who gives him suck.

To be human, what is that? Hobbes answers implicitly, in the
introduction to *Leviathan:* "life is but a motion of limbs." To Laplace, after Descartes, the living organism is a perfectly predictable
physiochemical system. The heart that animates this system "is a
piece of machinery." Of course William Harvey, whom I am quoting, is right. Only he is not sufficiently catholic. But more than
catholicity is involved. To the through-and-through scientific or
Platonizing temper, the "superficial" incarnation stinks in the nostrils. Gregory of Nyssa, the fourth-century Father and devotee of
Neoplatonic ideas, likens carnal involvement to an Egyptian bondage. He avoids from the beginning entanglement in life's desires
and cares. Carnality is a delusion, not merely in its narrow sense of
erotic attachment.[23] "You must have observed again and again,"
says Socrates to Glaucon, "what a poor appearance the tales of
poets make when stripped of the colors which music puts upon
them, and recited in simple prose." Colors and music are like carnality, or like the heart that is pregnant to good pity. A modern
commentator on Dante tells us gravely—it is as if he were an exegete of the Iron Age—that to go from the *Vita Nuova* through the
Commedia is "to progress from the *inter nos* to the *extra nos* to the
super nos of St. Bonaventura." We are to suppose a triple "ascending" away from the personal. The *Commedia* is infinitely more personal than the *Vita Nuova* and so, as we are faithful to the terms of
this asserted progression, it is the lesser performance. But Dante at
his best differs in kind from St. Bonaventura, who is the center of
the circle. Dante is not aloof from the substantial points on the cir-
cumference. It is where he lives. Quoting *Vita Nuova* XII: "Ego
tanquam centrum circuli, cui simili modo se habent circumferentie
partes; tu autem non sic." The seraphic visitor dwells in the center.

23. Gregory of Nyssa, *On Virginity;* Harvey, *The Motion of the Heart and Blood in Animals,*
1628.

He is equidistant from its circumferential points. "You, however, are not."

Rationality transcends our tactile explorations, it makes nonsense of growing and choosing in ways in which are implicit in the psychology of the mantic or intuitive man. The monad which is mind is a windowless structure. Empirical evidence is a contradiction in terms. "Nothing can be taught us the idea of which we have not already in our minds." To acknowledge the veracity of this idea, the soul only needs to be reminded. Locke, who asks how the mind acquires the materials of reason and knowledge, answers "in one word, from experience." [24] But the soul, says Leibniz, already possesses the truths which experience yields. He is expounding, in the more pretentious terminology of the modern age, the Platonic doctrine of reminiscence. The positions for which men dispute are evidently limited in number and the impulse to argue them endlessly recurrent. All men are born either Aristotelian or Platonic. The enduring side of us which is "Aristotle" craves a substantial presence. "Sine Cerere et Libero friget Venus." In the words of a minor Metaphysical poet:

> None, though Platonic their pretense,
> With reason love unless by sense.

This cheerful point of view is repudiated by the noetic or Platonizing temperament. In the hierarchies of being which are elaborated first by the mystics, matter is formed by successive privations of the impalpable One, which Plotinus locates at the apex but which he forbears to define. "What it is, we do not say." When radical Protestantism makes its initial appeal from the Crown to the country, it includes in a list of more odious abuses the practice of kneeling at communion. To kneel is to imply a real presence. Protestantism on its abstemious side is "Platonic." The Platonist knows intuitively that ideas are real and the universe an order or cosmos. The symbolic language he elaborates is the map of this cosmos which, to the Aristotelian, is perhaps only an old chaos of the sun.

---

24. *Essay concerning Human Understanding*, 1690, Bk. i, Ch. i.

The Nominalists, before they throw in their hand, are of the party of Aristotle. The realists are Platonic and have instructed us sufficiently in what it means to be real.

This perception suggests the unwisdom of taking at face value the modern or post-Baconian requirement that "names be made up of the definitions of things." Seth Ward, the Savilian professor of astronomy at Oxford, proposes the requirement as he wishes to be done with indigenous things and to supplant them with names or symbols, like x and y. Much of the greatest writing of the seventeenth century deals resolutely in the lower case. That is not enough to win it a favorable hearing. The hostile critic of this writing, who complains that he is put off "with nothing but rampant metaphors and pompous allegories and other splendid but empty schemes of speech," seems to be pleading the priority of the material world. (I am quoting Bishop Samuel Parker, a forward-looking churchman of the Restoration period, whom Marvell pillories as Mr. Bayes in the *Rehearsal Transprosed.*) The oldfashioned ecclesiastic, as epitomized by Jeremy Taylor or by the Cambridge Platonists, excites his indignation in that he is addicted "to discourse of the natures of things in metaphor and allegory." To gratify this addiction "is nothing else but to sport or trifle with empty words, because these schemes do not express the natures of things but only their similitudes and resemblances." [25] But the similitude is not empty. It is uncommonly concrete and that is the real ground of the complaint. From the plain style, things are progressively excluded. As he desires a total exclusion or transparency, Parker approves Ward's endeavor to create a universal language based on mathematics. Marvell in one of his letters speaks for the antithetical position: "I am so subject to be particular." What the linguistic reformers are reprehending is not a lack of concreteness but concreteness itself.

As propagandist or "bucinator" of new science, Bacon appears to reflect an affiliation to thingness in our more conventional sense. The *Novum Organum* stresses the importance of the inductive method. Heat is defined as a kind of motion. Bacon refers the defi-

25. *A Free and Impartial Censure of the Platonick Philosophy,* 1666; Ward, *Vindiciae,* C4v.

nition to empirical proof. But when William Gilbert in his treatise
On the Magnet (1600) brings together seventeen years of rigorous
experiment, his reception at Bacon's hands is negligent disdain.
Gilbert is not insufficiently faithful to the Baconian principles of induction. I think the contrary is true. Hobbes, who begins his career as secretary to the master and whose subsequent speculations
continue the Baconian tradition, seems to annul it. *Veritas in dicto,
non in re consistet,* he announces. But what Hobbes means is that
our knowledge of phenomenal fact is not genuine knowledge. We
call a common name, as opposed to a proper name, universal. But
the grandiose word corresponds to no reality in nature. It is only
the property and name of a name, "for the things named are every
one of them individual and singular." Reality is comprised in these
discrete entities, like the points in a painting by Seurat. The Ges-
talt or total configuration is our own idea. Hobbes creates modern
nominalism in England as he asserts that definition is an act of will.
Names are but "signs of our conceptions." We take them "at pleasure to serve for a mark." He is willing to suppose, he does not
much care one way or another, that "some names of living creatures and other things which our first parents used were taught by
God Himself." But he is adamant that these names "were by Him
arbitrarily imposed." [26] The manipulator of words can never reach
to the underlying reality. "I have proclaimed nothing," says the
despairing Virgil in the novel by Hermann Broch, "I have only felt
of the crag." That is what the classical scientist and the linguistic
reformer believe. It is the source of their dissatisfaction with language.

A different position is formulated by St. Augustine in his exposition on the Trinity and is canonical until the Renaissance. The
key words which embody this position are in the antithesis: *"non in
verbis . . . sed in facto."* I see them as endorsing—adumbrating,
anyway, a warrant for the integrity of language. Hobbes, deciding
that names "are not signs of the things themselves," is anticipated
and qualified by St. Paul in Galatians (4:22–26). When Paul dis-

---

26. Introduction to *Leviathan*, 1651; *De Corpore*, 1656; Pt. I, Ch. iii, sect. 7; *Computation,
or Logic* (in *Elements of Philosophy*, 1656), Pt. I, Ch. ii, "Of Names."

courses on allegory "he refers not to words but to fact: as when he shows that the two sons of Abraham, one by a bondmaid, the other by a freewoman (these are not words but facts), are to be understood as the two Testaments." The parenthetical phrase makes the difference. We are darkened in our reason, so what we utter is only a collocation of phonemes. But the word of God does really grasp the crag of truth, and men are privy to the word of God—the Apostle, no question, but also poets like Dante, employing the fourfold method of allegoresis in his *Commedia*. Nature, which takes her course from the divine intelligence, is a faithful showing forth of God's truth. But "your art," says Virgil to Dante in the eleventh canto of the *Inferno*, "follows nature as the scholar follows the master." This sedulous art is therefore "the grandchild of God." We see imperfectly ("quanto pote") and so must squint or labor. But seeing is not precluded. Nor is our captivity to metaphor a total captivity. Reality inheres in phenomenal fact, also in our expression of it. This is going to mean, whatever the strictures of Augustine and Aquinas, that style is of the essence. A Latin poet and preacher of the twelfth century gives us our text: "*Nomen enim verum dat definitio rerum.*" Style will logically preoccupy the writer who believes with Dante that "names are the consequents of the things they name: *Nomina sunt consequentia rerum.*" [27] But as the name has got to be true (*nomen verum*)—just this one, not another—infinite painstaking is approved. In fact it is required. There is no ready and easy way.

Primitive or superstitious man shares with the sophisticated lexicographers of the Renaissance and later a distaste for taking pains. The conjunction is surprising on its face. Primitive man elaborates the doctrine of signatures. If a drum head is made of the skin of a wolf, sheep will be terrified when the drum is struck. They recognize the sense in the sound. The equivalence is precise and apprehended without difficulty. This does not look like a tenable thesis. But Cusa, a prodigious intellect, comes close to affirming it. That man (or mage), he argues, who possesses the full signification of a name, possesses absolutely the thing for which it

27. *Vita Nuova*, XIII; Hildebert of Lavardin; Augustine, *De Trinitate*, XV, IX, 15.

stands. To take the radical force of this argument, on which the conceptualizing psychology of the Renaissance is founded, reverse the clauses and read: first of all possess the thing. Dante, writing to Can Grande, reverses the clauses: "A thing relates to truth according to the relation it has to existence." The ultimate source of the quotation is Aristotle in the *Metaphysics*. It is clear why his philosophy, his psychology rather, should be felt increasingly as off the point. In the closing years of the fifteenth century, the German humanist Johannes Reuchlin decides that names are more than arbitrary symbols. The decision does not suggest his kinship to Dante and Aquinas, rather to the new cabalism that marches step by step with the advent of new science. Names convey reality but not as we work or tease them. Letters are the things themselves.[28] How is that? Presumably as they are alive, the trembling receptacles of a charismatic power. In the Renaissance the Gnosticism of the early Christian centuries is conceded a new lease on life. Partly, that is what the Renaissance means.

Adam in the Garden, who receives his cue from on high, assigns to every creature a name denoting its essence. Milton makes him say: "I named them, as they passed, and understood their nature." The language of Adam is true, not simply *in verbis* but *in facto*. Perhaps we will feel, as words are our business, that Adam has not earned the right to employ it. His words are gratuitously given. Henry More, the Cambridge Platonist, likens them to "inscriptions upon apothecaries' boxes," where the master of the shop who inscribes his signature is the deity, and the humbler apprentice who reads and is instructed is ourselves. We are lucky as we are instructed. This ancient belief is still vital in the seventeenth century. The "signature" is not to be read as analogous. In the name of herbs is described "the very nature and use of them, not the mere name." Decoction of adder's tongue is sovereign for the bite of the adder. The quince is a hairy fruit and so it is efficacious against falling hair. A multitude of these correspondences-by-fiat are assembled in the herbal literature of the sixteenth century, as

28. *De verbo mirifico*, ?1494; *De arte cabalistica*, 1517; Cusa, *De mante* (*Works*, c. 1490), Ch. III.

brought together in my edition of John Hall's *Court of Virtue* (1961). They suggest to the superstitious understanding—More bespeaks it—that God "by natural hieroglyphics" is reading lectures on the natural world "to the rude wit of man." [29] It follows that knowledge of the origin of words—not semantic knowledge but cabalistic—is the key to coercing phenomena. Primitive etymology is spellbinding: the point of the title Isidore of Seville, writing after the eclipse of the Roman palladium and the triumph of the Visigoth kings, chooses for his encyclopedia of all learning, the *Etymologies.*

Modern or post-Baconian man believes, on the contrary, that to etymologize is to move in a circle. Conceded that etymology is the central concern of Horne Tooke and the philologists of the eighteenth century. In this later period, the attempt to classify language dominates philosophical inquiry into the universal character of words. Almost until the present, it dominates the scientific study of linguistics. But this diligent inquiring, like Bacon's dealing with phenomena, is felt in the last resort as preliminary. The philology of Horne Tooke is preliminary as it asserts that abstraction is elliptical. The detached word does not exist apart from the concrete fact it expresses (where expressing is creating).[30] If that is so, truth is partial and forever cleated to description. As we desire a plenary view, we will summon to our assistance not the descriptive but the philosophical grammarian. Genuine understanding accrues as this more comprehensive person intermits his concern for particulars (vermicular questions) and seeks to apprehend the subtleties of things, which are allowed materiality only as they are generic. In this way what looks to be Bacon's empiricism, running through Hobbes and Locke, begets the idealism of Berkeley. The function of words is to express the universal aspect. That is why Hobbes asserts that truth inheres only in words and why, in so asserting, he does not repudiate Bacon but fulfills him.

Not to sacrifice truth to coherence: if I am right in supposing that Augustine, Aquinas also, warrants the integrity of language, the warrant is certainly hedged. Only God or His deputy is able to

29. *Antidote against Atheism,* 1642, II, vi; 1655, pp. 98–99, 101.

30. *The Diversions of Purley,* 1786, Pt. I, Chs. i–iii.

vocalize what Donne calls the "naked enunciation." (Here the new Gnosticism of the Renaissance will enter its crucial demur.) In consequence of the razing of the Tower, human beings must take the long way around. The solipsist sees the journey or travailing as merely circular. "We are all ignorant men, incapable of the least, minor, vital metaphor, content, At last, there, when it turns out to be here." [31] Donne is not so despairing. For men to "comprehend the essence of the thing," no better way offers "than by a definition." The reservation is also an important concession. To the typical intelligence of the seventeenth century, the concession does not suffice.

The asserting of typicality in a discussion of this kind will always draw fire. Whatever matters is amenable to different points of view. Any writer who matters can be quoted against himself. Donne, who identifies language with hard labor, when he ascends the pulpit or watchtower places us in Abraham's bosom from which lucky station we look directly into truth. Only let our hearts be touched by faith, as opposed to the pedantry of being taught by the senses, and we are able to prosecute without further ado "that great search of the discovery of God's essence and the new Jerusalem, which reason durst not attempt." But Donne as we remember him best has little truck with that facile view of perception which is, on my reading, in the main line of seventeenth-century thought. "On a huge hill, cragged and steep, truth stands." The coincidence of names and natures at the beginning of the world is attested by this equivocal writer. He adds ironically that Adam, who is elsewhere so efficient, gave no name to himself. That is because "he understood himself less than he did other creatures." Like Milton, Donne believes that "names are to instruct us and express natures and essences." To hit on the name is, however, shrewd business. Scorn follows for that "enormous pretending wit of our nation and age"—it might be Bacon who is pilloried—for undertaking "to frame such a language, herein exceeding Adam," in which everything is denoted "by the most eminent and virtual property." Milton is more modern: cursory, facile. He agrees that, failing the gift

31. Wallace Stevens, "Crude Foyer."

of extraordinary wisdom, Adam "could not have given names to the whole animal creation with such sudden intelligence." But he sees this peculiar gift as our common inheritance. "Man being formed after the image of God, it followed as a necessary consequence that he should be endued with natural wisdom." [32] Abruptly, the legacy of Nimrod has been cleared.

In this summary resolution we recognize our intellectual beginnings. The position to which we adhere is characteristically and savingly Antinomian, whether or not the antique word is still part of our lexicon. In first and last things this position is not to be distinguished, as extremes confess their identity, from what looks to be the enervating determinism of Calvin. The seventeenth century, an age convicted of human depravity, blinks that depravity when human progress is in the cards. The man who receives his light gratuitously, from what Milton calls "the fountain of light," is exempted from additional labor. He does not win to truth, in writing or doing, by "recollacious" activity. St. Augustine, as often, is prophetic of the new psychology: God inspires the truth into our hearts. [33]

The word is the way to truth, also its repository. In the seventeenth century, the word is honored more than ever before or since. Concurrently, the diminishing of man begins and the subjugating of the word which makes him flesh. The ascendancy of man is celebrated with unparalled magnificence and magnanimity of spirit. And increasingly in this period the word is called in question. Communication is best reserved to yea and nay. The commenders of taciturnity are legion, though not always taciturn, and that is the gist of their message. "He that speaketh many words speaketh either false things or superfluous or both." Though the heart, not the brain, "is the fountain of speech," even speaking from the heart must be abridged. "Whatsoever is more cometh of evil." No man who is falsely accused need fear the end. His own word may prove ineffectual, "yet let him patiently commit his

---

32. *De Doctrina Christiana*, pub. 1825, Bk. I, end of Ch. vii; *Essays in Divinity*, "Of the Name of God"; *Second Anniversary*, ll. 291–92.

33. *City of God*, VI, iii; *Paradise Regained*, IV.289.

cause to God who in time will manifest the truth and bring it to light." Forensics are not to the purpose, for "the speech of truth is simple." Syllogizing and logic are only "a resumption of that which was known before." But not only are they gratuitous. The Puritan insists that preaching must not be conducted "with skill of speaking," for the "efficacy of the holy Spirit doth more clearly appear in a naked simplicity of words than in elegancy and neatness." Already Savonarola is incensed that the clergy should tickle men's ears with talk of Aristotle and Plato, Virgil and Petrarch. Why not cleave to one Book only, which contains the law and spirit of life! The next step is to exclude even the one Book. Milton takes this step in affirming that "the Spirit which is given to us is a more certain guide than Scripture." [34] Milton in his art does not often look hard at particulars.

Political persuasion has nothing to do with the new contempt for cerebral activity and ought not to be tied to the Puritans, who have enough sins at their door. King James and his retainer, Archbishop Bancroft, claim absolute authority for the ecclesiastical Court of High Commission. The King asserts the claim not as he is despotic but as the law is founded on reason, and "he and others had reason as well as the judges" who stand in his road. Sir Edward Coke, rejoining, distinguishes between the natural reason which is every man's possession and "the artificial reason and judgment of law, which requires long study and experience before a man can attain to the cognizance of it." King James, who is oblivious of the distinction, has the best of the argument, though it is not settled in his lifetime. Cromwell settles the argument.

Preoccupation with artificial reason and judgment, as against our endemic capacity, characterizes the more prosaic intelligence of the past. That is because the remoter past still sees itself as partly disfranchised. Donne in his essay on suicide makes the interesting coupling: "scholastic and artificial men." He likens the artificer to a chemist—the analogy is just right—who proposes to find the truth by resort to "school alembics, which are exquisite and vi-

34. Conflating William Perkins, *Direction for the Government of the Tongue*, 1615, pp. 2, 59–60, 84, 88; Agrippa, *Vanitie of Artes*, Blv; Webster, *Academiarum*, Ch. IV; William Ames, *The Marrow of Sacred Divinity*, 1642, pp. 180–82; *De Doctrina Christiana*, Ch. XXX.

olent distinctions." Anyway, the distinctions are exquisite. Now distinctions are felt as superfluous. Experience is replicative, study is dispensable. Already Reuchlin has exalted comprehension by faith alone. *Sola fide!* Faith frees us from the fear of Tartarus and the avenging furies. As time flies, it is not so much later that Jeremy Bentham is saying easily: "every man his own lawyer." This attractive dictum is an illegitimate but predictable extension of the Protestant dictum: "every man his own priest." Milton is his own priest and the god of his idolatry is the sufficiency of man. Sometimes belief in this sufficiency falters, even in the great Pelagian. As he reflects on the difficulty of inculcating the discipline of Presbyters and Deacons in the time allotted to him, Milton is a little dashed. Then, taking heart, he formulates a surprising proposition. Since the question in hand has got to be known "by every meaner capacity, and contains in it the explication of many admirable and heavenly privileges reached out to us by the Gospel, I conclude the task must be easy." [35]

The task is easy because it is already accomplished by virtue of the universal light which irradiates even the meanest capacity. The language of Adam which Juan Vives and company propose to retrieve from the Biblical past is "most perfect of all" as, attaching "names to things," it makes "clear the natures" of the objects described. Vives does not tell us how the just equivalence is forged. The metaphysical character of the proposition is apparent. The beauty of the Decalogue, like that of the epigram in the hands of a master like Juvenal or Ben Jonson, is in its summariness. In the Renaissance, the objections of the terminist philosopher are answered but by going beyond them to hypothesize a world he cannot assail as he cannot perceive its existence. The empirical investigations of the linguist and the new philosopher, brought to a halt, are driven back ineluctably on subjective idealism in order to take us out of chaos. Comenius, perceiving that "the multitude, the variety, the confusion of languages" is "a very powerful obstacle" between him and his homogeneous plain, obliterates the obstacle at a Word. Essentially he decrees his "Pansophic language, the univer-

35. *The Reason of Church Government*, Alv.

sal carrier of light." As it is "absolutely rational," it must be easily apprehensible. This supposititious reasoning informs the speculations—more precisely, the imprecations—of a contriver of the universal character like Cave Beck, a schoolmaster and clergyman of the seventeenth century. His common writing, "by which all the nations in the world may understand one another's conceptions," does not turn on the master's expertise but on the anterior knowledge of the pupil: and therefore "may be attained in two hours' space." [36] This dispatch makes us think of Giordano Bruno, whose fatal trouble begins as he boasts of his ability to teach the practice of "artificial memory" in one hour. In the event, his sluggish patron is disappointed and Bruno is handed over to the Church.

Only a few years after the martyrdom of Bruno, Webster is promoting what he calls the symbolic and cryptographic method of study as it is a "compendious way." He can dispense with "the tedious way of rule or grammar" because, as he tells us in a witty and suggestive phrase, the language of nature "is not acquisitive but dative." His scientism, like that of his clairvoyant and deracinating contemporaries, is rooted in an "affectation to simple and naked truth." He finds his counterpart in the scientifically benighted Samuel Howe, the preaching cobbler, who grasps the whole truth in an instant. Each is looking for a "new-light shorter cut" or some new key to "unlock nature's cabinet." The Renaissance schoolmaster proffers this key as he composes a manual in the style of Comenius in which the vulgar tongue is complemented by the universal language. "A child of ten years old," glancing from one to the other and "learning five sentences a day, may in four months' space be perfect in the whole Character." Joseph Priestley, the father of modern chemistry, who, as his mind is bent on loftier considerations, "never would acknowledge his daughter" (Cuvier), thinks that one month is sufficient. Leibniz, writing to his ducal patron of Hanover, argues that an alphabet of human thought can be acquired in a matter of weeks.[37] What has happened to lethargic or concupiscent man?

36. *The Universal Character,* 1657; *The Way of Light;* Vives, *De tradendis,* iii, i.

37. Letter of ?1679; Priestley, *Theory of Language,* 1762, pp. 5–8, 297–301; Beck, *Universal Character;* Thomas Hall, ridiculing Howe and Webster, *Histrio-mastix,* 1694, 06v; *Academiarum,* Epistle Dedicatory and Ch. ix.

Morbid talk of concupiscence is associated customarily with the narrow sectarian. But observe that this talk comes most readily from the preacher who is also an autodidact and rejoices in the inner light. Whether or not the contradiction is borne home to him, he abides it. The scholar, like the new Protestant, stands on his own two feet. Never mind who supports him. What he has to know is an ebullition. This revolutionary premise is apparent in the conventional and seductive analogy to applied science. In mechanical operations, engines which move of themselves—for example, clocks, levers, mills, and screws—confer most profit on mankind as they save time, labor, and money. So it is, says Henry Edmundson, with books of instruction. The most precious books are "easy and pleasant" to read, sequentially they are "clear and certain" in communicating knowledge, last—this is their principal value—they possess an almost magical power "whereby we may be made autodidact." The positing of this value defines the hope and spirit of the age. The Man of the Book is not simply learned but himself the inscription of learning. The plethora of letters, the many tracings of the cortex excite a pious frenzy in the truth-telling man, like John Dury, a Scotch disciple of Comenius, who intends "the ripping up of the hidden secrets of nature" and an abridging of the truths of Holy Writ. What Dury wants is "the marrow of the Bible, containing briefly the substance of that which is to be believed, done, and hoped for." [38] The word and the beguiling idea behind it are powerfully attractive to the mind and temper of the seventeenth century, which makes a fetish of titles like *Gospel Marrow* (1640) and the *Marrow of Ecclesiastical History* (1650)—or *Alchemy* (1654–55) or *Modern Divinity* (1646) or *Chemical Physic* (1669). To arrive at the marrow or essence of things not much address is required, as witness Sprat's belief that langugage ("a close, naked, natural way of speaking") unveils it; and that of the Puritan that the name of a man, anagrammatized, communicates his essential qualities; and that of the Quaker that to intone Scripture like an incantation without heed to the niceties of grammar is the surest way of getting to the truth of Christian theology.

Discourse, as it approximates the naked enunciation of Adam,

---

38. Dury in letter to Sir Cheney Culpepper, January 6, 1642; *Lingua Linguarum*, a2-v.

speaks to the comprehensive truth. In the seventeenth century this assumption becomes a commonplace. By virtue of the knowledge "insculpt" within him—inferentially within all of us—Adam is able to designate the animals and to give a name to Eve "suiting her original," a name "exactly conformable and configurate to the Idea in his mind." Webster laments the "pure language of nature" which Adam spoke and understood and which, in the vagaries of things, was "miserably lost and defaced." But grief is dissipated quickly in these men of good hope. The business of the seventeenth century is to effect "the recovery and restoration of the catholic language in which lies hid all the rich treasury of nature's admirable and excellent secrets." The enduring prestige of Latin suggests to lexicographers like Wilkins that it is the key to the treasure house. But the key fails to turn in the lock. Though Latin is more precise than other tongues, it does not always associate the specific term to the genre. Its words are "exceeding equivocal." There is "scarce one amongst them which hath not diverse significations." [39] The medieval glossarians, if we have the patience to read them, illustrate the validity of this critique. Servius discovers latencies in the *Aeneid* of which Virgil was certainly innocent. But the language he tortures makes love to its employment. Of course that is its glory. The ideogram, as elaborated by the Chinese, is in this sense Virgilian or "artistic."

Perhaps, Wilkins thinks, a more "rational" form of notation waits on the investigating of Hebrew. Rational means wraithlike. Hebrew is the language of angels, who have passed beyond speech. From mind to mind, thought moves silently. We remember the men of Shinar. Wilkins, like Pico della Mirandola before him, is attracted to Hebrew—initially, as to a false scent—because it has the fewest radicals. Whole sentences in this "compendium"—quoting Dalgarno, the tight-fisted Scot—are contracted to single words. The words themselves are forged in Heaven by the positions of the stars. The twenty-two letters of which they are compounded are not conventional or arbitrary but denote the parts of the universe and so possess, as we shift them in various combi-

39. *Real Character*, pp. 13, 385; *Academiarum*, Ch. III; Sprat, *History*, p. 113.

nations, uncanny authority. They are "the basis of the world and of all the creatures which exist and are named by them." But this is hearsay, maybe true, maybe not. Wilkins—unlike Agrippa, on whose *Occult Philosophy* I am relying in this discussion—has not come down from the mountain. He is not in his own view a vaticinal man. The universal character he invents or recovers is at a remove from cabalistic speculation. It does not signify words endowed with arcane properties and comprehensible only to the hermetic philosopher. It signifies things and is comprehensible to men of any language or station. Wilkins knows how this character may be made effable. I am using his vocabulary as I can. The naturalist John Ray, who collaborates with him by engaging to provide a classification of animals and plants, is not so sure. Neither is the chemist Robert Boyle, who wonders if the labor-saving language will prove like that subtle instrument much commended in his time for resolving all the mysteries of arithmetic. "I found it," Boyle says, "much more difficult to learn the uses of the instrument than the rules of the art." [40]

But the reservations which the scientist sometimes expresses are more practical than philosophical. Ray undertakes to translate Wilkins' *Essay* into Latin. Boyle's response to the *Common Writing* sent him by the Prussian emigré Samuel Hartlib is tinged with skepticism but pervaded with sympathy. He is like Milton in the tract on education who sneers at the projections of "modern Januas and Didactics" and dedicates the work to Hartlib, who is a prince of didactical projectors. The paradox in which he involves us is like that in which the preacher, despising our dross and exulting in it, involves us. Leibniz, annotating the Cartesian program for a universal language, communicated in a letter to the Abbé Mersenne, perceives that a meaningful lexicon cannot be worked up arbitrarily. If the characters are really to represent fundamental relations, a logical analysis of the contents of thought must come first. Nonetheless he insists that the analysis of ideas and the making of the *characteristica realis* can proceed simultaneously. "Although

40. Letter to Hartlib, April 8, 1647; Dalgarno, "Oratio Dominica," concluding *Lexicon Grammatico-Philosophicum* (*Works*, 1834).

this language depends on the true philosophy, it does not depend
on its perfection." Like most of us, he asserts for true what he
wants to be true. Already the new language is presented as like a
"new telescope" exploring the "inner nature of things, or else guid-
ing our reasonings as surely as an "Ariadne's thread." The optimism Descartes evinces is like this, cautious in the first place, finally irrepressible, therefore human. Descartes is skeptical as he
looks with his entrepreneurial eye at the task of formulating a
calculus in which the whole inventory of knowledge, refined to intellectual concepts, is to be digested in a fixed number of signs.
The ultimate equation, "taking each word for the true definition of
the thing," is not so easily compassed as the reformers imagine. Father Mersenne, who is the first to try for a universal language of
the Cartesian type, had better not be intemperately hopeful. But
Descartes does not break faith with his own prepossessions. Mersenne is instructed that the universal language is possible, also that
it will allow the rudest intelligence to judge of the verity of things.
Here the Brittany peasant makes his entrance as culture hero. In
deciding to express himself in the language of the people, Descartes appeals to human nature as he understands it. French is
preferred to Latin, the language of scholars, "because I hope that
those who make use of their own pure and natural reason will be
better judges of my opinions than those who believe only in ancient texts." [41] Descartes, who reins in the hopeful Mersenne, is
not hoping but affirming.

This simplistic division is affirmed also by the primitive
Church. St. Ambrose, the first of the Latin Fathers to be raised as
a Christian, has no brief for the practitioner of "dialectical disputation." Tertullian is willing to listen to the testimony of the soul "in
its natural state, plain, uncultivated, and simple." He closes his
ears against the educated soul as it belches merely academic wisdom. The optimism which enjoins a lack of learning is itself enjoined by a defensive hostility to the more lettered past against
which the Church is contending. But that is only part of the story.

41. Letter of November 20, 1629: (CXI in *Lettres*, 1657, I, 610–18; conclusion of *Discourse on
Method*, 1637. Couturat, *Opuscules*, p. 27, gives the comments added by Leibniz to his copy
of Descartes' letter to Mersenne.

The age which believes in the eschatine believes coincidentally in the ready and easy way. St. Benedict of Nursia, says his biographer Gregory the Great, grows "wise where he was not taught." Gregory is fortunate as the pentecostal dove is always whispering in his ear. On this side he prefigures Descartes. As optimism wanes, the *cognoscenti* get a better reception. As it waxes, learned men begin once more to affect a belief in *docta ignorantia*. King James supposes that nature is an open book unless willfully occluded, so he directs a moderately complicated treatise on prosody not to learned men but to those he calls "the docile bairns of knowledge." Innate perspicacity makes them receptive. "Who is going to decide what the truth is?" Bruno answers: "That is the prerogative of every careful and wideawake intelligence." This God-given prerogative is rendered less efficient by a needless resort to Latin as the universal medium of consequential discourse. Dante, who writes the *Convivio* in Italian, is apologetic. He sees his choice of the vernacular as a substantial blemish. The apology is equivocal and is elsewhere withdrawn. In the title *De Vulgari Eloquentia*, praise for the vernacular is implicit. Time passes, and the Tudor humanist Roger Ascham is arguing explicitly that the vernacular is no bar for wise speaking. Descartes, a little later, is unconcerned to palliate. "Good sense is of all things in the world the most evenly distributed among men." [42]

On this saying a spurious democracy, not political but intellectual, is erected. Latin is the privilege of the few and therefore enfetters good sense. So does the aureate terminology depending on it. But so does any utterance or representation of things not immediately graspable by the docile bairns of knowledge. That is why the Christian homilist, who is writing to the viscera, whatever he tells us, has labored deliberately to address the "understanding of the simple and ignorant rather than by poetical strains to please the ear and the eye of the curious learned readers." It is why Sprat and his followers are so intent on "bringing all things as near the mathematical plainness as they can" and why they prefer "the lan-

42. Descartes beginning the *Discourse;* Ascham, *The Schoolmaster,* 1570; Bruno, *De l'infinito;* King James, *Ane Schort Treatise,* 1584.

guage of artisans, countrymen, and merchants before that of wits or scholars." The perfect vision which is the birthright of the simple and ignorant corresponds to the facile truth hypothesized by Father Tommaso Campanella, "a single natural law imprinted in the heart of all men which no diversity can efface." To this monolithic law or "deep structure" all discourse, however tortured, will necessarily refer. In the words of the Silesian educational theorist Cyprian Kinner, "all natural things do like a tree concur and meet in the root and partake all of the same sap." They differ from each other only as boughs which spread in different directions. To Kinner, as to his master Comenius, it is clear that the various things overspreading the creation "were all at first and may yet be made by one general idea." [43]

The beginning of wisdom is the disputing of wisdom on its considering or "recollacious" side—in favor of an act of will. The seventeenth century asserts our native capacity or else it asserts, what is practically the same thing, that we are enabled by fiat. Its great men—Dryden, Bunyan, Newton, the Levellers and Diggers, George Herbert and his "atheistical" brother who reduces all religions to a featureless Deism founded on the instantaneous intuiting of truth—a disparate crew, certainly, are nonetheless to be taken together as we look back at them now. How they differ is obvious. What they have in common is their persuasion of grace abounding. The men of Shinar have only to possess their souls in patience.

43. *Summary Delineation . . . concerning Education*, 1648, B4v; Sprat, *History*, p. 113. The homilist is Simon Wastel, *A True Christians Daily Delight*, 1623.

CHAPTER TWO

The Word Made Flesh

IN his "School of Athens" in the Vatican Museum, Raphael imagines Plato pointing with a finger to the sky of thought. In terms of composition, the side of the fresco in which Plato dominates emphasizes verticality. Aristotle, with whom Plato is conversing, holds a book in one hand above the head of Heraclitus in the left foreground. Irresistibly the eye is drawn down. The other hand is extended and open, makes a horizontal plane and so a countervailing gesture. The Aristotle of the Stanze is receptive to the world and comes to conclusions as he explores it. In the seventeenth century, the open hand is rejected. We do not need it any more or it does not suffice us. Quoting St. Gregory Nazianzen: "For why should they keep a bodily fast who are cleansed by the Word?" [1]

Concurrent with the new Antinomianism is the rise of deterministic science, the growth of a self-abasing religion (Calvinism, mysticism), and a quietistic politics (divine right, then sequentially government by major-generals). These phenomena testify in similar ways to the extinguishing of capacity in the individual will. "The noises of Parliament are no longer in season" (Colbert). But the acceptance of determinism does not make for order. On the one hand it makes for supineness, on the other for an exaggerated willfulness which has no point as it can have no issue. If we are enfranchised by grace, we are freed from obeying the law. If events are predestined, it is idle for us to oppose them. Protestant nonresistance,

---

1. Following John 25:3 in "Fourth Theological Oration" (late 4th century), *Nicene and Post-Nicene Fathers*, Series 2, Vol. VII, p. 313.

which is the logical entail of predestination, begets the abolutism of the Stuarts. But in the last resort absolutism is anarchy: the rule of caprice. The new formulation reads: *L'état c'est moi*. Compare for the difference the judgment of the sixteenth-century ecclesiastic: "That city is at the pit's brink wherein the magistrate ruleth the laws and not the laws the magistrate." [2] Already Mazarin and Richelieu, only a hundred years later, are living in another universe. Bacon, who rationalizes physical phenomena, is also a prophet of the sovereign or despotic state which emerges from the Thirty Years War; so is Hobbes, the philosopher of mechanism.

The Protestant and the post-Tridentine Catholic, like the physical scientist, suppose the presence of a power in things that cannot be gainsaid. But this power is divested of particular lineaments, as by the mystic who declines to call it by name, or by the Calvinist to whom it is inscrutable. "Because God is in all things He has no proper name." That is Nicholas of Cusa. [3] "Indeed," says Faithful in the *Pilgrim's Progress*, "to know is a thing that pleaseth talkers and boasters, but to do is that which pleaseth God." The indigenous truth is suppressed. The corollary denies the torturing of discourse. To the natural philosopher authority is a paradigm of capital-letter abstractions, to the political philosopher it is a monolith like that stupendous figure which towers over the kingdom on the title page of the first edition of *Leviathan* (1651). Perhaps the King or the God is loved by His people but they do not know Him in palpable ways. Neither God nor King is expected to act in conformity to laws which ordinary mortals can interpret. In this way it happens that the seventeenth century, which establishes the rule of order in the physical universe, initiates in mundane business a terrible irrationality.

In the pamphleteering attack (1670–71) on the Royal Society mounted by the Greek scholar and physician Henry Stubbe, the shrewdest hit is at the latitudinarianism of Glanvill's *Plus Ultra*

---

2. John Aylmer in 1559.

3. *Of Learned Ignorance*, completed 1440, Bk. I, Ch. xxiv. Cusa is following Hermes Trismegistus.

(1668), partly a diatribe, partly a philosophical tractate, and written to commend the achievement of the new philosophers and to answer the question: "What have they done?" A piece of the answer—implicitly, Sprat allows it in his *History*—is that science effaces religious distinctions and makes them gratuitous. Stubbe is right in contending that as the barriers go down between one creed and another, the pretension of any single creed to primacy, at last to importance, will be denied. Sprat's irenicism follows. It is the counterpart, in religion, of Bacon's docility before the throne.

Docility is logical as forthputting activity is unnecessary, possibly wayward. Below the rush of phenomena is the comprehensive form. To employ a more ardent vocabulary: "The eternal God is thy refuge, and underneath are the everlasting arms" (Deuteronomy 33:27). The assumption of underlying law is as critical to the scientific renascence as to the purposed revolution in linguistics. Emerson, who is not called Transcendental for nothing, makes clear why that is so. The perception of identity with which he is favored "unites all things and explains one by another and insures that the most rare or strange is equally facile as the most common." On this perception equanimity depends and optimism follows. "But if the mind live only in particulars and see only differences (wanting the power to see the whole—all in each), then the world addresses to this mind a question it cannot answer, and each new fact tears it in pieces, and it is vanquished by the distracting variety." [4] The lynx-eyed man escapes distraction as he sees comprehensively. Chaos is

> The idle dayseye, the laborious wheel,
> The osprey's tours, the pointblank matin sun.

To resolve the multiplicity of forms and events, the circle is deduced:

> a shape of spare appeal,
> Cryptic and clean, and endlessly spinning unspun.

4. Emerson in his Notebooks, 1859, on "The Sphinx."

But the circle is not cryptic, unless to the skeptical poet (presented here by Richard Wilbur). It is divested of mystery as it remains forever the same.

To one notation analogous things are assimilated. We call them analogous. So all knowledge can be conveyed *more geometrico*. The proposition is advanced by Christian Wolf, the eighteenth-century mathematician and biographer of Leibniz. It is more willful than true, and indispensable to the thought and labor of the modern age. Reformation is contingent on narrowing the field in the interest of factitious form. Comenius organizes his *Way of Light* as a cluster of axioms and theorems. Phenomenal fact begins to come clear. The elder Mill is imitated, who sees himself destined to make "the human mind as plain as the road from Charing Cross to St. Paul's." It is the same Mill who is eager that "experience should be sacrificed to speculation." Wilkins accommodates under forty heads all intellectual concepts. The Scotch pasigraphist George Dalgarno breaks them down to seventeen, the schoolmaster Cave Beck to just three. Dalgarno is a "pasigraphist" in that his linguistic characters represent not words but ideas. He is on the right track, though he and we are unable to see it. A learned crank offers Parliament "a new and wonderful invention" for reducing to one index all the writers of merit in a given language. Comenius, who sends the tidings back to Poland, is ecstatic. "In this way it should be possible readily to ascertain and discover the opinions of divers authors on any specific point of interest." The opinions are isolated, the authors go unread. Leibniz to the same purpose promotes an encyclopedic *Index auctorum*. The informing psychology is struck off in a phrase by the poet Phineas Fletcher. We are not integers but man in the mass. Psychology itself is science or generalizing and

> like an index briefly should impart
> The sum of all.[5]

---

5. *The Purple Island,* Canto i, stanza 43; Comenius in letter of 8/18 October 1641; Mill, *Analysis of the Phenomena of the Human Mind,* 1829; Wolf, *Psychologia,* 1732, pp. 216–17.

As language is attenuated to the bare bones, extreme compression becomes possible.

> We now may Homer's *Iliads* confine,
> Not in a nutshell, but a point or line.
> (Richard West, 1694)

The construction is, however, derivative. In unexpected ways, Nature and Homer are the same. All that Nature does, in the opinion of Leonardo, is achieved "per la via brevissima." The Renaissance, as it strives to imitate Nature, takes the shortest way with the wisdom of the ages. Circumstantiality is narrowed to the saws and sayings of the *florilegia*. In the lives of the philosophers and poets which are the staple material of these popular collections, the protagonists themselves take a back seat. The real man is important only as a *point d'appui*. The medieval logician Walter Burley, the *bête noir* of William of Ockham, is a favorite contributor. Burley extracts homilies from his rifling of the past. Biography does not detain him, He reads experience under the aspect of a crapulous realism.

Material things forfeit their status, then the words which pretend to denote them. The function of words is not to distinguish particulars—that is Donne, asserting the obsolescent point of view—but to transcend particulars. Whatever is not transcendent goes to the dustbin. "In our definitions we meddle not with the inconstant but keep entirely to the constant." Individuals, says Christian Wolf, "are no objects of science." A scientific study of linguistics or natural phenomena is practicable only as it endorses this proposition. So far, that is what everyone knows. The codicil is something new as it withholds integrity from the crude stuff on which the study is supposed to depend. "Every cold empiric"— Dr. Johnson gives his character in the *Preface to Shakespeare*— "when his heart is expanded by a successful experiment, swells into a theorist." The empiric, says Johnson's contemporary, the scholar-politician James Harris, neglects "the sublimer parts of science, the studies of mind, intellection, and intelligent principles." He acts "as if the criterion of all truths were an alembic or an air-pump" and judges "what cannot be proved by experiment . . . no better than mere hypothesis." Harris, who typifies the linguistic and scientific abstractor, "would not be understood . . . to undervalue experiment." Only he would add that "the man who acts from experience alone, though he act ever so well, is but an empiric or quack." Implicit in the definition is the praise Harris confers on arithmetic and geometry, artistic studies as they do not rest on experience. When experience is sacrificed to speculation, "the empiric quits his name for the more honorable one of artist." [6]

A few weeks before his death, Einstein is asserting that everything which emanated from the great mind of Lorentz, the scientist he admired above all others, "was as clear and beautiful as a good work of art." Einstein himself is supremely the artificer, whose most important endowment he describes as "the gift of fantasy." When finally he breaks his long allegiance to the empiricism of Ernst Mach it is because, for Mach, science is no more than the sum total of the relationships which exist between the data of experience. But that, Einstein thinks, is a bad point of view. "What Mach created was a catalogue and not a system. To the extent that Mach was a good mechanic he was a deplorable philosopher." Science is not fact grubbing nor a "fetish of the concrete intelligence." The American poet Laura Riding, who wants us to think so, is propagating a vulgar error. Art is more prosaic than science "since the greater part of sciences deals only with ideal beings." The bizarre perception of Rudolf Raspe, the creator of Baron Munchausen, has in it this scintilla of truth, that the construction or *fictio* which the scientist sponsors depends at last on imagination. That is partly the ground of its enormous appeal. To a far greater extent than poetry, it has the power "of pleasing our fancy." [7]

When Rousseau undertakes his imperial (scientific) survey of world history, he begins with the words: "Commençons par écarter les faits!" We are at a beginning only as we brush the facts aside. Rousseau is not impervious to facts. But they bore him. Bernard

6. Harris, *Hermes*, 1765, pp. 351–52; Wolf, *Logic*, 1770, pp. 46, lxxi; Donne, *Essays in Divinity*, p. 23.

7. Raspe, *A Critical Essay on Oil Painting*, 1781; R. W. Clark, *Einstein*, pp. 622, 288, 87.

Palissy, the sixteenth-century potter of Périgord, employs the apt phrase, "Science with the teeth," to characterize his faithful observations of the physical world. But Palissy, who really does set himself to canvass topography, geology, natural history, is applauded in his own time only as a sport. He is not a modern man but atavistic. Descartes suggests what it means to be modern in his critique of Galileo, who has "merely looked for the causes of certain particular facts, building thereby without any foundation." [8]

The search for the "groundwork or foundation" haunts the linguistic reformer (unless he thinks he has discovered it) in his effort to frame "a new perfect language and a universal or common writing." I am quoting Francis Lodwick, a Dutch merchant living in London and a fellow of the Royal Society. In the seventeenth century the political and legal theorist appeals to the foundation: Grotius, not least in his speculations on religion, Edmond Wingate in his treatise on the common law. "The Generals must go before and the Specials must follow after." The law student who takes this prescript to heart will be gratified "in noting the same key to open so many locks." (Already Pico has detected in the Cabala the one key to the mysteries.) Consult, but only summarily, the bewildering number of pleas; hold fast to the "one ruling axiom" that resolves them. [9] Copernicus can assimilate the unthinkable, "that the distance of the earth from the sun, though appreciable in comparison to the orbits of the other planets, is as nothing when compared to the sphere of the fixed stars." It is easier—the word he uses—to concede an infinite universe "than to let the mind be distracted by an almost endless multitude of circles, which those are obliged to do who detain the earth in the center of the world." Modern man shies at the obligation. The proliferating of epicycles or adjustments offends his esthetic sense. Hence the unified Field Theory with which Einstein seems literally entranced. This is not to suggest that we return to a geocentric cosmology or remove Copernicus and Einstein from the Kremlin Wall, only that we open our-

8. Œuvres de Descartes, 1898, ii, 380; Palissy, Admirable Discourses, 1580; Rousseau, Discourse on Inequality, 1755.

9. Wingate, Maxims of Reason, 1658, pp. 261, A4-v; Grotius, De Veritate Religiones, 1627; Lodwick, Essay towards an Universal Alphabet, 1686.

selves, as once before, to the idea of an endless multitude of circles.

Efficiency is at stake, also a more frugal perception of the nature of truth, in the reconciling of diverse functions or the hoarding of infinite riches in a little room. But to look deeper is to be persuaded that compulsiveness plays its part in the insistence on boiling down. Unaccommodated man is man divested of personality: whitened or purged. The view from the watchtower makes for this divesting, so does microscopic analysis. That is Gulliver's discovery. It is anticipated by the German Jesuit Athanasius Kircher, who publishes an account of the tiny organisms which infest the blood of the plague-stricken man (1671), and undertakes concurrently to reduce to statistics the perplexing variety of the world of brute fact. In the tables and definitions of the *Ars Magna Sciendi* (1669), which offers an alphabet of esoteric lore, phenomenal knowledge is subdued. Bruno, dedicating the *Expulsion of the Triumphant Beast* to Sir Philip Sidney, a compatible spirit, plumes himself on having "numbered and arranged [the] seeds of his moral philosophy." The end is not truth to nature but the assuaging of a fierce personal need. Mersenne, the Minorite father and the author of a universal geometry (1644), resolves the corpus of learning to an "Opus Theologis, Philosophis, Medicis, Jurisconsultis, Mathematicis, Musicis verò, & Catoptritis" (1623). I read the last item in the series as emblematic. The precious stones, signified by the curious word out of Pliny, are docketed and assigned their proper place as in a rock museum or jeweller's tray. Hereafter these stones—like the stuff of theology, medicine, law, and music—are tractable.

The Renaissance in its passion for encyclopedic representation is not embracing the world. It is hammering the world. Its violent order is a great disorder. Mersenne's *Quaestiones in Genesim* (1623) endeavors to explicate various cruces in Holy Writ, it impugns the errors of the atheist and deist, it vindicates the Vulgate text from the calumnies of heretics, and like the work of Paracelsus it is involved at the same time with cabalistic dogma. But the governing principle is to fine down. Ramus illustrates this principle in his commentary on Christianity (1577), which looks like an antique treatise dealing with the seven liberal arts but is really a drastic narrowing of what it treats. That is true of the great bulk of those Renaissance books which pretend in their titles to a representation that is *totius* or *universalis*. The Renaissance writer prepares a digest, his predecessor makes a speculum mundi: Ordericus Vitalis, Walafrid Strabo, Durandus, Honorius of Autun. John Ray, in his cataloguing, discriminates; Vincent of Beauvais, who is called *librorum helluo*, devours at random. To Rabanus Maurus, in his *Allegory on Holy Scripture*, everything means everything. One example only: the word *cadaver* signifies Christ, but also—as Rabanus pursues it from one context to another—the man lapsed in sin, the sin itself, the devil, our prayers, and the pains of damnation. This ninth-century Father does not help us transcend the world but negotiates our surrender to it.

In Kircher's "Paradigma ex Jure Canonico, Theologia positiva & morali," the more expeditious way of the Renaissance encapsulators is suggested. Paradigm is the operative word. It describes the Baconian enterprise, summed up in the *Advancement of Learning*, also the achievement of the Swiss naturalist Conrad Gesner. As he wishes to elucidate the ghostly paradigm of things, Gesner proposes to render the Lord's Prayer in twenty-two different tongues (1555). It is a linguistic version of the Tree of Jesse, except that the common root is still to seek. Boiling down is Gesner's métier. He produces an edition of Martial's epigrams (1544) and at the other end of the spectrum a *Bibliotheca Universalis* (1545). The underlying strategy is the same. Gesner's manual of medicine and chemistry declares it. This work, in which the author undertakes to divulge all the "secrets" appurtenant to his craft, is applauded by its English editor as an excellent labor of "distillation." [10] It is as if one were reading in a phylactery where the deepest thoughts and "requirements" of the age are written down. Gregorius Reisch, making a gathering of the arts and sciences, likens his work to a compacted stone "richer than all his tribe." The title is *Margarita Philosophica*. By fiat the single pearl contains within its narrow verge "Totius Philosophiae Rationalis Naturalis & Moralis." Ges-

10. Preface to *New and Old Physicke*, 1599.

ner, a few decades later, seems more apprehensible or modern. Scientific botany originates with him, he is prospectively the author of a natural history of the world. But the world is a sponge and the problem is to squeeze or express it. Expressing means abstaining, as when we speak of the Expressionist Theatre of the twentieth century which dispenses with flesh and blood. Einstein's interest in science, as he confesses to Solovine, is restricted to the study of principles.

Beginning in the middle of the sixteenth century, Ramus sets out to methodize everything under the sun. The drift is to quantification. Caesar's writings boil down to a science of war and ethics. The *Bucolics* and *Georgics*, when the assayer is done with them, are reduced to a science of physics. Geometry becomes the art of measuring well (*ars bene metiendi*). Logic is resolved to suavity. "What is Dialectica?" Ramus inquires, and answers: it "is the art of disputing well and in that sense is called logic." The more ample (elusive) character of the oldfashioned logic is implied by Sir Thomas More, who girds at the medieval dialectician for his scrupulous distinctions between "Leo animali est fortior" and "Leo est fortior animali." This dismal hilarity associates More with his adversary Tyndale to whom the author of the *Utopia* is an artificer of "painted" fiction, therefore not so different from the niggling logicians at whom he is poking fun. "One holdeth this, another that. One is a real, another a nominal. What wonderful dreams have they of their predicatements, universals, second intentions, quiddities and relatives." [11] But Ramus in his obsession with the Least Common Denominator, the greatest fiction of all, is the dreamer. As he must do what he dreams, he brings much trouble to the world.

Ramus is the sixteenth-century Bentham. His vade mecum, as with the new philosophers of the seventeenth century, is application. It functions to obliterate the visible world. "Method is the parent of intelligence, the mistress of memory." It might be Sidney, the faithful acolyte, admonishing us to set down in a "table of

---

11. Tyndale, *Obedyence of a Chrysten man*, ?1536, C 3v-4; More, mocking Peter of Spain's *Parva Logicalia*, in a letter to his friend Martin Dorp; Ramus, *Dialectica*, 1632, B2.

remembrance" each pregnant passage we encounter in our reading. "When you read any such thing, straight bring it to his head,
not only of what art but, by your logical subdivisions, to the next
member and parcel of the art." Keep a table, or make a storehouse
of inviolate bins, "as either military, or more specifically defensive
military, or more particularly defensive by fortification, and so lay
it up." In the resort to one's tables from which all trivial fond
record is wiped away, the psychology of Polonius is anticipated:

> And these few precepts in thy memory
> Look thou charàcter.

Hopefully, the drums that beat to dissolution are muffled. Some
monstrous burden is assumed in this intense concern to bring what
matters "to his head." It is one way to coerce experience. The
other way asserts that experience is a lie. John Willis, who tutors
his readers in the art of memory, thinks that the great imperative,
before which pleasure is negligible, is numbering and arranging
the seeds. As venery distracts the book of the brain, the use of
"Venus" is forbidden if we like it too much or propose to enjoy it
on a full stomach or when sleep does not follow, "for it is requisite
that the loosened members of the body be refreshed." Too much
hair on the head is disagreeable as among the "things that debili-
tate memory." [12] Nothing escapes the remorseless eye of the classifier.

    I think we see why "Aristotle" is cast as the great antagonist to
the modern age. As his temper is unremittingly catholic, he distracts us with impertinent matter. Campanella's advice to Galileo
goes unheeded: "Leave for heaven's sake all other business and
think only of this one." To the encyclopedic man, who is to be distinguished from the winnowers and sifters, nothing is alien that
is mundane. Like Raban the Moor he puts questions that are endlessly fecund—but not of answers. Aristotelian logic agitates the
truth, and that is why Ramus rejects it as "a mere art of disputa-

---

12. Willis, "A Treatise of cherishing Natural Memory," 1621, L1 (annexed to first English
edn. of *Mnemonica*—the Art of Memory—1618); Sidney, letter of 1580 (Feuillerat, XLII).

tion" and seeks to replace it with a logic "on natural foundations" (1543). The adjective is of course contentious. Natural means mutable. Ramus has something else in mind. He puts us off in suggesting that Aristotle "closed the door of dialectic, which was never after opened until our day." [13] The peripatetic philosopher throws open the door, also the windows. Discrimination goes out the windows. The genus is felt as insufficiently constraining. The species is intractable and to the front.

To take order with the species, modern science is invented. Mathematics makes up the vanguard. The mathematician quantifies the species, hence, on my reading, the appeal of his discipline to the great humanist collectors of the fifteenth century like Bessarion and Duke Frederick of Urbino. Number, says the Tudor mathematician Robert Recorde, is the key to divinity, law, physics, and astronomy. [14] The key resolves these studies, it segregates and fixes them. In the gymnasium founded at Strasbourg (1538) by the humanist Johann Sturm, mathematics occupies the central position. That is because it banishes controversy in favor of "clear and settled significations." Ramus, who is Sturm's premier disciple, explains. "Like heaven," this science gives us power "when wandering blind in darkness, to number all things in the widest light. . . . When shaken, to remain steadfast!" In the Latin edition of Euclid (1545), again in a treatise on the art of arithmetic (1569), Ramus communicates his enduring purpose to fix or petrify the truth. He is the philosopher of petrifaction, and in him the antidiscursive tendencies of humanism are finally triumphant. When Ramus dies in the Massacre of St. Bartholomew's Day his eminence as a geometrician is exceeded only, among his countrymen, by that of François Vieta. His chair of eloquence and philosophy in the University of Paris is replaced by a chair in mathematics, constituted by Ramus himself in his will. Thus the progress of the age, from vermicular questions to the perfect calculus which decides them.

13. Preface to *Dialectique*, 1555 (according to Ong, *Ramus: Method and the Decay of Dialogue*, pp. 47–48). Edn. of 1555 is not in BM; quotation does not occur in two later editions I have looked at.

14. *Whetstone of Witte*, 1557.

The search for the calculus, like the scientific revolution it announces, begins in the thirteenth century at the height of the medieval achievement. It is the wick or snuff that lives within the flame of love. But science in its beginnings is not to be associated with Thomist Aristotelianism, mind speaking to mind and sponsoring a new departure, rather with the emotional and fundamentally anti-intellectual Augustinianism of the Franciscans. St. Francis opposes intellectual pursuits on two grounds. Study, as it requires books and a place in which to read them, interferes with absolute poverty. But study interferes with humility also, for the learned man is respected who should be counted among the dregs. Moorman says, in his *History of the Franciscan Order,* "the ideal friar was to be *idiota et subditus omnibus,*" humbled to all things. But St. Francis, who deprecates learning for love, numbers among his followers Duns Scotus and Alexander of Hales and St. Bonaventura, the Italian philosopher and head of the order of Friars Minor, a man worthy of the steel of Aquinas. In each of these men the intellectual faculty is highly developed. They are, however, true Franciscans, as opposed to true Dominicans like Aquinas, in that they emphasize against the intellect the primacy of will. The world as they interpret it is not a subject for analysis. It is affirmed. In their endeavor to represent natural phenomena, they are likely to rely on mathematical terms. The humility they profess does not mean that they are patient of things.

Duns Scotus, the Torch who throws a light for the scientific future, is devoted to mathematics. So is Robert Grosseteste, the Bishop of Lincoln and first lector to the Franciscan friars at Oxford. Mathematics, he argues, anticipating his pupil Roger Bacon, is the one possible foundation on which to build a philosophy of nature. "Natural phenomena must be explained by geometrical lines, figures, and angles." That is because "Nature acts always in the mathematically shortest and best way possible." The Renaissance, personated by Leonardo, is predicted. Nature is remade in the image of the abstemious man. He decides—quoting Hugh of St. Victor, the author of a general theory of science—that though the derivative streams are many, the fountainhead is one. So he raises the thrilling question: "Why do you follow the windings of the stream? Lay hold upon the source and you have all." [15]

Einstein locates "the key to the understanding of natural phenomena" in "purely mathematical constructions." [16] He has his medieval counterpart in Roger Bacon, for whom number is "the gate and key" to the secrets of nature "which the saints discovered at the beginning of the world." Number is superior to experience because it is not subject to time and change. Gregory of Nyssa identifies beauty with the life of the Supreme or immutable Being. "Every desire ceases with the possession of its object except the desire for Beauty. It is Beauty alone that the insolence of satiety cannot touch." Down the ages, the eloquent statement reverberates. The young Francis Bacon inquires, more than a thousand years later: "Are not the pleasures of the intellect greater than the pleasures of the affections? Is not knowledge a true and only natural pleasure, whereof there is no satiety?" The priority assigned to mathematics in the Augustinian or Platonic psychology is menaced by the rise of Aristotelianism in the second half of the thirteenth century. Aristotle is execrated by the chiliastic philosopher who misreads or mistranslates the text of Holy Writ and so expects the imminent ending of the phenomenal world. But he responds enthusiastically to the simplistic and abstracting language of mathematics. In this he announces his affinity to the new Montanists of the seventeenth century. Descartes, who abolishes the world of phenomena, establishes coincidentally the notion of imaginary roots. The faith to which the new philosopher adheres—like Wilkins or Bedell or Comenius in his *Via Lucis*—is that the final revelation is at hand. A distaste for small beer is the logical consequence.

Aristotle is not indifferent to mathematics and in fact takes more pleasure in that study than Francis Bacon. He is no more convinced than Plato that transubstantiation is truth, nor is he less committed than Plato to the searching out of first principles. The

15. *Didascalion*, 12th century, III, xi.

16. "On the Method of Theoretical Physics," the Herbert Spencer lecture, Oxford, June 10, 1933.

Aristotle who figures in this discussion is partly a metaphor of my creating. Plato needs his antagonist. Jaeger and others have demonstrated conclusively how Aristotle platonizes and is indebted, not less than Plato, to an intuitive vision of reality. Aristotle begins, however, not with the general but with "this thing here." He differs from Plato as from the Platonizers of the Renaissance and later in maintaining that "we should rationally assert only what we see occurring" (De caelo). The legendary character he is made to assume partly mirrors the fact. Pliny adumbrates this character in his account of Alexander the Great, collecting animals and plants while campaigning in Asia that the master may scrutinize real data as a prelude to generalization. In the Metaphysics Aristotle argues that "when length and breadth and depth are taken away, we see nothing left." He is unwilling to accept, what Galileo and Descartes will proclaim in laying the cornerstone of new science, that matter alone is equivalent to substance. That is impossible for substance is identified by "separability and this-ness." Galileo and associates do not really require the keenness of sight which denotes the lynx-eyed Argonaut from whom they take their name. It is only to convince his Aristotelian opponents, says Galileo amusingly, that he resorts to experiment. These myopic opponents are always insisting on the evidence of the senses. But the archetypal pattern is sufficiently obvious, except to the prisoner of distracting particulars. That is why the Lynceans announce as the purpose of the new Academy their resolve "to fight Aristotelianism all the way," and why Webster, like Bacon, desires "that the philosophy of Plato may be brought into examination and practice" and "the rotten and ruinous fabric of Aristotle and Ptolemy rejected and laid aside." [17]

The obloquy that attaches to Aristotle is inherited by Scholastic philosophy. "A Schoolman," says Joseph Glanvill, "is the ghost of the Stagyrite in a body of condensed air, and Thomas but Aristotle sainted." We do not find St. Thomas congenial today and have banished him by and large from our curriculum—the Thomistic philosopher like Gilson who knows his business and loves it is rare—but not because we are irreligious. The Schoolmen are ex-

17. *Academiarum Examen*, pp. 103, 106.

ecrated from the seventeenth century to the present because they are agnostic. Their solutions are not really solutions but distinctions. (Bacon is rejecting them in the *Advancement of Learning*.) Their resort to scruples and cavilling breeds "one question as fast as it solveth another." Like Saul, the son of Kish, of whom the chosen people require an answer, they are forever hiding themselves among the stuff. Their pronouncements are riddling. The untranslatable language to which they are prone—untranslatable because insistently ad hoc—is "ambiguous" or "equivocal" or—citing Webster on the language of the Schools—it is like "that black humour poured forth by the cuttle fish, under which lying hid she escapeth catching." The eye with which they survey experience is intense but not penetrating. Bacon says, giving the devil his due, it "openeth and revealeth all the terrestrial globe." But as it is riveted there "it obscureth and concealeth the stars and celestial globe." It is preoccupied—in the teeth of what we have been taught—not with essence but with the mundane city. Illuminating natural things, "it darkeneth and shutteth up divine." Given his bias, Glanvill's indictment is just. The Scholastic philosopher has muddied the fountain of certainty and platted the head of evangelical truth with a crown of thorns.[18] It is a great phrase, almost worthy of the unflinching commitment it denigrates.

J. V. Cunningham distinguishes precisely the "fault" of Scholasticism, which ought to be attractive to the hunters of archetypes like Bacon and is not. "The commonest and most available source of Neo-Platonic ideas in the sixteenth century was the scholastic doctrine of the Christian God, who is only protected from utter Neo-Platonism by an unceasing vigilance in qualification." This vigilance describes the empirical scientist for whom the physical world is sufficient. Donne on his Platonic side likens him sourly to the builders of the Tower of Babel. They might have considered that

> All this whole solid earth could not allow
> Nor furnish forth materials enow.

18. *Vanity of Dogmatizing*, pp. 151, 166–67; Bacon, *Works* (1859 edn.), VI, 122–23, 96; *Academiarum*, p. 62.

The materials are exiguous and crumble at a touch. The rebuilding of the Tower demands a sturdier foundation. This foundation is strong against the depredations of time and place exactly as it is not palpable. Galileo, who really does see as he looks through the telescope, is anticipated by Copernicus, who does not see at all but hypothesizes. The discoveries of Galileo are corroborative. It is not from the fact-riveted intelligence that "new Towers rise, and old demolished are." [19] The Tower of Babel is demolished in the beginning as it takes support from what we miscall "this whole solid earth." To focus attention on sensory data, as by numbering the streaks of the tulip, is to lose ourselves in the umbrageous world of opinion.

The new philosophers from whom we derive are too avaricious, also too queasy, to accept the proposition that knowledge comes through the senses. Their fabulous ambition is to intuit the mysteries of the universe and inscribe them in the tables of law. Their embodiment is Marlowe's Faustus. The mystics of the fourteenth century are their fuglemen. Hence the language of the Papal Bull in which Meister Eckhart is condemned: "He wanted to know more than was fitting!" Hegel speaks for them toward the end of their ascendancy when, introduced to the writings of Eckhart, he exclaims: "Here we have exactly what we want!"

The anathema pronounced against Eckhart is, however, formulaic. He is derelict not as he wants to know but as the knowledge he covets is perfectly aseptic. Hence his appeal to the denaturing or death-dealing philosopher. To make life into art, where art is the dissolving of intransigent particulars, that is what he wants. Like the blind seer Tiresias in Pavese's story, things affront him like a blow. Beneath the earth is the rock, the bluest sky is the emptiest. The goal before which his inquisitors stand, warning him off, is the abolition of diversity in which the adult life is defined. The summons of the new infantilism, interdicted by the Catholic hierarchy exactly as it is mundane, is to recover the rock, to resume the *tabula rasa* not yet blotted with hateful permutations, "to

19. Donne, *Second Anniversary*, ll. 417–20, 262; Cunningham, " 'Essence' and the 'Phoenix and Turtle,' " p. 268.

destroy all language, to destroy all names, so that again there may
be grace" (Hermann Broch).

Early in the sixteenth century the German mystic Sebastian
Franck redacts the old and spurious Fifth Epistle of Clement, a
fertile source of communist doctrine. That is only a fact and does
not matter any more. What matters is the comment the redacter
adds to the work. The first age is catholic. Then "Nimrod began to
rule, and then whoever could manage it got the better of the other.
And they started dividing the world up." Mine and Thine make
their entrance. "Yet God had made all things common, as today
still we can enjoy air, fire, rain, and sun." The second age is announced as the primal unity gives place to separability and this-
ness. Quoting St. Anselm: "Once man ate the bread of angels,
which now he hungers for, now he eats the bread of sorrow which
once he did not know." The fall of man is accomplished, also beto-
kened, as he puts on the muddy vesture of decay. Like Narcissus,
he loves his physical reflection in the water and mingles fatally with
it. Marsilio Ficino identifies the reflection with Nature. But Nature
is irrational form. The definition summarizes the thought of the
Corpus Hermeticum, which the young Ficino translates in the
1460s at the instance of Cosimo de Medici. Hermes Trismegistus,
the prehistoric mage on whom these apocryphal writings are fathered, is called thrice great "because he was preeminent as the
greatest philosopher, the greatest priest, and the greatest king."
That is what Ficino says. But his importance to the Renaissance
and hence to our context depends on the pernicious supposition
that man is at first and ideally, like the God who sponsors him,
disembodied *nous* or mind. We are conceived as by parthenogene-
sis, a joyless activity and so commending itself—as the wheel of
ideas comes round again—to the austere feminism of the 1970s. As
man takes a body to couple with Nature, "the bond that united all
things was broken by the will of God." This is an even more lugubrious version of the Fall in the Garden or the destruction of the
Tower of Babel.

The body is evil because it is occlusive. That is the philosophical position. For the personal or fastidious considerations that
prompt it, we must read between the lines. Plato, the generic

source from whom the anonymous compilers of the *Corpus Hermeticum* take their tenuous ideas, was born, says a Renaissance wit, of
a virgin and the phantom of Apollo. Whoever "cherishes the body
that issued from the sin of love, that one lives in darkness, suffering
in his senses the things of death." As the body brought death into
the world and all our woe, we are redeemed as we slough the
body. But the "as . . . so" sequence is a blind, logic masking rhetoric. The world is a head and the trunk that should support it is
nowhere. That is how the grammarian James Harris depicts that
other Hermes to whom he assigns the inventing of letters and the
regulating of language. Hermes is a head without limbs. For trans-
acting important business, only the head is required. In the opinion of Pimander, the *Nous*-God—Bacon might be writing the
script, more readily than he wrote Shakespeare—"mind does not
exist until it has laid aside the deceptions of the senses and the
mists of fancy." [20] The hermetic rule holds good for astrology,
magic, and alchemy, none of which are empirical studies. (Subtle
in his laboratory is only passing the time.) The common denominator which associates the occult with anti-Aristotelianism and new
science is a hatred of the word made flesh. I take as a type-figure
the French humanist Lefèbre d'Etaples, who despises the Philosopher, translates the Bible into the common tongue—like Descartes
he is appealing to "pure and natural reason"—and writes on mathematics, music, astronomy—the more rarefied disciplines—sequentially on esoteric lore. "Science with the teeth" does not engage
him.

Two ways of approaching experience are at issue and often
they are conjunctive in the same man. Leonardo, as he believes in
the possibility of boiling down, is modern. "Truth has only one
term, which being declared the dispute is ended for all time." But
Leonardo partakes also of the "Aristotelian" or fact-riveted intelligence—who in more sumptuous ways? "Write," he adjures
himself in a memorable passage—it is as if he were recalling a medieval poet like Dante, scrutinizing the figured pavement on the
terrace of pride—"Write the tongue of the woodpecker and the jaw

20. Ficino's Argument to *Pimander;* Harris, frontispiece to *Hermes,* 1765.

of the crocodile. Write the flight of the fourth kind of chewing butterflies, and of the flying ants, and the three chief positions of the wings of birds in descent." Webster hypothesizes an anterior truth (the light shining out of the darkness) which we perceive by divination—and insists that "we should from particulars proceed to generals," discovering the truth by "laborious trials, manual operations, assiduous observations." Philip Melanchthon, whose voluminous writings advance the cause of the new mathematics, still venerates Aristotle as "the one and only master of method." Sprat sees that to arrive at truth is a painstaking business which requires that we add little by little to the store of fact. Aristotelianism dies hard, even in the historian of the Royal Society. But Sprat thinks it "almost impossible" that our words should not be "perspicuous" when our thoughts are clear and untroubled "and the thing to be spoken of is thoroughly understood." How do I understand a thing until I have written it? The question does not arise. The job of words is only to "denudate nature's hidden operations." [21] The new philosopher is like Napoleon who declared at St. Helena that he had fought sixty battles and learned nothing he did not know at the beginning.

Galileo creates the science of dynamics, which conceives of bodies as matter in motion. Their real properties, like density or mass, are mathematical expressions. We cannot apprehend this science, we cannot read the universe "if we do not learn first to understand the language and interpret the characters in which it is written. It is written in mathematical language." As we fail to parse this notational language, to which words are like nuggets, we are consigned to "aimless wandering in a dark labyrinth." But Galileo as he leaves for Rome to face the Inquisition asks inconsequently why we should begin with words instead of works. "Is the work less noble or less excellent than the word?" Bacon is, however, the connoisseur of contrarities. On the one hand, the proper business of mankind is the cultivating of particulars. Quoting from the *Advancement of Learning:* "He that cannot contract the sight of his

21. Sprat, *History*, pp. 115–16; and *A discourse to the clergy*, 1696; Webster, *Academiarum*, pp. 34, 68. Melanchton is quoted in Taylor, *Philosophy and Science*, p. 26; and Leonardo in Santillana, *Age of Adventure*, pp. 67, 70.

mind as well as disperse and dilate it wanteth a great faculty."
Maybe the quotation is equivocal as perception is glossed in terms
of the sight of the mind. There is nothing equivocal in this, from
Sylva Sylvarum: "the nature of things is commonly better perceived in small than in great." Bacon is the martyr to the inductive
method who, as he was "desirous to try an experiment or two,
touching the conservation and induration of bodies," catches his
death while stuffing a chicken with snow. The story is apocryphal
and makes a valid point. The kind of induction Bacon requires
must be used, however, "not only to discover axioms but also in the
formation of notions." Comparison is indicated to the "things or notions" the new language must express. But this kind of induction
has never yet been attempted, "save only by Plato." [22]

The opposition between "Plato" and "Aristotle" persists in the
seventeenth century. Of what century is this not true? Seeing so
much, one is tempted to argue that there are no beginnings or
endings. But the seventeenth century is a beginning, the matrix in
which the modern world is formed, as the enduring opposition is
envenomed and partially resolved. Now and henceforward, the
Platonic or synthesizing temper is in the ascendant. Seth Ward,
laying the foundation for a universal character, prefers intellection
or intuition to other modes of discovery because he assumes—like
Plato, like Einstein—that "induction is ridiculously applied to
mathematical truths." The adjective is superfluous, also misleading. When the operations of nature are followed up to first causes,
"the use of induction will cease and syllogism succeed in the place
of it." [23] Plato is vindicated in the preferring of the deductive
method. His quarrel with language turns on its indifference to "notions" and its stupid fixating on things. The latter have only a
dependent existence. If we see them, we are looking askance. "The
mother and receptacle of all created and visible and in any way
sensible things . . . is an invisible and formless being" (*Timaeus*).
Descartes will observe that our senses perceive nothing that is cer-

22. Bacon, *Novum Organum,* Aphorisms I, cv; letter to the Earl of Arundel; Galileo, letter to
Elia Diodati (January 15, 1633).

23. *Vindiciae Academiarum,* p. 25.

tainly and permanently true of a thing which changes as (for example) it is heated or cooled. Its essential qualities are abstract, like extension and flexibility. That is Plato in the *Timaeus*, precisely. "Anything which we see to be continually changing, as . . . fire [or water], we must not call 'this' or 'that' . . . nor must we imply that there is any stability in any of those things." They are "too volatile to be detained in any . . . mode of speaking which represents them as permanent." Stability inheres only in "the universal nature which receives all bodies." But this natural recipient of our impressions, though it "appears different from time to time by reason of them," is "unperceived by sense and apprehended only by the mind."

The preferring of form to substance is apparent in Plato's profound devotion to mathematical methods of reasoning, as in his insistence that the study of philosophy depend on a prior training in mathematics. This insistence is resumed in the writings of Origen, the teacher and chief of the catechistic school of Alexandria. The cosmology of Origen is Platonic as it repudiates the testimony of the senses. It is millenarian as, after Plato, it makes geometry fundamental to philosophy. Plato, who banishes poetry from his cosmos as it is substantial, is credited with the construction of integral right triangles. The basic particles of the *Timaeus* are not physical substance but mathematical form. The deity who manipulates these particles creates a world that is insubstantial, and paradoxically more enduring. It is the same deity who will reign on earth a thousand years.

The rage for a static and homogeneous universe and the abstracting turn it takes denote the man who despises his portion. Intense numerology is a recoil or palliative. The ideal is the immutable and eternal. To bestow the ideal "in its fullness upon a creature . . . [is] impossible," since whatever is indigenous is subject to accident. "We ourselves too are very much under the dominion of chance." To escape from this dominion, Plato decrees an image of everlastingness independent of the whimsicalities of language or flesh and bone and "moving according to number." Plato's God, like the fastidious Creator hypothesized by Descartes or the logicians of Port-Royal, does not create by planting a garden eastward in Eden and stationing there a man formed of the dust of the ground. "Who is stupid enough," says Origen, the faithful disciple, "to believe that God like a gardener made plantations in Eden, and really placed there a tree named the tree of life which could be seen by the bodily eye?" God has no commerce with the eye or ear. Having integrated matter and spirit with an intermediate essence "and out of three made one," He proceeds to divide this abstract construction. His labors cease, not on the seventh day but with the seventh part, "which was twenty-seven times the first." This consorting of digits does not yield a palpable or particular issue to stain the unity in which eternity resides. As the Creator goes about His spectral business, it is unlikely that any bodily creature, however wheyfaced, will be engendered. The definite article, all that is parochial, therefore endearing, has been dispensed with.

God, the real maker of a real chair, deals in indefinite articles or notions. The carpenter, who copies the chair, necessarily distorts it. Greater distortion attends the miscreations of the painter or the bookman, who imitate things as they appear. "Words are no substances," says Sir Giles Overreach, a prophet without honor, in the play. The monkish writer Cassiodorus, whose pleasure in words is unalloyed, is oblivious of the problem. "A chair," as he defines it in his *Commentary on the Psalter*, "is a form composed of matter, suitable for seating, which receives our curves softly from behind and like a cunning receptacle enfolds us, bent into its lap." Plato is not indifferent to suitability for seating. His appeal is, however, to an ampler criterion of value.

The artist, by whom the word is made flesh, is responsible only to the shadows which dance before his eyes (*doxa*). Perhaps his poem, muttered in the old days, is rhythmically preserved *paideia*. But the "real" content of the poem is thin because the narrative by which its home truths are borne home is time-conditioned. Perhaps the oral culture he inhabits dictates particularity for mnemonic reasons. With the inventing of the alphabet, the eye is summoned to the aid of the ear. The repudiating of a concrete style becomes potential. Still the poet, even with the triumph of literacy, remains parochial. His indigenous learning is gathered out-at-doors. Here the metaphor shifts from that employed in discrediting the Idols of the Cave. The point is to sublunary things. Inside and outside are the same. Even the Platonic poet—Sidney or Milton—not less than the Homeric singer or *scop*, is indebted to foraging and cannot get free of opinion. Content is controlled by the poetic strategy he elects at first and is felt as ancillary in terms of that initial choice. Form is there by imposition. Style, whatever the pretense of form, is paratactic, a sequence of coordinates in which genuine sequence is denied. The summarizing statement which Plato, like Bacon, requires is achieved by resort to hypotaxis, the subordinating of one clause to another as in the proper sequence, "since . . . so"; or more efficiently by forsaking syntactical relationships altogether for the mathematical equations which describe immutable form.

Conventional language is not immutable. That is why there are so many books instead of the one book, the thesaurus of the Library of Babel, or the wordless communication of angels. A noun is not the consequent of a thing. Dante is deluding us. A noun is an attack on a thing, where the latter is conceived as monistic or real. The practitioners of language in its ordinary acceptance "copy images of virtue and the like, but the truth they never reach." Virgil, as Broch presents him, determines to burn the *Aeneid.* "Even were the sole and final task of poetry to be that of exalting the name of things," even were it to succeed in looking into the fountain of speech "beneath the profound light of which the word for the thing is floating," still the poem would fall short as the act of creation takes place in the duplicated world. Milton epitomizes the embittered attempt of the seventeenth century to transcend the duplicated world. He stoops to examine things only to disengage the radical meaning they invest. He employs language only to enunciate the idea. But even so austerely committed a writer is confronted always with this danger, that the facade may come to seem preeminent. The beautiful chains of language, quickening with a life of their own, dispute the integrity and primacy of the idea. Aspiring to more than a neutral or secondary function, they "entangle the distracted god in the flesh."

> Belles chaînes en qui s'engage
> Le dieu dans la chair égaré.

As a gloss on this distich of Paul Valéry's and an exemplification of it, see the sonnets of Shakespeare in which the form makes head constantly against the kingdom of meaning.

It is intolerable to Diogenes the Cynic, if not perhaps to Valéry the poet, that meaning should be exhausted in form. The Cynic philosopher, who ranges himself on the Socratic or Platonic side, is chary of language because he is aware that its hegemony is always potential. "Words, like the imagination, can be the cause of grave and multiple errors unless," says Spinoza, "we put ourselves on guard most vigorously against them." [24] He sees the hegemony of language as asserted in two ways. The form, as tough as adamant, may decline to countenance his meaning. Or the form, as weak as water, may blur and refract it. Rhetoric makes meaning. Connotations distort. The comic despair of Dickens does not seem comic to him. "What words can paint the Pecksniffs in that trying hour? Oh, none: for words have naughty company among them, and the Pecksniffs were all goodness." He desires to avoid this naughty company, as he can. Hence his search for a purely notational language. For he understands, what Pater perceives in the essay on "Style," that "the ornamental word, the figure, the accessory form or color or reference, is rarely content to die to thought precisely at the right moment, but will inevitably linger awhile stirring a long 'brain-wave' behind it of perhaps quite alien associations." He is, however, fearful of the imprecision endemic in words and their relation, not only or even chiefly from a pettish concern for the autonomy of what he has to say but because he believes that his apprehension of knowledge, if grasped absolutely, will avail. Modern man is not so ennuyé, which means at heart so pessimistic, as to see neither any need nor fruitful possibility in examining "the abstract question what beauty is in itself" or knowledge, of whatever variety, in itself. As he honors the Socratic injunction: Know thyself, by extension the real or suprasensory world the self is supposed to inhabit, he requires a wholly rational personality, freed from the spell of language.

In the realist philosophy, matter is uncreated. "So then it is neither fire, air, water, nor earth, which we call elements, of which

24. *Œuvres complètes*, 1954, p. 189, para. 88.

this visible world is composed." St. Augustine, deprecating the testimony of the senses, harks back to Socrates and Plato and is a
precursor of Galileo and Descartes. After Plato, he is the master
psychologist to the modern age. Finally he parts company with
Plato because he does not honor the word made flesh. But Augustine, to whom the Incarnate Word is the central fact of the Christian dispensation, seems to me to confront it with disgust. Not
always. Augustine, like Donne, is quotable on either side of a
question. Here is one side. Nothing in Heaven has its origin from
seed. The fool who licks the picture of a crust insures that he will
always go hungry. He turns "the glory of the incorruptible God
into the similitude of the image of a corruptible man." God is indivisible, "not to be pictured," not temporalized, not confined. Con-
finement argues corruption. In the mind, which is unique in its
ability to come to terms with "intelligible things," there is no body,
only its likeness. But "the body's likeness revolved in the mind"
has no reality either. It is an imposition, like the air-borne dagger
that presents itself to Macbeth. To perceive the shape beneath the
skin or duplicated world is everything. Perception is the work of "a
far more excellent interior sense" which has nothing to do with
"the eye, the ear, the smell, the taste, nor the touch." As it functions, the conceptualizer knows his being. "Hidden harmony," says
Heraclitus, who is bearing witness against himself, "is better than
manifest." The materialist, in his preoccupation with the surface,
rarely gets so far. As he attributes integrity to matter, he forfeits
that inward and intimate knowledge—the phrase is Dalgarno's—
which alone makes possible a unifying view of the event. That is
why Augustine exclaims irately: "Let Thales depart with his water,
Anaximines with his air, the Stoics with their fire, Epicurus with
his atoms," and all those "who placed nature's origin in bodies." A
millenium later, as the old disaffection recurs, Glanvill scorns the
gross conjecture that "a thousand might dance on the point of a
needle." It is as plausible to allow the soul the use of wings "as a
proper *Ubi*" or localized place.[25]

25. *Vanity of Dogmatizing*, p. 108; Dalgarno, *Ars Signorum; City of God*, VII, xix, xxx; IV,
xxiii, xxxi; VIII, v, vi, ix; XI, xxvii; Romans 1:22–27.

Robert Hooke, in his description of minute bodies as seen by the microscope, begins with the observation "of the point of a sharp small needle." One thinks of Aquinas and the famous question imputed to him, always derisively. Hooke's questions are prolegomenary. "We must first endeavor to make letters and to draw single strokes true before we venture to write whole sentences or to draw large pictures." Hooke is meticulous and yet wants to get on to the larger picture. Aquinas in the meantime is still consulting the point of the needle. As one reads him and his kind—as one looks at the stone carpeting of the Cosmati—one feels that the *Summa* can wait. Ulteriority is decisive in distinguishing between the achievement and psychology of the Roman *marmorari* like Magister Jacobus, a poet who works with his hands, and that of the new philosophers four centuries later. Convention imputes to the former a distaste for cerebration. "Poetry" is impressionistic and wrought in the half light of the cave. "Since feeling is first"—see the whole work of e. e. cummings—the syntax of things does not matter. The poet, like Richard Eberhart, as he cudgels his brains is understood to dwindle.

> And in intellectual chains
> I lost both love and loathing,
> Mured up in the world of wisdom.

But that is a false dichotomy. The scientist of the heroic or classical age is the implacable foe of the poet, not as he is more thoughtful but as he considers experience under a different aspect.

This grand opposition between the two kinds of temperaments is inferred by the chemist Robert Boyle (1627–91). Necessarily, he is committed to experiment. But the commitment is felt as provisional. In ridiculing those he calls "sooty empirics," Boyle catches in a phrase the indifference of classical science to brute fact. Materialism is defined in the derogating of materiality. The winged horse on the signboard before the public house where Gradgrind and Bounderby confer, like the painting which hangs behind the bar, as they are indigenous are sure to give offense to those promoters of the concrete exemplification. "Stick to Facts, sir!" cries

Mr. Gradgrind, who is the quintessential idealist. Edmund Halley, for whom the comet of 1680 is named, presents a different type of the natural philosopher. As he is agreeable to weighing and measuring, Halley to a point resembles the poet. When, attempting to catalog the stars of the Southern Hemisphere from his mountain peak on St. Helena, he is prevented by bad weather from continuing his observations, Halley turns to the perusal of whatever else is curious in that unfamiliar place. But this devotion to matter of fact is qualified. Halley on the process of evaporation is instructive. "We took a pan of [salt] water," he writes, "about 4 inches deep and 7 $9/10$ inches diameter, in which we placed a thermometer, and by means of a pan of coals we brought the water to the same degree of heat which is observed to be that of the air." But the rest of the passage need not preoccupy us, only the gist. To be summary, like the natural philosopher himself: the means is incidental to the end. This end is the proposition that the surface of the ocean is lowered in twelve hours at the rate of one-tenth of an inch.

The scientist, from his lofty station in the watchtower, is able to perceive the coming together of particular experiences to form a consistent design. "Standing on the top of them," he ranks "all the varieties and degrees of things, so orderly one upon another." [26] Giordano Bruno gives the character of this far-seeing man, in his dialog on intellectual love. "He is dead to the world, free from the prison of matter. The walls are now cast down; with full unobstructed vision he looks out upon an unbroken horizon. He is beginning to see the whole as a unit." Contemplation, as of this liquid or this solid, does not suffice. Like Stevinus or Pascal he is concerned to demonstrate that the pressure exerted by a fluid against the vessel which contains it is the same in any given direction, or like Newton, that a spherical body of uniform density throughout attracts a foreign body to it as if its entire mass were concentrated at the center. The twelfth-century exegete Stephen Langton, reflecting on a text of Numbers, discovers that the manna with which the children of Israel were sustained in the desert "was as coriander seed" (11:7). The fact is of no importance when weighed

26. Sprat, *History*, p. 341.

against the progress of the chosen people from Egypt through Sinai
to the promised land. To the Biblical scholiast, however, the
means and the end are equally engrossing. "We could discourse
lengthily on this," he comments, "if only the nature and quality of
coriander seed were known to us."

I want to suggest, in citing this medieval glossarian who was
famous once, that the perusing of detail need not subtend a specific
purpose. Dante in the fourth canto of the *Purgatorio* forces his way
upward through an opening even smaller than that which the peasant stuffs with a forkful of thorns to protect his grapes from the
weather in the ripening time. The simile is neither especially congruent nor is it essentially decorative. Dante is remembering "la
vita serena." He often remembers. It is the warrant of his implausible journey, which might otherwise pass belief. In canvassing for
truth he resembles the ancient *retiarius* who swings his net from
side to side as he advances. This net is efficient along a wide arc.
But its yield is apt to signify only to himself. Affectionate curiosity
describes him. Like the God of the Psalms, "Who counteth the
multitude of the stars and calleth them all by their names," he is
the master of the enumerative style. Or he is, in Sprat's contemptuous phrase, the true "empiric in philosophy." He has a great
collection of particular experiences but he knows how to use them
only "to base and low ends." As a setoff to Dante the pilgrim and
his roving eye, here is the Jacobean pilgrim Joseph Hall. "Those
that travel in long pilgrimages to the Holy Land, what a number of
weary paces they measure!" When they get to their destination
what do they find "but the bare sepulchre wherein their Savior lay
and the earth He trod upon, to the increase of a carnal devotion?" [27] Bishop Hall is on the road to the "celestial Jerusalem."
Dante, I think, is travelling in circles. Bertrand de Born still
engages our horrified attention, there, with the lantern in his hand.

The unregenerate cause which is our salvation has no affiliation to matter. Dante puts his salvation in peril. Virgil, seeing so
much, reproves him in canto xxx of the *Inferno* for his attention to

---

27. "Third Century" of *Meditations and Vows*, ed. P. Wynter, *Works*, 1863, No. 34, vii,
500; Sprat, *History*, p. 341.

the apes of nature. Agrippa of Nettesheim is more prudent as he shuts his eyes and ears. Agrippa wants us to throw out the pictures, the sacred vessels, the lights and bells, after that to burn down the church. "It is a wicked and a cursed thing to shut the gods within walls." [28] Luther's colleague Andreas Carlstadt, as he is covetous of taking captive the thing itself, repudiates whatever is not of the spirit as a clog. Painting and sculpture, music, whether sacred or secular, are forbidden. Zwingli at Zurich strives for essentiality in the same astringent ways. Nearsightedness afflicts him. It is the appropriate disorder. "Images," he confesses, "are able to delight me less since I cannot see them well." Images and relics are abolished, the organ in the cathedral is smashed. But Zwingli continues to honor the classics and has even a word to say in admiration of the visual arts. So he is rejected as insufficiently draconian, for example by Balthasar Hübmaier, the Anabaptist preacher and martyr, who condemns all "books of men" and resolves to admit nothing corporeal between himself and his maker. He is like Jacob Boehme the mystic, who laments that "the Temple of Christ was turned into temples made of stone." The capital letter denotes the one habitation which is everywhere and nowhere.

As the inborn "principles of truth and light," not refracted but blent in a single beam, are understood to be "above all particular examples and texts" (Benjamin Whichcote), the multifarious truth is denied. Milton, who exalts before all temples the upright heart and pure, reaffirms this denial in demanding that the doctrine of the gospel be "winnowed and sifted from the chaff of overdated ceremonies." The Protestant casuist is contemptuous of ceremony as it is "an outward action." By design it refers "to some other thing, to the substance whereof it is neither a cause nor a part." The cause, Augustine thinks, always goes before the seed, but the seed never generates the cause. "I am what I am." That is all his taciturn deity is willing to say. [29]

The philosophical grammarian is the bedfellow of the divina-

28. *Vanitie . . . of artes and sciences,* Y1-3, z-3v.

29. *City of God,* VII, xvii; William Ames, *A Fresh Suit Against Human Ceremonies,* 1633; Milton, *Of Reformation in England,* 1641.

tory man and the scientific conceptualizer. He intermits his concern with *grammaire particulière* in favor of *grammaire générale,* which is nothing else—on the word of an eighteenth-century encyclopedist—but "the nature of language put out in the open or exposed to plain view." This naked enunciation or linguistic substrate dictates the form of every human utterance. The general grammar which describes it "is therefore a rational science of those immutable and general principles of language, any language, whether spoken or written." The underlying generative system is our birthright, also our fence against change. The substrate or syntax of an expression is not the same as the superficial form. There is, however, no need to take alarm so long as we agree that the form is superficial. Only, we have to modify the dictum of Leibniz that language mirrors the mind. The mirror is not immediately or not obviously a faithful reflector. It is a concave glass. The signification of the word is basic; belying it is the multiplicity of sounds or linguistic signs. Adverbs and prepositional phrases are such signs. In deep structure the tendency is to succinct resolutions, in consonance with the instinctive desire attributed to us by the grammarians of Port-Royal "to abridge what we say." [30] The saluting of this desire attests the enduring vitality of Ramus and the new Laconians of the sixteenth century in the history of bad ideas.

On the glozing surface, the prepositional phrase is one possible mode of expression—for example: *cum sapientia, in hoc die*— but so are the adverbs: *sapienter* or *hodie,* which break it down. The verb also admits of alternative constructions. Deep structure, as it registers the native impulse to abridgement, implies but suppresses the copula. Although in the physical utterance it engenders different forms are potential, in the kernel sentence these options are collapsed. Affirmation is there, as regarding "the person who is spoken of." So is the act of affirming, as regarding "the person who speaks." The sentence, *Petrus affirmat* looks like itself alone. But "*affirmat* is the same thing as *est affirmans.*" The *coincidentia oppositorum,* beloved of the mystics, is realized in this comprehen-

---

30. Nicholas Beauzee, *Grammaire générale,* 1767, pp. v–vi, xv–xvi; Leibniz, *New Essays Concerning Human Understanding,* 1696, iii, vii, 368 (in Langley trans.).

sive structure. Hence the once-celebrated *Logique* of Port-Royal
refers insistently to it. A sentence may appear to be exclusively affirmative. That is only, in the view of Antoine Arnauld, its ostensi-
ble or grammatical form. To say that "there are few pastors in the
present day who are ready to give their lives for their sheep" is also
to say, beneath the surface, that many pastors nowadays are unwilling to do so. The affirmative sentence contains the negative sentence within it.[31] Deep structure is compendious, also catholic.
Synecdoche, the glimpsing of the world in the part, like a will-o-
the-wisp lures on the linguistic reformers.

"The perception of identity unites all things": as in "the works
of your modern Raphaels," says Charles Surface in Sheridan's comedy, "who give you the strongest resemblance yet contrive to make
your portrait independent of you, so that you may sink the original
and not hurt the picture." The philosophical grammarians and the
makers of the universal language are committed first to the representing of this total picture. Athanasius Kircher announces on his
title page: "Omnia in uno sunt & in omnibus unum." He is imputing to himself a supernal power "to see the whole—all in each."
That is Giordano Bruno before the Venetian tribunal which dis-
patches him to Rome to be burned in the Campo dei Fiori. As he
asserts the *coincidentia oppositorum*, Bruno assimilates particulars
in the tepid bath of enveloping oneness. Suspended forever in a
neutral emulsion, the hard opposites or integers which give so
much trouble to the manipulator of language do not signify any
more. *Quodlibet in quolibet:* everything in everything, says Nicholas of Cusa. He is paraphrasing Ramón Lull. The simplifying or
reductive temperament cultivates synecdoche as it declares the
omnipresence of the substrate. The phenomenal world delights in
difference. A finite line is divisible, in the last resort it is discrete.
But a plurality of distinct exemplars is absurd, Cusa thinks. "Each
would be to the objects modelled on it the infinitely true exemplars, but infinite truth can only be one." So he posits an infinite line which has no parts and in which the myriad potentialities

---

31. Arnauld and Lancelot, *Grammaire générale et raisonnée*, 1660; *Port-Royal Logic*, tr. T.
S. Baynes, 1854, Pt. II, Ch. ii, p. 110; Pt. III, Ch. ix, p. 210.

of the finite line (phenomena, equivocal words) are actualized. The infinite line is the explanation of the finite. "The diversity of things or of lines is not essential, for there is only one essence, but accidental." [32] It is a tremendous affirmation and preliminary to the reconstituting of language, as to the triumphant progress of new science.

Comprehensiveness and concision seem to be antinomies but are the same. As he grasps this truth, anyway as he affirms it, Kircher, elaborating his dictionary of the artificial language, is able to contract to numbers and symbols all the words in a single language group. In his spare and yet sufficient vocabulary, Roman xxvii, arabic 36, and a capital N distinguished by a loop on the upper right hand vertical designate the English name Peter in Latin, Hebrew, Arabic, Italian, French, Spanish, and German. Eight languages, by ordination, are reduced to one. Milton is agitated because "the tenth part of a man's life, ordinarily extended, is taken up in learning, and that very scarcely, the Latin tongue." Milton wants to remedy this "tardy proficience." But the sinewy grammar he composes, in which "the long way is much abbreviated and the labor of understanding [made] much more easy," requires first the denying of eccentricity. Maybe Latin is eccentric per se. Its jagged contours are smoothed in George Dalgarno's *Lexicon Latino-Philosophicum*. Dalgarno, like King James, is writing to the docile bairns of knowledge. Words like *absolvere, absurditas, academia* are mysterious, except to the scholar. All the world, Dalgarno thinks will take the sense of their more effable equivalents: *kon shon sis, shib prem softos, dadtem fantem dadtis*. The new pedagogy of Comenius repudiates the complex world in favor of "simplicity and plainness." Looking out on the unbroken horizon—it is lowered in place from the flies of a hectic imagination—Cyprian Kinner proposes an abbreviated course of instruction when "all things necessary to be known may be instilled" into our hearts without labor or books or dictation. [33]

---

32. *Of Learned Ignorance*, Bk. ii, Ch. ix, i, xiii, xvii. Kircher is quoted on t.p. of *Polygraphia*, 1663.

33. Kinner, *Summary Delineation*, A4-v; Milton, *Accedence Commenc't Grammar*, 1669, A2.

The "language of the whole world" which Joseph Priestley is pursuing is remarkable for its freedom from the "superfluities, defects, and ambiguities, either in words or structure, with which all languages actually abound." Like the syncretizers of Port-Royal, Priestley supposes that we can achieve this freedom by reconciling apparent contradictions in the base structure or set of "natural principles" on which every language depends. He is having it both ways, a nice exemplifying of the *coincidentia oppositorum*. But how do we delineate the natural principles and where do we find them? The answer is vaticinal. In the heart is the language of specious analytics, which attenuates the names of things to identifying characters. The proscribing of "verbal analogies" by the scientist and lexicographer is supposed to be therapeutic. Priestley sounds like a reformer seeking redress, as when he tells us that much absurdity in Greek philosophy, also in Christian hermeneutics, depends on the confusion of the word. But to chase the plain style, by preferring Demosthenes to Cicero or even by giving primacy to the language of artisans and mechanics, is not finally efficacious. The search for more lucid forms and patterns in the poetry of the Renaissance, like the reforming labors of the early orthoepists or mere tinkers of language, must be read as prolegomenary. Priestley, as he sees this, does not propose to clarify the word. He proposes to replace it with a "universal character which shall represent ideas directly without the intervention of any sounds." He is looking to the day when language will "contribute to its own extermination." [34] Felicities of speech, or cilicisms and solecisms, are equally indifferent as each is involved with the surface.

A seventeenth-century proponent of the universal language apologizes for what he calls the "harshness of the style" in which the new language is couched. But his apology is muted since the thoughts he is intent on expressing, however baldly, "tend to the advancement of knowledge." Einstein says to a desponding young woman—he is trying to cheer her up: "Whether you write this or

34. Priestley, *A Course of Lectures on the Theory of Language, and Universal Grammar*, 1762, pp. 5, 7, 297, 302.

that article yourself, or whether someone else writes it, makes very little difference." [35] The point is valid so long as Einstein is standing on his own ground. During Newton's retirement from Cambridge to escape the plague of 1665–66, he engages in the mathematical experiments which result, subsequently, in the invention of the Newtonian calculus (fluxions). It is unlikely that, had Newton died of plague, the sequence of discovery would have remained broken forever. Calculus is common property, or truth. Shakespeare also had his brushes with plague, notably in the early 1590s when his work as a dramatist was temporarily intermitted. But Shakespeare's death, as the work is idiosyncratic, would have entailed a permanent loss. This is not to treat of value but kind.

The *characteristica universalis*, as Leibniz presents it in his more hopeful account of the human understanding—the *New Essays* on that subject in answer to Locke—is by intention the reverse of idiosyncratic. Leibniz compares it to a "universal mathematics." First comes the discovery of the few basic primitives which are put for the gamut of thought. The job of the primitives is to compartmentalize. This job accomplished, the primitives are combined. As the combination is effected, "the fruit of many analyses will be the catalog of ideas which are simple or not far from simple." Even the "divine Plato" is not so monistic. Plato is not so Platonic as his epigones. His theory of forms has therefore "to be completely discounted, for there is but one infinite form of forms and of it all forms are images." The quotation is from the *City of God*. [36]

In the semiotic tables of the seventeenth century, a lexicon of signs does duty for equivocal words. Classification comes first, for the real character is "founded upon science." The vocabulary which expresses it is marshalled in categories. Sidney's prescription is honored as everything is brought to its head. Each category bears a distinguishing symbol. As the symbols are modified, the specific word within the generic class is made to acknowledge its descent. In the new orthography the First Commandment is written, "leb

---

35. Clark, *Einstein*, p. 192; Francis Lodwick, *A Common Writing*, 1647, A3r.

36. VIII, xi; Leibniz, letter of ?1679; *New Essays*, IV, xvii.

2314 p2477 pf2477." But what is written may be spoken. Honor thy father and mother, says the Lord. The linguistic reformer makes Him say: "leb toreónfo, pee tofosensen, pif tofosensen." The men of Shinar are getting their own back. Sonority gives place to brevity, plainness, and facility. Wilkins illustrates in his transcription of the Lord's Prayer.

1 2 3 4 5 6

Hoi coba oo ril dad

(Our Parent who art in Heaven.)

Brevity is not so obvious here. The rendering in real character is incontestably more plain than the time-honored invocation it engages to replace. It is also nearly as prolix.

Dalgarno is perhaps anticipating this criticism in an alternative version. "Pagel lalla tim bred Nammi, 1.," he writes, but already his verboseness is apparent.[37]

Dalgarno, who is the author of a "Deaf and Dumb Man's Tutor," refers persuasively to his own experience in working with defective children. The labor of three decades at a private grammar school in Oxford is enough to convince him that communication is likely to fall on deaf ears. So he is led to consider how a language "may be attained by reading and writing when it cannot be attained by speaking and hearing." A first essay in the making of this effable language is the Latin treatise called the *Ars Signorum* or "Sematology," to which Leibniz assigns a pioneering role in the development of symbolic logic and logistic. The language of symbol is the ultimate shortcut, but one. It is more auspicious than "the old beaten path"—mellifluous noises, however we refine them—as it conducts to the truth with less diffuseness, also with greater expedition. This is question begging. But I am paraphrasing here.

The rediscovery of shorthand in these years, to the end that words may be expressed "compendiously" and "by a short character," enacts the program of linguistics and new science to pierce to

37. *Didascalocophus*, 1680 ("Consonants"). The description of the real character conflates Wilkins and Beck.

the marrow. The quotation is from John Willis, who offers "a very easy direction for . . . secret writing" in which the prolixity of letters gives way to a terser lexicon of signs. Timothy Bright, whose motto is "every character answering a word," perceives the greater gain in economy attendant on strict notation, more niggarding than the abbreviated longhand with which his contemporaries in the later sixteenth century are satisfied. Considering "the great use" of an alphabet compounded "of few characters," Bright works up his ideographic system of "short, swift, and secret writing." His successors, who want to overgo him in celerity and concision, are mostly not worth retrieving any more, except to document the argument. There are a lot of them—that is the point to take hold of—and so they bring home to us the augmented vigor of the impulse to boil down. Not More but Less is the watchword of the seventeenth century. There are just "seven means" to ascertain the learning of English orthography. That is Richard Mulcaster, the Schoolman in duodecimo. More peremptorily—this from Comenius—there is only "the one straightforward way." Vives makes it "essential to the welfare of men that there should be one single language which all peoples should use." [38] Why is it essential?

The commitment of the New Model Army is to unmanacle "the simple and pure truth of the gospel." The commitment of the new philosopher is to shear with quick fingers the "cunning cobweb-contextures" he identifies with the parochial learning of the past, spinning an endless multitude of circles.[39] A common intention, implacable and blind to itself, more implacable because at a remove from the reason to which it appeals, links together this brisk disposing of the older metaphysics, and the confident strictures of religious reformers like William Perkins and Decalogue Dod, and the enthusiastic projects of Urquhart and Wilkins. The intention is to cut the Gordian knot—physicality, the laborious concatenating of sentences—at a blow. The last word is the abrogating of the word. Bishop Wilkins pronounces it. In his "Se-

---

38. *De tradendis*, beginning of Bk. III; Comenius in preface to *Way of Light;* Mulcaster, *Elementarie*, 1582, Ch. XVI; Bright, *Characterie*, 1588, A2-v; Willis, *The Art of Stenographie*, 1602.

39. Webster, *Academiarum*, p. 88.

cret and Swift Messenger" (1641), he purports to show us how "a man may with privacy and speed communicate his thoughts to a friend at any distance." It is the angelic discourse or new language of Cilicia, which is ideally no language at all.

CHAPTER THREE

The Enclosed Garden

IN conventional discourse, synonyms or antonyms disclose no necessary relation to each other. That is as the word is made flesh. Understanding depends on the prior knowledge of a vast thesaurus of discrete words and phrases. In the semiotic language the word hoard is resolved. I should say it is dissipated. As corporality is banished, only a phantasm remains. Bishop Ward, taking him as typical of the reductive temperament, proposes to enter in his notational lexicon "all the sorts of simple notions." The symbols which present them make it possible to communicate "without any other pains than is used in the operations of specious analytics." [1] The adjective denotes to the mathematician communication by means of letters or signs. The primary meaning is, however, residual as the instrument the symbologist employs is divested of integrity. We do not wait avidly on what he has to say. He supposes that words and notions still acknowledge their integrity as a small number of radicals are subjected to successive permutations. But the acknowledging is only formal. The hidden harmony or resemblance is always apparent, the radix is always there in its derivative. It is not enough to say that the whole is more than the parts. There are no parts, or not as they pretend to autonomy.

For the history of linguistic reform in the Renaissance, the impulse to simplification is decisive. The same impulse governs in the history of Renaissance science. King Lear is in his time an eccen-

1. Quotation and discussion of Ward here and in the following pages derives from *Vindiciae*, C-D2.

tric personality, as when he retorts on his persecutors: "Reason not the need." In new science and linguistics more than nature needs, at an absolute minimum, is rejected as superfluous. The goal of Renaissance mathematics is to reduce to one the eight principle formulae of the quadratic equation, or to summarize equality in the pairing of horizontals, or the concept of ratio in a collocation of dots, four of these in William Oughtred, only two in Christian Wolf. Progress is recognized in the achieving of the LCD. The definition of progress remains mysterious. The epistolary writer who is introducing Thomas Urquhart's "Exquisite Table for Resolving All Manner of Triangles" likens it to a "sea voyage in regard of that by land betwixt the two Pillars of Hercules, commonly called the Straits of Gibralter, whereof the one is but of six hours' sailing at most and the other a journey of seven thousand long miles." [2] In the overland journey, conventional discourse is figured. Against this circuitous way algebraists like Thomas Harriot and Robert Recorde urge the claims of notation and simplification. Harriot replaces the capitals of the *logistica speciosa* with lower-case letters of the alphabet. Recorde, who composes the first English treatise on algebra (1557), introduces the modern signs for plus and minus. Multiplication is symbolized, as by the hydrographer Edward Wright in his translation of Napier (1618). Division, to Vieta or John Pell, is expressible as a fraction line; addition as a Maltese cross. The mathematician John Wallis, who is born in the year of Shakespeare's death, is more niggardly than Shakespeare (perhaps he is more elegant) in representing infidelity by a stroke of the pen. The fascinated attention to spareness—it is economic or rational and independent of reason—is exemplified further in the vogue of the ideogram which gets rid of the word altogether, or in the abridging of the word by the omission of letters or the displacing of syllables by signs in printed books and manuscripts. See the bewildering array of examples collected by Capelli in his dictionary of Renaissance abbreviations (1949). A straight line, or *tilde*, is the shortest way home.

The putative superiority of notation is, however, obscured so

2. *Trissotetras*, 1645, A3v.

long as it remains indebted to language. "The trouble of words" is that the mind, beating on them, "neither sees the consequence so clearly nor can so swiftly make comparison as when it is acquitted of those obstacles." Concision is wanting where the unknown quantity and its powers and roots are signified by *res* or *Coss* or *cosa*. Particularity describes and vitiates the mathematical researches of the Bavarian astronomer Christopher Clavius (1537–1612) as he relies on the rhetorical formulae of the cossistic system. To break free of ambiguity and periphrasis it is necessary first, as Ward perceives, to abandon "that verbose way of tradition of the mathematics used by the Ancients, and of late by almost all (such as Clavius and the like) who have written huge volumes of particular subjects." The volumes are huge as they are particular. This suggests to me that concision and truth are not the same. The heroic couplet when it does what it ought to do makes memorable statements that are neither true nor false.

An early mathematician like Girolamo Cardano, working in the first half of the sixteenth century, is notably periphrastic and therefore ambiguous in his description of the unknown quantity. Cardano does not denote. More circumstantially he writes of "rem ignotam, quam vocamus positionem." In consequence, a simple formula like $60 + 20x = 100$ must be rendered "60.$\bar{p}$. [for plus] 20. positionibus aequalia 100." Copernicus, in his account of the revolution of the heavenly orbs (1543), fails for a long time of a hearing partly, I think, as he scants the use of algebraic symbols. (The book of nature, as the modern age construes it, is written in these symbols.) That is true at first of François Vieta (1540–1603), with whom the mathematics of the baroque period begins. The process of multiplication is expressed in words; so is the concept of equality; so are the powers of quantities. Encapsulating is a casualty of this roundabout manner. So far, the chance for communicating by means of a semiotic language remains elusive.

The through-and-through conceptualizer thinks he has answered to the problem as he reduces language to that efficient paradigm which Pythagoras had glimpsed in the beginning. "All things are numbers." The Evangelist is controverted, also the philosopher of indeterminacy. As number replaces conventional dis-

course, certitude, the portion of the Deity alone, becomes potential. The faith of Ramus is approved in Bertrand Russell's hopeful
saying: "mathematics is the manhood of logic." The congeries of
number to which the conceptualizer appeals is possibly deficient in
the power of appealing to the senses. That is, however, a small
price to pay for what Glanvill calls "the uncontroverted certainty of
mathematical science." Glanvill is partial to mathematics as it is
"built upon clear and settled significations of names which admit of
no ambiguity or insignificant obscurity." Shakespeare is circumstantial, he is necessarily ambiguous and obscure as he locates inequality in the differing conditions of the King and the Beggar
Maid. His contemporary Thomas Harriot finds a better way in juxtaposing the points of right angles. To Webster the superlative excellence of the mathematical sciences lies "in their perspicuity,
veritude, and certitude." He would like to know "who can be ignorant of the admirable, easy, and compendious use of all sorts of
symbolisms that have but any insight into algebraic arithmetic."
Cusa before him commends the use of mathematical signs because
of "their indestructible certitude." Since "mathematical demon-
strations are so convincing," as opposed to the inconclusive attesting of the word, it is evident to Christian Wolf that "the mathematical method is applicable to other subjects as it is the natural
manner of thinking." [3]

The possibility of application is not lost on the truth-telling
man. The mathematical research of John Wallis anticipates the discovery of the differential calculus. But the discovery of the real
character is also implicit in this research. The line of reasoning
derives from Priestley. The "one philosophical language" on which
he is bent is "rational," like mathematics; it is therefore "universal." By and large, the seventeenth century accepts the equation.
As there exists "already an universal mathematical character, received both for [the practitioners of] arithmetic, geometry, and astronomy," it seems plausible to suggest a universal character for
the rest of us. The sequence is recapitulated by Burnet in his life of

3. Wolf, *Logic*, tr. 1770, pp. lxxxii–iii; Cusa, *Ignorance*, I, xi; Webster, *Academiarum*, pp.
20–21, 24, 40; Glanvill, *Vanity*, p. 160.

William Bedell, the Bishop of Kilmore. Bedell is not so energetic as Wilkins. Having blocked out "a scheme of the whole work," he hands it over for refining to one of his presbyters.[4] The underlying truth, which the crude sematology of the Irish bishop engages to render, is everywhere apparent. "He standeth behind our wall, he looketh forth at the windows, showing himself through the lattice."

The facile correspondence of the chemist or astronomer or mathematician witnesses to this immanent presence. The invention of logarithms (1614) puts an end to controversy in the navigating of ships at sea, hypothetically to controversies in metaphysics and morals. The frontispiece of the *Universal Character* (1657) by the schoolmaster Cave Beck depicts a sober Englishman, a turbaned Oriental, a black man, and a red man seated around a table and engaging in amicable and apparently intelligible discussion. Prefatory verses enforce the connection to Napier's bones. "Here [are] logarithms [be]yond what Napier finds, That teach by figures to uncipher minds." Francis Lodwick looks to the physician "whose medicinal weights are alike characterized, whether in French, English, or Latin authors," or else to the arithmetician "whose numerical characters are still the same, although described by those of differential languages, as the figure of five (5) is still alike described, whether written by a Dutchman, Englishman, Frenchman, etc." Lodwick thinks his common writing will be "legible and intelligible in all languages whatsoever" as it has "no reference to letters or their conjunctions in words." It is quantified, hence free from idiosyncrasy. Boyle's opinion tallies. "I conceive no impossibility that opposes the doing that in words that we see already done in numbers." Boyle, who divulges this opinion in a letter to Hartlib, goes on characteristically in his role as projector: "As for the pneumatical engine. . . ." Technological progress is much on his mind. The resort to number, as it is instrumental in forwarding progress, "will in good part make amends to mankind for what their pride lost them at the Tower of Babel." [5]

4. Gilbert Burnet, *Life of Bedell*, 1685, p. 79; Priestley, *Lectures on the Theory of Language*, pp. 5–7; Wallis, *Arithmetica Infinitorum*, 1655.

5. Boyle quoted, Birch's *Life*, 1744, p. 73; Lodwick, *Common Writing*, 1646, A2-v.

But the vision proves chimerical. It holds for chemical symbols, which every man can parse "though they be always the same and vary not." [6] For number it does not hold, or more precisely it is irrelevant. Number is always the same but like the pebbles on the sand. In this context, it is as mischievous as rhetoric. Each is inimical to meaning, where the latter is exhausted in an aperçu or declarative statement. The old-fashioned *logistica numerosa* designates each increment by number in an endless and apparently random progression. The stenographic systems of the seventeenth century, like the conventional proposals for the universal character, lean heavily on number. The arithmetical symbols which take the place of words run on, Ward complains, to infinity. He understands, what is not always clear to his contemporaries, that there is a double end and motive in the inventing of symbols. The end on the one hand is "the avoiding of confusion or perturbation of the fancy made by words," but on the other the "preventing [of] the loss of sight of the general reason of things by the disguise of particular numbers." The end is really one. It is to tear away the disguise which the consensus opinion associates with particularity, whether imposed by rhetoric or by the *logistica numerosa*.

To look into the seeds of things we require an instrument efficient "against language and its servant grammar" and able at the same time "to oppose the use of numbers" as this use is inordinate, therefore subversive of design. Leibniz illustrates the contention of number and manifest truth in the early *Dissertatio de Arte Combinatoria* (1666). Already he has persuaded himself—reflecting on Descartes's letter to Mersenne (November 20, 1629)—that "we should be able to reason in metaphysics and morals in much the same way as in geometry and analysis." Calculus is sovereign for the investigation of mathematical problems, also "where the correctness of a chain of reasoning is at stake." [7] So Leibniz utilizes numbers to express the relationship of general ideas and the primitive constituents which underlie them. Simple concepts are denoted by prime numbers: 3 is "rational," 7 is "animal." The combination of two such concepts is expressed by the product of the

6. Webster, *Academiarum*, pp. 25–26.   7. Couturat, *Opuscules*, p. 27.

numbers. Man, who is the rational animal, is simply the product of 7 times 3. But simplicity is burked as the numbers proliferate. So extensive is "the number of several [separate] characters" that to learn them, Ward observes, must be "either impossible or very difficult." As he contemplates this unending procession, the abstemious man is temporarily baffled.

Bacon sees the way to resolve his dilemma. Bacon turns an indifferent eye on the old-fashioned mathematics. He is alert to its prolixity, also to its involvement with the word. So he calls, like Ficino, for the inventing of a real character, capable of rendering "whole figures of plants, trees, and animals." Ficino is the antithesis of the scientific investigator, and Bacon the bucinator of new science. Here, they seem more similar than different. I think the scientist is another version of the mage. Each posits a little man or homunculus hiding in the deep structure or innermost self who converts visual images to percepts and makes the welter of sensory information with which we are assaulted conform to what we know already about the world outside the self. The conforming is expressible, the expression is plenary. The scientist and mage argue for absolute equivalence between the phenomenal fact and its intellectual representation or "whole figure."

But how can pictures designate or names denote absolutely? Ficino explains: "the power of a natural object reaches through the senses to the imagination, through the imagination to the intelligence itself by which it is apprehended and enclosed in a name." The apprehending agent he calls Dialectic, that art of the intelligence which concerns itself not with words but things, the latter understood as "real" or essential and partaking of universal truth. Maybe man is a husk beneath which lurks an incorporeal kernel—or stickler or régisseur. I don't know. My concern, hostile in the event, is with the psychological effect of endorsing this ancient bifurcation.

A pattern for the real character to which the mage and the scientist are looking is supposed to be available in the picture writing of the East. "In China and some other oriental regions," says Webster, "they have certain characters which are real, not nominal, expressing neither letters nor words but things and notions," and so efficiently "that every nation can read and translate a book written in these common characters." Webster is remembering an influential passage in the *De Augmentis Scientiarum* (1623), Bacon's expanded Latin version of the *Advancement of Learning*.[8] The philosophical position which Bacon promulgates is murky, like that which informs the allegorical art of the seventeenth century. The whole figure of a plant is like no plant in nature and therefore "catches just because it is stereotyped and formal the unchanging environment, and makes one feel that he is reading, not verse about things, but rather closing with the things themselves" (C. S. Lewis in his defense of *Paradise Lost*). The appeal to the ideogram or hieroglyphic—generically, the appeal to pictorial language —does not depend on the venerating of particulars. It depends on the need to transcend them. Francis Lodwick, supplementing his alphabet of symbolic cartoons with a phonetic notation (1686), is willing an end to diversity. He levies on symbols to free the mind from provincialism.

The Novum Organum is, in Lodwick's phrase, "a hieroglyphic representation of words." The representations are neither discrete nor peculiar. The conjunction of letters and words is displaced by the conjunction of hieroglyphics, each of which is subtended by its distinguishing number as in a series of half-pictorial fractions. As the hieroglyphic in which the radical word is figured has its signallizing character, so do the derivatives which "bear the character of the radix of their descent." Lodwick is saying that differences have been composed. As that is so two strangers, though not understanding one another's language, "may communicate their minds one to another." The language they bring to this meeting of minds is supererogatory. It is ironically the first chapter of the Gospel of St. John which Lodwick elects to render as a model of his symbolic writing. "In the beginning was the word." But the Evangelist has got it backwards. Anterior to the word, which divides man from man, is the instinctive perception of homogeneity.

As the variety of tongues is reduced to a perspicuous alphabet

8. Bk. VI, Ch. 1, in *Works*, I, 650–55. Ficino is quoted in the *Philebus Commentary*, ed. Allen, pp. 143, 219.

of symbols, all the world is turned into a plain (Comenius). The cultivating of Egyptian hieroglyphics by fifteenth-century Neoplatonism illustrates the requirement of a static or isotropic psychology. There is ideally but one way to represent thingness. This is the reverse of saying that each thing is itself. Ancient Egypt had preferred to letters the carving of one iconic picture for one thing. Plotinus in his *Enneads* is the authority. "Thus each picture was a kind of understanding and wisdom and substance and given all at once, and not discursive reasoning and deliberation." Ficino, translating Plotinus and commenting on him, proposes that God's knowledge of things—with luck and assiduity, our knowledge—does not depend on complex discursive thought but manifests instantly the simple and steadfast form. The Egyptian priest, employing hieroglyphics, is able to comprehend an entire discourse in one stable image. This perfect comprehending is like the common tongue which lapses with the fall of the Tower.

The prospect of retrieving stability by resort to pictorial language is vivid to the science and linguistics of the Enlightenment. It still beckons today in the ideographic notation of symbolic logic. Joseph Priestley resumes Bacon's interest in the transferrable characters of Chinese "which is said to be understood by several nations inhabiting the eastern parts of Asia, though they speak different languages." [9] But Priestley is skeptical, with reason. For every new idea, a different character is needed. As the ideogram displaces the morpheme—the word or word-part—rhetoric is eliminated, also the *logistica numerosa*. Hypothetically, this is to the good. In the hieratic language of the Egyptians, the number 1 is denoted by a vertical staff or the number 1,000,000 by the picture of an astonished man. But pictorialization on so vast a scale begins to approximate conventional discourse. It is insufficiently terse. More critically, it is open to confusion. One Egyptian papyrus represents the squaring of a number by a pair of legs walking forward, in another the identical ideogram functions as the sign for addition. The fifth-century *Hieroglyphica* attributed to Horapollo (1st edition 1505) identifies temperance with a penis pressed by a hand. Wasps

9. *Lectures*, p. 34.

are identified by the drawing of a dead horse. "For from a dead horse, many wasps are born." Perhaps these correspondences do not follow inevitably. The same objection can be ventured of the emblems of Alciati and his numerous successors. We need the adept to supply us with his meaning.

Bacon, who anticipates these objections and overrides them, is as often cavalier. But it is he, not the cossists or the practitioners of the *logistica numerosa*, who has looked into the future. It is a fortunate chance, though lamented by Bishop Ward, "that my Lord Bacon was not skilled in mathematics, which made him jealous of their assistance in natural inquiries." A language of signs that does really communicate is the surprising consequence of the jealousy or suspiciousness of the possibly benighted man. The amplitude of the communication is another matter. In the future is the language of logistic. Significant progress in that direction begins with the preferring, not only to the word but also to the number, of a spare and extensible symbol. Ward fathers "the symbolical way" on the mathematicians. It was "invented by Vieta, advanced by Harriot, perfected by Mr. Oughtred and Descartes." I think the credit, if credit is due, goes first to Bacon in his familiar character of Moses the imperfect divinator, who prescribes for the kingdom though he does not enter on it.

In terms of logistic, the irreducible mimimum is realized as ordinary sentences are replaced by a series of propositional variables which stand indifferently for any proposition. The variables acknowledge their equivalence as they are associated by a triad of horizontal lines. Truth is denoted by the letter T or the number 1, its obverse by F or zero. The truth-functional expression, which describes the joining together of the variables by linking words or logical constants, does not require the intervention of language. This compendious way allows the substance of volumes to "be brought into the compass of a sheet or two." But Ward discerns a further virtue in symbology. As it abridges, it insures that "the things thus reduced" are made "more comprehensible and manageable." Already in the sixteenth century and concurrent with the old obeisance to the word, the possibility of reduction, which is manageability, begins to be glimpsed. Cardano apparently is attempting to get free of his fetters. In the *Practica Arithmetica* (1539), he abbreviates plus and minus to $\bar{p}$ and $\bar{m}$ or denotes the cube of an unknown quantity (x^3) by the notation *cu*. It is, however, Vieta who challenges decisively the hegemony of the word. That is appropriate. Vieta is the student of Diophantus (edition of 1575), the last great mathematician of antiquity. The ancient past is sending signals to the present.

Observing the constant repetition in the algorithmic formalism of his master, Vieta attempts to define this repetition. He perceives it as a pattern. Bacon's pictures or symbols are nominalistic. On the discovery of the pattern or substrate, the development of the universal character depends. Vieta, as he wishes to emphasize recurrence and sameness, is led to employ letters, and not too many of these, for numerically undetermined algorithmic quantities. In his lexicon consonants denote known quantities, vowels those that are unknown. The immediate result of the *logistica speciosa* is the discrediting of "that verbose way of tradition of the mathematics." The ultimate result is the discrediting of language itself. The "designation of quantities by species or of the several ways of managing them by symbols" will bring not an advance "but an elevation [evaporation] and uselessness upon language and grammar." Ward salutes the issue as he identifies conventional discourse with the long way around. The identification is just. Only the hostility is malapropos. Quoting Emily Dickinson: "Tell all the truth but tell it slant." As the injunction is honored, certitude gives place to dubiety. But dubiety is where we live.

The new logic is free of language and number, free also of the arbitrariness which disables the hieroglyphic systems of the past. It is a mode of communicating at once symbolic and rational, and it suggests to the makers of the *lingua universalis* the practicability of resolving all discourse to an abbreviated language of signs. First, by analogy to the stipulating of "known quantities," the range of simple notions is determined. To each notion a symbol is affixed. A complex of "simple elemental notions" is represented by an aggregating of symbols. Ward's objection to the tediously ramifying alphabet of signs, as elaborated by contemporaries like Kircher and Beck, is met by an implicit confession of faith. I express this act of faith as follows. The basic notions are self evident. To speak of complex notions is partly a contradiction. So the linking together of symbols to denote them poses no difficulty: "the reason of their composition [will be] easily known and the most compounded ones at once will be comprehended." Truth, says Jonson in his commonplace book, is "plain and open." If for all simple notions symbols are put, "those will be extremely few in respect of the other." There is a kind of Decalogue which exists before time, and then there is the myriad of gratuitous terms which circle around it. The limited repertory of characters from which the new lexicon is drawn—limited, as we reason the need—"will represent to the very eye all the elements of their composition and so deliver the natures of things." Multiplicity is vanquished, it is only an illusion, and the journey of seven thousand miles to Gibraltar abridged to a few hours' sailing.

I see the quest for abridgement as primarily the result of the ordering or logistic treatment of life. The science of logistic employs as its instrument the ideographic language of symbolic logic, which purports to delineate the most general principles of intellectual activity by laying bare their relationships to one another. The relationships are expressed as on a demographer's chart. The questions posed are rhetorical questions. As the deductive method governs, the matter to hand derives not from the world but from what is posited of it. In the logistic investigation of types of order, there is an element of creativity. Plato envisions this science in the *Republic* and *Philebus*. Socrates, who is the presenter in the latter work, a dialog of old age, is putting down that mundane, hence inferior kind of science—he compares it to ciphering or mensuration, the arithmetic of the vulgar—which contemplates objects "that come into being and perish." Opposed to it is "the geometry and calculation practiced by the philosopher," which "deals with being, reality, the eternally self-same" and bestows its attention on objects that neither begin nor cease. Truth can hardly reside in "things none of which has ever been, ever will be, or is at this present in any self-same condition" but must be sought for in that which is "uncontaminably itself" (*Philebus*, 56–62). Contamination is inseparable from actual things. The mind, as its nature is realized, makes use "only of Forms and conducts its inquiry solely by their means." The analogous practice is that of the mathematician, who also repudiates thingness and assumes the validity of the data with which he begins. He feels no call to give an account of this data. Starting out from the received proposition he goes on until he comes, "by a series of consistent steps," to the conclusions which he set out to investigate at first. This assumed and impalpable world, where pure being replaces process or becoming, is like the *hortus siccus* of the symbolic logician. It is identified with "all that unaided reasoning apprehends by the power of dialectic . . . never making use of any sensible object but only of Forms, moving through Forms from one to another, and ending with Forms" (*Republic*, VI, 509–11). The logician acknowledges only those objects which "are ever immutably the same." He is the "man who thinks of righteousness as it verily is and has discourse answering to that insight" (*Philebus*, 61–62). This man is Leibniz.

As Leibniz perceives that the logistic treatment of any subject is essentially mathematical, he translates the Platonic vision to fact. The imposition of order is the goal of his universal mathematics or *calculus ratiocinator*. It is contingent on the "implicative function." As he assents to the formal proposition: if p, then q, he is transported, in the phrase of Augustus De Morgan, to "the higher atmosphere of syllogism." De Morgan regrets that the ancient geometer "did not think it necessary to throw his ever-recurring *principium et exemplum* into imitation of *Omnis homo est animal, Sortes est homo*, etc." [10] The imitation is feasible only as the aberrant thing is denied. Leibniz enacts the denial in the *Specimen calculi universalis* (1679). Outlining the principles of the calculus, he proposes that "whatever is concluded in terms of certain variable letters may be concluded in terms of any other letters which satisfy the same conditions." If it is true that all ab is a, it will also be true that all bc is b, and that all bcd is bc. The cohesive force which ties the variables to each other is the narrow range of significance—the one property they have in common—imputed to them by the logician. Whatever lacks this common property is excluded from consider-

---

10. Concluding a paper on relations, *Cambridge Philosophical Transactions*, X, 358.

ation. The resulting universe of discourse is therefore perfectly homogeneous. The logician has insured that it will be.

The grammarian James Harris makes mathematics almost primary among sciences. He argues, however, that as it is employed "not to exemplify logic but to supply its place," a crepuscular world is interposed between the investigator and the fact. That is to turn against the realist philosopher—whose position Harris elsewhere endorses—his own critique of reality. Everything does not inhere in everything, as the mathematician (like Cusa) affirms. The abstract way is not "the natural manner of thinking" nor is it endlessly applicable (the supposition of Christian Wolf). When "men come to attach themselves for years to a single species, a species wholly involved in lines and numbers only, they grow insensibly to believe these last as inseparable from all reasoning, as the poor Indians thought every horseman to be inseparable from his horse." This caveat suggests the limitation in scope of the philosophical language, also the naïveté or coarseness of mind that promotes it as all in all sufficient. Oughtred values "symbolical arithmetic" not only as it is succinct but as it offers a "theorem for the solution of the questions in other quantities." The adverbial phrase makes the difference. Harris thinks, conversely, that the symbol which pretends to assimilate the individual fact is imperfectly catholic. As the fact is inviolate, it is not to be subsumed in the general statement. This means that provincial language is vindicated exactly as it is provincial. To assert "the necessity of enlarging our literary views" is not to enter the sentimental plea of the mere belle lettrist. The enlarging is necessary "lest even knowledge itself should obstruct its own growth." Extrapolating is growth but like a buccaneering foray, and performs "the part of ignorance and barbarity." [11]

The point is to the value of the eccentric instance, the innumerable configurations by which matter is recognized and described. The symbologist entertains a different conception of value. The world is abraded to lines and numbers. Geography, says the German physician Varenius (1622–50), is only "that part of mixed mathematics which explains the state of the earth." This state is im-

11. Harris, *Hermes*, 1765, xiii–xv; Oughtred, *Key of the Mathematics*, 1694, pp. 4–5.

palpable, so it is empty of things. Descartes, who casts himself in the role of the maker, does not expect that the work of creation will detain him for long. "Give me extension and motion," he cries, "and I will construct the world." The world Descartes constructs is hermetic and abstracting, like the world of symbolic logic. The formulae which express it are "well-formed," not as they are true to life but as they are "meaningful" or "permitted." They depend for their comeliness on ignoring the content of the propositions to which they refer. With respect to the creation of an alphabet of human thought, Leibniz is more hopeful even than Descartes as he omits to consider "extensional" or indigenous things. Individuals are rejected in favor of sequential variables like x and y. Only the point of view of intension or connotation is honored. Leibniz is putting on blinkers. He takes as definitive the specific property common to the members of the class or aggregate with which he begins. As p implies q, and q implies r, the law of the transitivity of implication requires that the final variable be implied by the first. The parts or variables which make up his universe are denuded of peculiarity, so it is possible to subject them to permutations as in a game of tick-tack. To juggle the letters within the several terms changes nothing: ab is identical with ba, "rational animal" with "animal rational." The repetition of a letter is not a genuine increment but only a tautology.

You and I, who are oblivious of the principle of composition, are committed to working with an infinite repertory of things. The logician collapses this repertory (or series) to a single proposition by joining all the subjects in one subject and all the predicates in one predicate. The equation he proposes is just but perhaps it is not perfect, as between the compound predicate and subject. To this objection Leibniz is immune. The principle of division instructs him that from any proposition whose predicate is composed of more than one term, more than one proposition can be made. He concedes that the range of significance is arbitrary. The domain or universe of discourse comprises only that limited area, a, b, c and their properties and relations, which he has agreed to survey. A formula is "satisfiable" within the domain if it is coherent and consistent. An axiom set will manifest these characteristics. It is held to be complete if the addition of any further formula destroys the coherence of the whole. Ostensibly, the logician is content with the superficial equivalence his variables express. All the same, he pretends to catholicity. Look the other way and he is immediately annexing contiguous territories, this on the unsupported ground of ethnographic similarity. Self preservation suggests that we call his bogus science in question.

The clay with which he is working—for example a pair of contrary names, like *man* and *not-man*—represents, says De Morgan, "everything imaginable or real in the universe." It is, however, not practicable to include in one category everything that is *not-man*. The recitation of names or kinds would last out a night in Russia when nights are longest there. So the contraries are made to embrace "not the whole universe but some one general idea." Still the logician wants to have it both ways. He boils down, then announces that "the whole idea under consideration is *the universe* (meaning merely the whole of which we are considering parts)." [12] We are radically impoverished as we accept the equivalence. A modern symbologist like Jean Effel is confident of his ability to render any human utterance as he believes, with Leibniz, that "all our reasoning is nothing but the relating and substituting of characters, whether these characters be words or marks or images." [13] Suppose the utterance to be rendered is not discursive, or that its parpahrasable content does not really communicate the total configuration it makes? The symbologist declines to entertain the possibility. Thought is reducible to a series of expanding rings, the convention of the cartoonist. A curved line above them converts the noun to a verb. Already the saying of Descartes: "I think, therefore I am," is within range of ideographic notation. Poetry also is a collection of phonemes or letters. As such it is amenable, not less than philosophy, to symbolic representation. If nothing is gained and nothing is lost in the substituting of characters, it is possible to codify Hamlet's lines beginning: "To be or not to be." The concept of being is essentially the same in Hamlet's soliloquy as in the philosopher's dictat, except that the verb subject is wanting.

12. *Formal Logic*, 1847, p. 37.   13. New York *Times*, Nov. 27, 1967, p. 18.

That is the proposition. The copula is nearly equivalent in Shakespeare and Descartes. It has the same truth-value as the following paraphrase is approved: "To think is to be." Patently, the equivalence is only skin deep. In the truth-table, as the eye attests, one notation squares with another. *Omnis homo* is identical with *animal*, the Cartesian postulate with any other whose grammatical form is the same. There is in these observable complementarities not so much information as we might desire. Shakespeare, from the point of view of the symbolic logician, surfeits us with information.

Shakespeare is himself, also the great exemplar of an enduring psychology or temperamental bias, and that is how he figures here. He is critical to this discussion as he represents in his work everything the conceptualizer denies or ignores. I take him, therefore, as the protagonist who has the right of it in the matter of "Shakespeare versus Shallow." His interest, despite Dr. Johnson, is not in "just representations of general nature" but in the indigenous thing. Making little of this interest is the symbologist, like Quine in our own day, in the seventeenth century like Webster, to whom man is a capital-letter abstraction. An asterisk, Webster thinks—he epitomizes the point of view of classical science—is enough to denote it. He employs one sign to "serve for one notion to all nations." [14] Shakespeare does not filter but engrosses the babel of contradictory signs. Man is the paragon of animals, also a quintessence of dust. Who can say where this leaves us. The important opposition is not, however, between poetry and science. It is between the abstracting temper and that more provincial and less imaginative temper which is rooted, even stolidly, in the here and now. Shakespeare, as the imaginative faculty is underdeveloped in him, is willing to characterize only what he has analyzed or explored. He is disinclined ultimately to infer. In the general premise which emerges from his analysis, there is no pretense to inclusiveness, as with Boyle or Torricelli or the characteristic poets of the Augustine Age. Each fact is sui generis. "Here's Wart!" says Falstaff. Hamlet is witness to the feckless behavior of the Queen,

14. *Academiarum*, p. 26.

whose behavior and person are understood to be particular. So he frames a comment that is in the last resort to the woman alone. "Reason panders will." It is true that the comment reverberates. It pleases us to suppose that Shakespeare, through Hamlet, is speaking from the chair. But it is partly convenience that engenders the supposition, not a warrant from the dramatist that can be produced on demand. Avogadro, enunciating his hypothesis, proposes to characterize the behavior of all gasses under pressure. Shakespeare is more modest and more nearly scientific. It is by no means clear that what he demonstrates today will hold tomorrow. The view of the world he appears to express does not lend itself to codification. Unequivocal judgments are seldom on his lips. He has no horror of contradiction. He is proficient in analysis but he does not see the end as a precipitating out of the truth, rather as the maintaining in a kind of stasis of immiscible things. The unlikely emulsion he produces is exciting or magical, like legerdemain. It is not enlightening, except on its own parochial ground.

The logician George Boole (1815–64) is parochial in his willingness to admit propositional functions, which depend for their validity on circumstantial definition. There are statements, he concedes, that are true under some circumstances and yet may be false under others. The more thorough-going conceptualizer repudiates this tentative reading. His penchant is for absolutely determinant propositions. If x is not true, then x must be false; if x is not false, it has got to be true. Certainly it cannot be both. For the successful operation of a calculus of propositions, the Law of Non-Contradiction is basic. "In the Institute in Copenhagen"—it is Niels Bohr who is reminiscing—"we used, when in trouble, often to comfort ourselves with jokes, among them the old saying about the two kinds of truth." To one kind of truth belong statements "so simple and clear that the opposite assertion obviously could not be defended. The other kind, the so-called 'deep truths,' are statements in which the opposite also contains deep truth." The conceptualizer is successful as he is able progressively to eliminate these contradictory truths. The movement is to ratio. Shakespeare contends against this movement. He differs from Bacon in that the tables he brings down from Sinai are felt as true or false only for the moment. The inconstant ardors of Lysander and Demetrius are not less tenable or true than the absolute constancy of Romeo and Juliet, which wears out the everlasting flint. It is a disjunctive intelligence, proper to the undiscriminating collector of particular experiences, which observes of love that it "alters not with his brief hours and weeks," even as it resembles the impress of love to a figure

> Trenchèd in ice, which with an hour's heat
> Dissolves to water and doth lose his form.
> *(Two Gentlemen of Verona)*

This Shakespeare, the sympathetic protagonist in the contention I am seeking to dramatize, is a weathercock or else a chameleon. It seems to him, as to Dante in the *Vita Nuova*, that "certainly the lordship of Love is good, seeing that it diverts the mind from all mean things." But it seems to him also and concurrently that "certainly the lordship of Love is evil, seeing that the more homage his servants pay to him, the more grievous and painful are the torments wherewith he torments them." His love is like a rose and simultaneously a canker. In his plays, the same character grieves because he lacks advancement, and could be bounded in a nutshell and count himself a king of infinite space. It is, says Laplace, "the generality of . . [Newton's] discoveries respecting the system of the universe . . . [which] will insure to the *Principia* a lasting preeminence over all other productions of the human mind." An apophthegm from Pope or Johnson would serve as well to make the point.

Johnson complains with justice that Shakespeare's principles drop from him casually. That is partly a result of their affiliation to a particular context. Galileo, who is credited with the discovery of the principle of the parallelogram of forces, is not so casual as Shakespeare in that he has got beyond the provincial instance. As he is intent on proving that any object when thrown obliquely into the air will describe a parabola, he undertakes first of all to enforce anonymity on the object and its milieu. But the process is susceptible of schematization. Let the line LMNOP represent the horizontal path the object would travel were it solely obedient to the principle of inertia, and the vertical MQRST the line on which it would fall as in obedience to gravity alone. But the object, mediating between these two contending principles, finds out the curvilinear MUVW, where $OV = 4.NU$ since $MO = 2.MN$, and since the distance the falling object traverses varies as the square of the time. That is a way of apprehending and interpreting experience. It is incompatible with the kind of thinking I predicate of Shakespeare, the type of the contextual writer. One can speak, I hope usefully, of his poetics, where the Aristotelian word denotes recurring patterns in the work. But in last things he has no poetics.

In the enclosed garden of the philosophers of rarefaction, truth is independent of its correspondence with perceived objects. It depends on interior coherence—what Spinoza calls the "adequacy" of ideas—in a unified system or design. The enveloping context, as it is extramural, does not signify. Relations are "external attributes." They do not belong to the object *an sich*. That is Johann Lambert (1728–77), the German astronomer and mathematician, who requires that bloodletting come first in the development of a calculus of logic. "I see it now," says the great Denier:

> The intellect
> That parts the Cause from the Effect
> And thinks in terms of Space and Time
> Commits a legalistic crime,
> For such an unreal severance
> Must falsify experience.

Adam and Eve, the abstracted, bitter refugees of Auden's poem, are committed henceforward to the syllogistic sin as they taste of the poisonous fruit.

De Morgan, in a paper on the logic of relations, is attempting to nail down the circumscribed consequences of whatever we do. "Is not logic the science of the action of the machinery?" Then he puts the question: "What is the *act*, as distinguished from the *acted on*, and from any inessential concomitants of the action?" Polonius is acted on, Hamlet also, in thrusting his sword through the arras. Much bloody business follows on the act itself. But these concomitants or external attributes "are of the form, as distinguished from the matter." [15] Shakespeare, to adopt the terminology of the logic of relations, fails to distinguish between formal and material elements. The cease of majesty, on his reading, dies not alone. But the act, which ramifies forever, has no material equivalent. I think that is the abiding truth dramatized in the fiction of Henry James. The efficient use of syllogism is frustrated by the mode of operation or apprehension which considers events in this light. The opposition of "Shakespeare" and "Shallow" is a natural consequence. Shakespeare deals typically in what the logician calls the singular proposition. This rudimentary form of discourse is distinguished by the use of proper names or particular identities. Genera are admitted only on a provisional basis. Truth-functional connectives (logical constants) are no necessary part of this writer's equipment. Neither are inclusive words, like *all* or *none* or *every*. In the language of Ockham, signs of quantification—*omnis* or *aliquis* or *nullus*—are dispensable. Shakespeare is not likely to say: *Omnis homo est albus*. He omits the constants or "syncategorematic" terms. Mostly, his interest is confined to the variables or "categorema": *homo* and *albus*. His resort to signification is restricted. Simple (or peculiar) appellation describes it. "You are the Queen, your husband's brother's wife": that is a singular proposition. It is not open to analysis in the sense that further propositions can be generated from it. Analysis begets only the concrete terms of the proposition itself. The poetic statement resembles the particular quantifier of symbolic logic. It is reserved to the point of taciturnity. There is Gertrude, the consort of Denmark. The logician, as he contemplates this tentative assertion, does not feel that it takes him very far.

A general statement seems to admit of analysis, as when we read in our volume of Elegant Extracts: "Frailty, thy name is woman!" or "The hand of little employment hath the daintier sense." The critical terms are apparently distributed. The propositions in which they occur speak apparently to the whole of the class: woman, or the slothful man, to whom the terms refer. But

15. *Camb. Phil. Trans.*, x, 177n.

the propositions are verifiable only in the finite domain which is the play or poem, and perhaps they do not hold even there. The logician is characteristically more venturesome. His mathematical bias inclines him to suppose that if a formula is satisfiable within a finite domain, it is satisfiable with the infinite domain as well, where the sequence of positive integers runs to no perceptible conclusion. This leap Shakespeare is unwilling to take. Only in the world of mathematics, he thinks, does the exponential curve ascend to infinity. In his world, it is likely to saturate or fall. The syllogistic term, as he construes it, is always undistributed. The proposition he frames is always a particular proposition. His commitment, in the irritable phrase of a modern logician, is to "entities of zero type, viz., sequences of individuals." [16] His description is extensional. Points hypothetically in common to the various members of the class are not determinant but are counted just once. The horses in *Macbeth*, as they tear each other, are unnatural. So is the regicide, whose unkindness they recapitulate. The resemblance is, however, circumscribed by the context of the play. This circumscribing is the death of generalization.

The baffling of generalization by writers of Shakespeare's persuasion suggests to a supporter of Galileo's "an emblem those pedants could put on their shingle." The suggestion is mooted in a letter of 1611, the year of the *Winter's Tale* and the *Tempest*. In the image of a fireplace with a stuffed flue, and the smoke curling back to fill the house in which there are assembled people to whom dark comes before evening," the ambiguous nature of Shakespeare's art is struck off. Shakespeare, as it happens, is born in the same year as Galileo. In nothing else does the one man resemble the other. Shakespeare darkens the truth. Galileo intends, by dispelling the darkness, to cast the truth in bold relief. To fulfill this intention, he requires a clue or key to negotiate the labyrinth of particular experiences. Father Campanella speaks to this requirement in a letter to Galileo from the Neapolitan dungeon in which the Inquisition had lodged him. "It is impossible to philosophize without an assured system of the world as we expect it from you." Galileo, as

16. W. V. Quine, *Journal of Symbolic Logic*, I, 4.

the type of the abstracting intelligence is realized in him, does not frustrate expectation. The assured system he elaborates is founded, however, like the universe of symbolic logic, on abstention. "Leave for heaven's sake all other business," says Campanella, "and think only of this one." Shakespeare swears by the inconstant moon. His personality and temper are feminine. The double vision by which he is recognized is at a total remove from that of the systematizer and so disables him from handing down the law.

As the legislating temper reenters history in the Renaissance, opposition quickens powerfully to conventional discourse. It dilates, it dwells. Circumstantiation is immaterial to the new philosopher or a gauntlet thrown down in his way. He could recite if put to it the different steps transacted by Georg Simon Ohm with his battery and compass and wire. But he finds it more congenial to speak tersely of Ohm's Law, still more congenial to recite the formula: $E = I \times R$. The early settlers of Australia, in negotiating the purchase of sheep, are forced to acquiesce in a tedious ritual. That is because the Bushmen with whom they are dealing do not grasp the possibility of an aggregate purchase. It is necessary, therefore, that the buyer hold his coins or trinkets against a single sheep, the very one he is supposed to desire in the present moment. As the bargain is struck, the sheep is driven away. And so with all subsequent bargains. Arithmetic reduces these many transactions to one. Symbolic logic allows of the same kind of reduction. The intractability of the integer is coerced. If P is a valid formula and Q is a valid formula, under the Rule of Adjunction PQ is valid as well. Shakespeare is like the Bushman. Having enunciated a proposition, he considers the consequences depending on it: he drives the consequences away. Then he begins again. His memorable commonplaces are contingent, hence the despair of the syllogist. "What is a man?" Hamlet inquires, as he contemplates the ardent activity of his rival of Norway. But that is not a question. To levy on contemporary jargon, it is the metonym of a question. As the environing context is decisive, it is only the inscription of an interrogative utterance.[17]

17. Paul Ziff, *Semantic Analysis*, pp. ix–x, 89.

My criticism of the symbolic calculus in the hands of irridentists like Leibniz and his followers to the present is that reality, so far as we can know it, inheres only in the metonym or concrete inscription. It is argued of poets like Milton, Spenser, or Dante that their assumption of an invisible world makes a crucial difference for our assessment of their poetry. I suppose this argument to misconstrue the nature of poetry which, as it succeeds, never assumes. Always, validating comes first. I think the same criticism applies to the science or pseudo-science of linguistics. To classify is to extrapolate. Whatever we utter is characterized by what the linguist describes as an intonation contour: italics, punctuation marks, or tone, or primary and secondary stress. The utterance is therefore and inevitably a "suprasegmental morphological element," and that is the perennial vexation of the classifier and the final barrier against which he drives. Insofar as he is truthful, he has got to admit that his saying will be true of only one idiolect or speech of a single person. If he is really to grapple with a problem—for example, "What does the word 'good' mean in New England American English?"—he sees that he will have to consider every idiolect of the speech of the tribe. He is like the Bushman, or plodding Shakespeare. Resort to ad hominem computation is the defeat of his science. Were description to consider "only one idiolect at a time, then the task of structural linguistics would not only be inexhaustible . . . but its results would be trivial and hardly worth the effort." [18]

The word, like the willful electron, remains elusive. So the word is disfranchised, as by the grammarians of Port-Royal. The goal of Cartesian linguistics is the reduction of language "to certain definite classes." James Harris, from whom I am quoting, shows us how the reduction is achieved. As we accept that intellectual activity is more than polite causerie, we will want to watch him closely. He agrees that if the syntactic units by which we communicate differ hopelessly "in their stamp and character. . . . they can be no objects of rational comprehension." But fruitful inquiry into language depends on the possibility of comprehending (constraining).

18. F. de Sassure, *Cours de linguistique générale*, p. 20; Ziff, pp. 6–8.

Here the inquiring man throws his magic powder in the cauldron. He wills an "expedient" to reduce the infinitude of sentences, and so performs the unconscious act of faith which associates the scientific renascence to the occult investigations of the past. Two classes, of Assertion or Volition, are hypothesized. The denominating words are just right. To one or the other of these classes, every sentence is referred. Speech is "divided into its constituent parts" as by a deific stickler, or else "resolved into its matter and form." Now what is called Philosophical or Universal Grammar, which sets forth or reconciles "these different analyzings or resolutions," is potential. The end of conceptualizing, says Teilhard de Chardin, is "to construct a synthesis of the laws of Matter and Life" to insure that the world will be seen "in the same coherent perspective by the whole of mankind." The end is that of the pansophical writer, like Comenius. It is "the establishment of an equally common form, not merely of language, but of morality and ideas." [19]

Experience instructs us that homogeneity is a lie. So experience also is discounted. The face of things, in art, in language, is formal—Coleridge, who employs a different vocabulary, says it is "mechanic, when on any given material we impress a pre-determined form, not necessarily arising out of the properties of the material—as when to a mass of wet clay we give whatever shape we wish it to retain when hardened." The more substantial class is organic and innate. "It shapes as it develops itself from within, and the fullness of its development is one and the same with the perfection of its outward form." To account for the disjunction between inner and outer, the thesis needs modification. The metaphor of the distorting glass answers to the need. "Each exterior is the physiognomy of the being within" but the true image is "reflected and thrown out from the concave mirror." [20] The being within, although we cannot see it, makes a homogeneous configuration. We have been taught by question begging to call this interior being the "base system." Language, as it is analyzed or resolved, is presented as its faithful reflector.

19. *Phenomenon of Man*, p. 79; *Hermes*, edn. of 1751, pp. 2, 14–15, 17.

20. "Lecture-Notes and Other Fragments," I, 198, in Everyman edn.

The dichotomy developed by Cartesian linguistics between organic and simulated form seems to move linguistic theory in a direction contrary to determinism, hence contrary to law. Harris says: "In the brute, nature does all; in man, but part only." The communication of animals, as they are dominated by instinct, is mechanic or predetermined. It is given from the outside, as by God, and "appears to tend in each species to one single purpose—to this, in general, it uniformly arrives, and here, in general, it as uniformly stops." Descartes, in a letter to Henry More (1647), observing that no "animal has arrived at such a degree of perfection as to make use of a true language"—he means any sign or utterance "which could be referred to thought alone rather than to a movement of mere nature"—sees in this want of capacity the prime difference between man and beast. "All men, the most stupid and the most foolish, those even who are deprived of the organs of speech, make use of signs, whereas the brutes never do anything of the kind." Man speaking, creates. But this does not make him autonomous or vagrant. For the determinism to which the animal submits is only less complex than that which governs in the rational kingdom. Human speech is ascertainably capable of taking "infinite directions—is convertible to all sorts of purposes—equal to all sorts of subjects," but even this more ample range or spectrum, Harris thinks, is finally amenable to analysis.[21] If the infinite variety of signs and sayings—lumped together as "surface construction"—is the "image reflected and thrown out from the concave mirror," it will be the business of the linguist to delineate the mirror and to distinguish its imaging from what lives on the surface. Descartes, quoting again from the letter to More, commits his followers to this arduous business in defining the word as "the sole sign and the only certain mark of the presence of thought hidden and wrapped up in the body." The impelling idea is to discover the legislating or directing force. To paraphrase: the idea is to free the thought of its cerements.

Three centuries later this disrespectful commitment, which

21. *Treatise the Third . . . Concerning Happiness*, 1741. In 2nd edn. of 1765: Pt. I, pp. 160–62.

turns its back on the world we inhabit, engages the respectful attention of the contemporary linguist in his collateral effort to formulate a theory of transformational generative grammar. Cartesian linguistics endeavors to locate the regularity that underlies variety and belies it. The goal of modern linguistics is reminiscent. It is to locate "the *kernel* of the language" or "the fundamental underlying properties of successful grammars." The modern linguist attempts to say how organic form or deep structure is manipulated, as by supernal fingers, to engender the physical utterance we hear. He assumes, like his predecessors in the seventeenth century, that language is not the mechanical sum of phonemes but a rational system and conformable to law. His task is to ferret out the law or "universal schema to which any particular grammar conforms." Every sentence can be represented not only as a finite sequence of phonemes but also as a finite sequence of "such 'higher level' elements as morphemes," so the task is negotiable. Analysis, stripping away the cerements from these primary patterns, makes possible a theory of language which is "a theory of linguistic universals." [22]

The descriptive grammarian thinks that the task is accomplished with the ordering of his data into fixed classes. For the philosophical grammarian, this ordering is only a start. To employ a word of which he is conspicuously fond, it is essentially "trivial." His interest is not exhausted in the superficial category. It hardly detains him. He is looking for the Urform or primal category. In his terminology, he is more sophisticated and appears to take us further along the road. His generic resemblance to the descriptive grammarian is, however, established in that each construes the means as contingent. As he prosecutes the end, the grammarian makes his own rules. He is unlike the empirical scientist, like the symbolic logician. He decrees that " 'mental' factors . . . whatever their place in literature or religion, are [to be] excluded, as nonphysical." [23] Physicality is, however, a red herring. It does not mean existence in time and space. What it means is predictability.

22. Chomsky, *Syntactic Structures*, pp. 13, 18, 45; *Cartesian Linguistics*, pp. 11, 26–27, 38–39; "Explanatory Models in Linguistics," p. 536; N. S. Troubetzkoy, *Psychologie de langage*, p. 245.

23. L. Bloomfield, *Linguistic Aspects of Science*, pp. 21, 56.

The confusion is certainly unconscious. It is also suggestive, as when the ideal constructions of new philosophy are commended as matter of fact. Discussing grammars of the form, which describe the utterances they generate, Chomsky suggests that the issue can be clarified by analogy to chemical theory. The theory generates "all physically possible compounds just as a grammar generates all grammatically 'possible' utterances." [24] In the process of titration, assuming satisfactory technique, an emulsion will yield only the one precipitate, now and forever, as a specific reagent is introduced. The macrocosm, as classical science perceives it, is determined in similar ways. "It is like a rare clock, such as may be seen at Strasbourg, where all things are so skillfully contrived that the engine being once set a-moving, all things proceed according to the artificer's first design" (Robert Boyle). The comparison to qualitative analysis, also to the wonderful clock, an affair of wheels and springs and metallic figures which appear on the hour, is misleading. The ponderable thing, as it is an integer, makes against efficient design.

It is apparent and distressful that if a proper name may or may not refer to a particular entity in time or space, semantic analysis "simply in terms of spatiotemporal referents cannot even begin to get off the ground." A science of linguistics is practicable, by extension any activity that purports to be truly scientific, only as it transcends these referents, which means as it assimilates them to classes or kinds. That is why James Harris performs his sleight of hand. Success is not simply description but "fruitful generalization." It is menaced by the particolored nature of truth. So Ramus, in the sixteenth century, proposes to assimilate all forms of discourse to the paradigmatic discourse of science. The referent is ostracized. It pretends to thingness in itself. The language employed by these ostracizing writers is barbarous as they have divorced themselves from things. "There are semantic regularities or projections pertaining to virtually all syntactically nondeviant whole utterances." [25] The adverb allows for the exclusion of the deviant utterance. Modern linguistics announces its provenance, also its psychology, as it participates in this exclusive and possibly dishon-

24. *Syntactic Structures*, p. 48.   25. Ziff, pp. 76, 91, 113.

est employment. The success the modern linguist is hunting is certifiable only as he can specify "the correct structural descriptions with a fairly small number of general principles of sentence formation." [26] He is standing on the shoulders of Bishop Ward and Vieta. The principles he discovers or affirms must be few and their writ acknowledged through the kingdom of discourse. What looks to be complex or incorrigibly simple is subject to codification.

Linguistic science in its less assured beginnings forbids "Shakespeare" access to the kingdom. He presents the flecked surface as never the same way twice. To let him trouble the surface, as the oldfashioned linguist is candid to admit, "would have complicated the writing of grammars." [27] The contemporary linguist is more assured. He recognizes and deplores the circularity of poetry, which is not finally to be construed in terms of what it means. Still he insists "that at least part of the characteristic sense of unity which a poem projects is imparted by the special use and exploitation of ordinary language factors." As they function recurrently "to unify the texts in which they appear," the poem is open to analysis. [28] The statement is true but the analysis is trivial. Roman Jakobson and his collaborator promise much in their anatomizing of Shakespeare's sonnet 129, "The expense of spirit in a waste of shame." Really what they give us is descriptive grammar titivated in the idiom of linguistic science. "The phonic affinity of *perjurd* with *purpose* is supplemented by the confrontation of the latter word with *proposd.*" You can make criticism out of these complementarities but not an assured system of the word. For poetry is analyzable linguistically only in terms of its phonemes and morphemes. In the sonnet beginning, "When to the session of sweet silent thought," recurrence is indubitable. It is of the essence of the poem. For instance:

> I summon up remembrance of things past,
> I sigh the lack of many a thing I sought.

26. Following Chomsky in "Explanatory Models," p. 533; and *Syntactic Structures*, p. 61.

27. S. Saporta, "The Application of Linguistics," pp. 84–85.

28. S. Levin, *Linguistic Structures in Poetry*, p. 60 (and pp. 9, 52–54).

But the predicates are not semantically equivalent. A rule or "expedient" restricting them to co-occurrence with the succeeding words in the two lines is not a viable expedient. The "procedure would have to be repeated in hundreds of other instances in order to accommodate other lines occurring in poetry." To establish and define a meaningful equivalence, it is necessary to "resort to an extra-linguistic reference." [29] If science does not suffice, fiat suffices.

Sometimes the problem appears to be tractable, as when the words in question are composed of identical phonemes. At least twice in the Sonnets, the friend of the poet is presented metaphorically as the perfect flower. The point of view is that of intension.

> For nothing this wide universe I call,
> Save thou, my rose.

But the substantive with which Shakespeare's line concludes denotes elsewhere a particular woman, for example in *As You Like It*, and so nullifies the chance of semantic regularity. "Such a use of 'name,' " says the schematizer plaintively, "may make for good poetry but it makes for bad philosophy." [30]

The function of ordinary language is to work its extinction. We employ it, says Webster, "in order to a further end." [31] Once we grasp what is said, "the language is replaced in our minds by what it has signified." This is the triumph of linguistic science. In poetry, the case is altered. The otiose quality of poetic language "is that it lasts." [32] Poetry menaces the referential role of language as it attenuates the character of words as designation. Figures of speech do not only fuse but separate words from their meanings. Rhyme and metre undercut denotative meaning by directing attention to the word as sound. A pun asserts that phonetic likeness, the fortuitous collocation of homophones, establishes intellectual likeness. Hence the contempt for punsters evinced by Augustan critics like Johnson or John Dennis, or like Addison, who was "desirous to get

29. Levin, p. 32; Jakobson and Jones, *Shakespeare's Verbal Art*, p. 18.

30. Ziff, p. 86.   31. *Academiarum*, pp. 20–21, 24.   32. Levin, p. 60.

out of [their] world of magic, which had almost turned my brain." [33] Magic or intransigence make impossible the facile communicating of truth. The syntagms or propositions of which poetry is constructed generate particular paradigms, these in turn generate syntagms, so we are led back to the poem. "Put another way, the poem generates its own code, of which the poem is the only message." The refusal of the poem to submit to a perfect translation will be matter for praise or blame depending on the ax one has to grind. Valéry makes it a point of praise that poetry "tends to get itself reproduced in its own form: it stimulates us to reconstruct it identically." [34] But compare Hobbes on the untranslatable language of the Schools.

The critique of language we get from Hobbes is spelled out in action by more purely literary writers of his generation and earlier. This is not surprising. Art in the Renaissance imitates nature, also and with increasing respectfulness the powerful art of new philosophy. In the fiction of Sir Philip Sidney, the name is absolutely denotative. There are no latencies or contradictions. Sidney's hero in *Arcadia* is all fire and glory. He translates, he is Pyrocles. Sidney's heroine is all sweetness. She is Pamela. The name defines what she is to the tittle. Sidney's Musidorus, who is the gift of the Muses, as he translates so fluently may strike us as peculiar. Richard III, though a monster, is more human as he is himself alone. But it is not Sidney's work that looks peculiar but Shakespeare's, when set in its time. In the waning years of the sixteenth century, more vividly in the century that follows, the modern maker endows his protagonists with specific ornaments or garments or denotative names. He is Red Cross or Merecraft the great Projector. More simply he is Wrath, running up and down the world and wounding himself with a case of rapiers. Not unexpectedly, Shakespeare bears witness to this preference for the general formulation. That is partly by virtue of his endless hospitality to whatever is going. In the late plays, he tends "to decompose human nature into its constituent factors" or to produce "symbols, allegories, personifications, of qualities and abstract ideas" (A. C. Bradley). But

---

33. *Spectator*, 63.   34. *The Art of Poetry*, pp. 65, 71–72; Levin, pp. 41, 60.

the *Tempest* is not really a morality play, nor are Prospero and Ariel definable except by the dramatist himself. Neither are they heteronomous or compelled. "I'll be wise hereafter, And seek for grace," says Caliban in the close of the play. Unlike the kind of artist who guards and flaunts his own integrity, unlike the costive and more fastidious Ben Jonson, Shakespeare is a bay in which all ships may ride. Abstraction is in the air he breathes, so it is observable in the plays he writes. But Shakespeare—and in this he differs from most of his colleagues in the writing of the new drama, who are seen to be his satellites only in retrospect—is not greatly given to honoring the universal before the thing.

In the characteristic plays of the Jacobean and Caroline masters, truth is not for an age but for all time. The ideal hero is Everyman. His behavior is predictable and therefore determined. It rises unswervingly from a common nature, which is analyzable and responsive to law. The language spoken by this generic hero is, at least by design, an uninflected language. Ideally, it is a language such as all men do use. The new drama takes for its governing precept the Latin tag, *Universalia ante rem.* Like baroque mathematics or like the new logic and linguistics, it is seeking to free itself from the delimiting case. Often in the plays of Marlowe, who is the *fons et origo* of Renaissance drama, the noun is displaced by the adjective, the generalizing quality substitutes for the localizing detail. The Jacobeans sink the person in what they think is representative about him. Webster, in the *Duchess of Malfi*, sees his hero-villain not as a murderer but as a notorious "murder." Tourneur's Revenger is not simply blunt but a "bluntness." To Ford, in *Perkin Warbeck*, a frenzied earl is a "frenzy," a scandalous cleric a graybearded "scandal," a pompous official a wise-seeming "formality." But what is exciting about these seventeenth-century writers is that the very nature of their vision, not merely the words they use, is generalizing and abstract. Shakespeare may name his characters Grumio or Borachio or Aguecheek, Perdita, Miranda, or Marina. But almost always they are more than their names. Compare his persons, however, with what are essentially the lurid cartoons of Webster (who, as he is making a semi-historical drama, is confined to historical names),

or the explicit cartoons of Tourneur and Jonson (whose imagina-
tions beget, not Falstaff and Hamlet but Sir Epicure Mammon
and Languebeau Snuffe), or—most curious of all—the emblematic
puppets Ford manipulates in such a play as the *Broken Heart* (in
which "the names of the speakers [are] fitted to their qualities").
It is hard to figure Shakespeare as creating Euphranea and calling
her Joy, or describing Philema as a Kiss, or Calantha as the
Flower of Beauty.

The denotative or classifying habit is increasingly congenial to
Shakespeare's contemporaries, not only his literary contemporaries. The classifier, although his hegemony is not confirmed until
much later, reaches for it already in the closing decades of the sixteenth century. The world he inhabits is a spectrum of primary colors. Chiaroscuro is anathema to him. His ambition is to assimilate
the esoteric in the catalog of common things. He would do this, not
because he is averse to beauty but because he is covetous of truth.
Only he sees the truth as an entry in the truth-table. He knows
that the table is in jeopardy as the word is made flesh. So he pro-
vides against the possibility. The perspicuous language or "purely
rational sematology" he sponsors is mortified, hence aloof from the
contamination outside the walls.

CHAPTER FOUR

Mysticism
and the Scientific Doom

$\mathbf{A}$ S new philosophy is hermetic and abstracting, it ought to look with indifference on the world and its business. But new philosophy is everywhere engaged. It conceives mathematics as an intentional study, even the selfsatisfying art of the Cabala. "Everything of both the cabalists and the Pythagoreans is of the same sort." Johannes Reuchlin associates the two disciplines, superficially so dissimilar. "Both lead back ultimately to the salvation of man." [1] I want in what follows to support this paradoxical truth, then to suggest what it means.

In mustering exemplary cases I begin with Agrippa, the revenant who hates and rails without discrimination and nonetheless deserves our honor as he is seeking for his fellows the true felicity which consists "not in the knowledge of goodness," hypothetically a sterile preoccupation, "but in a good life: not in understanding but in living with understanding." The same gingerly praise belongs to Peter Ramus. It is dust and ashes to read him, except as he is ennobled by an impersonal zeal for our salvation. Ramus undertakes to reform the logic of Aristotle because it fails, he would say, to touch us where we live. The governing question is "how I should put the logical arts to use." The end or yield of religion, it seems to me, is esthetic. Better to be an Italian Catholic than an Irish Cath-

---

1. *De arte cabalistica*, 1517.

olic or a Southern Baptist. The end of religion, Ramus thinks, is "usus et exercitatio." A sixteenth-century hand has underlined these two nouns in the text from which I am quoting and scribbled in the margin: "doctrinae finis." [2] In the annotation the psychology of this equivocal reformer is comprehended.

In the often wooly rhetoric of Giordano Bruno, the enduring constant which retrieves it all is his devotion to our mundane claims and aspirations. Bruno is the hermetic philosopher par excellence, but the matter of you and me is always at his fingertips. He despises the "heretics of England and France" as they exalt faith above works. By industry we approximate the divine. He is ambitious of our divinity. "The trees that are in the gardens of laws are ordained by the gods to bear fruits," not that men may admire their beauty but that men may "feed and nourish themselves" and offer at the heavens at last. The empery of Leisure in the Golden Age is deplorable to Bruno as it forfeits this possibility and insures that men were more stupid than beasts (*Lo Spaccio*). From his cosmos, Leisure is banished and driven down to Hell. This rigorous sentence is a function of Bruno's interest in the common good, austerely construed.

The rhetoric of Sir Francis Bacon is marred by insincerity, the career by self indulgence. It is painful to hear his denunciation of Essex, worse to watch him feathering his nest. But Bacon the false friend and peculator is infinitely less memorable than the altruistic Bacon whose goal is the "restitution and reinvesting of man to the sovereignty and power which he had in the first state of creation." The Utopian community he envisages in the *New Atlantis* is dedicated to "the knowledge of causes and secret motions of things." That is to paraphrase Virgil in the *Georgics*: "*rerum cognoscere causas.*" Now this knowledge becomes contingent. The Wiseman, as Bacon represents him, stipulates as its purpose "the enlarging of the bounds of human empire to the effecting of all things possible." While Bacon was commorant or resident in the university, says his chaplain and biographer William Rawley, "he first fell into the dislike of the philosophy of Aristotle," finding it "only strong for

2. *Commentariorum de Religione Christiana*, 1577, A3v; Agrippa, *Vanitie of Artes*, B3.

disputations and contentions," hence "barren of the production of works for the benefit of the life of man." [3] The "unfruitfulness of the way" inflames the new philosopher, in whom the humanitarian personality is enlarged. Bacon, like Moses, is profferring to us the tablets which admit to the kingdom. It is as a lawgiver to the chosen people that he "led us forth at last":

> The barren wilderness he passed,
> Did on the very border stand
> Of the blest Promised Land,
> And from the mountain's top of his exalted wit,
> Saw it himself, and showed us it.
>   (Abraham Cowley)

If the vision is chimerical, that does not lessen the heroic involvement of the man who entertains it.

The critique of academic learning formulated by John Webster is purblind. He bundles together and rejects as inert constructions "grammar, logic, rhetoric, poesy, politics, ethics, economics." Webster is the type of the draconian personality, the reason I include him in this litany of reformers. He is like Tertullian, where Bacon presents St. Augustine. The nice discriminations of metaphysics serve in his view "no other use than bare and fruitless speculation." He supposes that "in vain is power to speculate if it be not reduced into action and practice." The labors of new science are applauded as they "clearly appear to be practical." Then follows the portentous question: "Is he only to be accounted *Felix qui poterit rerum cognoscere causas?*" If the end is only to understand, it is just to conclude that "our philosophy is made philology from which we teach to dispute, not to live." Webster sees how "hugely profitable" the universal character would have been to mankind had our ancestors brought it to perfection. People of different languages might then have exchanged their different ideas and "more easily had commerce and traffic one with another." Our profit engrosses this bigoted man and we should be grateful for that. An

---

3. *Life,* 1657, p. xxxiii.

academic moralist like Robert Anton of Magdalen College, Cambridge, is in his strictures dead wrong, also unforgivably fatiguing. If we submit ourselves to his fuligenous style, our reward is to see what he thinks he is up to. Like Descartes, he prefers "art and nature without their ugly periwigs." [4] He identifies the latter with the gratuities of language. He wants us to discern the real lineaments of things. His business and pleasure is "the salvation of man."

The impatience with finery or excrescence is on one side pragmatic. The literature of the age, not least the underground literature, puts the point beyond dispute. In some of these writers of the seventeenth century, as for the silent majority in their time who are given tongue in the doggerel verses of Joseph Waite and Nathaniel Smart, this impatience is pragmatic first and last. Sprat looks forward to that likelier age when the "beautiful bosom of Nature will be exposed to our view," because he perceives that when Nature is denuded we shall be able to "enter into its garden and taste of its fruits and satisfy ourselves with its plenty." This metaphor occurs to Cowley in announcing that "the orchard's open now and free." His contemporaries, as they "behold the ripened fruit," are not willing any longer to settle for a specious approximation. They are like Jonathan who puts the honey to his mouth, "and his eyes were enlightened." The benevolent design is by cleaving the surface, in this case the dross of words, to effect a "turning of the now comparatively desert world into a paradise." That is Joseph Glanvill, who thinks it anomalous that the profitless chaffering of metaphysicians, "of no accommodation to the use of life," should make up "the burden of volumes and the daily entertainment of the disputing schools, while the more profitable doctrines of the heavens, meteors, minerals, animals, as also the more practical ones of politics and economics are scarce so much as glanced at." Like the Port-Royalists, Glanvill pits his reason against the importunate witnessing of the senses. Their province is matter. But Glanvill is a great contemner of the liberal or discursive arts. Their province is mind. Yet their canvassing is only "of notion and dis-

4. *Vices Anotomie*, 1617, B1; Webster, *Academiarum*, pp. 24–25, 87.

pute which still runs round in a labyrinth of talk but advanceth nothing." [5]

The apparent non-sequitur is at the heart of my subject. The man who is impatient of the liberal arts—Bacon the scientist, the logicians Arnauld and Nicole, Bernard Lamy—does not deride them as "intellectual," like a modern philistine, but as insufficiently intellectual. Maybe he is benighted. But I think we grant that he is logically consistent. Still there seems to be in his position a radical inconsistency and with it we must ultimately come to terms. The inconsistency lies in his willingness to espouse "the more profitable doctrines" of technology and sociology, which are quite as gross as the pictures or plays he explicitly condemns. The new philosophy Glanvill champions is surely corporeal. How else is it going to promote "the ways of useful knowledge?" It looks as if his role of skeptical philosopher is temporarily in abeyance. This confusion or fissure pervades the thought of the seventeenth century. The skepticism of Hobbes falls away as he contemplates a technocratic future when all ratiocination will be comprehended in two operations of the mind, addition and subtraction. By ratiocination Hobbes means computation. This miserly yet immensely sanguine definition inspires Leibniz to address himself to the making of the universal language. Like Newton, or the mathematician Cardano a hundred years earlier, Leibniz admits to no unanswerable questions, or he sees their resolution as imminent. "If controversies were to arise there would be no more need of disputation between two philosophers than between two accountants." Leibniz, whose windowless monads ought to make ciphering gratuitous, nonetheless adjures his disputants "to take their pencils in their hands, to sit down to their slates, and to say to each other . . . Let us calculate." [6]

The analogy to accounting is instructive. Prose is "certainly the most useful kind of writing" but not the convoluted prose of Jeremy Taylor, rather, Sprat thinks, the discourse of businessmen

5. *Plus Ultra*, 1668, I; *Vanity of Dogmatizing*, Ch. XIX, p. 182; XVIII, Sprat, *History*, p. 327.

6. Bertrand Russell, *Exposition of Leibniz*, p. 169; Hobbes, *De Corpore* in *Works*, trans. Molesworth, I, i, 2.

and factors. The transpicuous style to which he is looking meets
the need to express an exact equivalence between commodities.
Beck emphasizes as the great gain accruing from a universal character (if "contrived so as to avoid all equivocal words, anomalous
variations, and superfluous synonyms") that it "would much advantage mankind in their civil commerce." Banal verses commending
his treatise and more pointed for their banality express the hope
"that diverse languages no longer may Upon our trading such em-
bargoes lay." The author makes no question that "if the world do
but its profit mind ('Twere strange it should not), thou success wilt
find." The parenthetical phrase is striking as it is so laconic. Henceforward the end envisaged is profit. This tenet is implicit and not
open to argument. The speculative intelligence begins the work. It
is crowned by the man of application.

> Great Bacon's soul, my friend, divides with thee,
> He found the plat and thou the husbandry.

The precedence that goes to Bacon the philosopher is *pro forma*. It
is the practical issue of the philosophizing that Bishop Wilkins has
in mind. Dedicating his *Essay Towards a Real Character* (1668) he
observes that the boiling down of language will put an end to controversies in religion, that it will prove of excellent use to states-
men and soldiers, most of all that it will facilitate "mutual commerce amongst the several [different] nations of the world."
Charles II is like the Christian missionaries of a later time, promoting the Bible and incidentally the Empire, as he predicates of the
common language "singular use for facilitating the matter of communication and intercourse between people," by the way for "increasing traffic and commerce." Not less enthusiastically than the
scientific projector, the King asserts his belief that the humanitarian scheme for which he acts as presenter will be efficient in "re-
pairing the decays of nature." [7] Like the others, he is intent on
finding his way back to the Garden.

7. King Charles in Dalgarno's *Ars Signorum*, A4–5v; Joseph Waite in praise of Bacon; Beck
"To the Reader" in *Universal Character*, with prefatory verses by Nathaniel Smart; Sprat,
Life and Writings of . . . Cowley, 1668, c1.

Partly the impulse to linguistic reform is an eleemosynary impulse. To take off "such taxes or burdens" as the people "chiefly groan under" Edward Somerset, an aristocratic projector of the Restoration period, compresses the alphabet to a "Cipher and Character so contrived that one line, without returns and circumflexes, stands for each and every of the 24 letters." The Lords and Commons of England on whom Somerset bestows his compendious alphabet are assured that, as it is put in practice, "His Majesty shall not only become rich but His People likewise." The good will of the projector extends to the inhabitants of countries less favored than his own. He creates a universal character not only "methodical and easy to be written, yet intelligible in any language." If it is employed by "a Frenchman, Italian, Spaniard, Irish, Welsh," even by "a Grecian or Hebretian," each "shall as perfectly understand it in their own tongue as if they were perfect English." Thomas Urquhart describes his version of the "new idiom" or "universal tongue" as agreeable to the "furtherance of industry" and "conducible to all manner of other virtuous undertakings." What is at stake for the scientist or "Pythagorean," also for the crank, is a locating of "the key of lucriferous" or money-bearing inventions, not knowledge for its own sake but knowledge for "opening treasures." The writer is Sir William Petty, the friend of Hobbes and fellow of the Royal Society, who is reflecting on the uses of the universal language in a tract addressed to the ubiquitous Samuel Hartlib. "Being not at leisure to frame utopias," Petty is succinct in ticking off the labors his contemporaries are to accomplish. On celerity and terseness a more handsome accrual of profit depends. So children must be taught not only to write in the conventional way "but also to write swiftly and in Real Characters, as likewise the dexterous use of the instruments for writing many copies of the same thing at once." To implement these precepts, Petty sponsors the invention of "double writing." He is hostile to foreign languages not for chauvinistic but for economic reasons, and thinks their employment "would be much lessoned were the Real and Common Characters brought into practice." As his concern is to show us how to make a living, he requires the compiling of a history of trades in which the different methods or keys "whereby men raise their fortunes may be at large declared." [8]

It is hard not to conclude that the contempt which new philosophy visits on the sensory world is only formal. If this conclusion is false, how do we rationalize the practical bent of seventeenth-century science? Sprat seems to crystallize its temper. He is dedicated to unravelling "the mysteries of all the works of nature" apparently as knowledge is the means to an end. His coworkers of the Royal Society do not suffer their observations to lie idle but "use them to direct the actions and supply the wants of human life." Much of Sprat's history of the earlier years of that body is occupied with accounts of the greater sophistication it achieves in the refining of saltpetre, or the recoiling of guns, or the method of agriculture or viniculture, or the dying of fabrics. With this sentence the great work is brought to a close: "While the old [philosophy] could only bestow on us some barren terms and notions, the new shall impart to us the uses of all the creatures and shall enrich us with all the benefits of fruitfulness and plenty." Sprat is willing to concede that "the light of science and doctrines of causes may serve exceeding well to promote our experimenting." But he thinks "they would rather obscure than illuminate the mind if we should make them the perpetual objects of our contemplation." Here the analogy is to the light of the sun which, though beneficial in directing our hands and feet, "would certainly make us blind if we should only continue fixed and gazing on its beams." The sun, like knowledge, is for use. The main purpose of new philosophy is "bent upon the operative rather than the theoretical." The door to which knowledge is an efficacious passkey opens not on the mind but the world. We read philosophy, says Christian Wolf, only for its "usefulness in future life." Use, says Dalgarno, the humanitarian Scot, "is the sovereign lawgiver to all languages." The reason for being of physical science is to bring what it knows "to the uses of human society." [9] The reiterated word is like a bell, heralding the onset of the technocratic civilization in which we are living today.

8. Petty, *Advice . . . to Hartlib*, 1648, pp. 10, 15, 18, 23; Urquhart, *Logopandecteison*, Bks. III–VI; Somerset, *Century of the Names and Scantlings*, 1663, B-Clr.

9. Dalgarno, *Consonants*, 1680; Wolf, *Logic*, p. lxxvii; Sprat, *History*, pp. 257, 342, 395.

But the paean to use is not only predictive of the future. It is reminiscent of the classical past. The seventeenth century resumes the psychology of Socrates, an active personaility who sought, in Sprat's phrase, to make his teaching "immediately serviceable to the affairs of men and the uses of life." Socrates in youth had "a prodigious desire to know that department of philosophy which is called the investigation of nature; to know the cause of things, and why a thing is and is created or destroyed." But at last he finds himself "utterly and absolutely incapable of these inquiries" (*Phaedo*). Natural philosophy is only justified as it affords a basis for the ethical life. This basis is not discoverable in the world of phenomena. As his interest is practical, Socrates disputes the testimony of the senses. That at least is what he says to Cebes the Pythagorean. The humanist, like Juan Vives, is committed to the abrading of phenomenal fact. The commitment engenders his interest in abstract science as the key to simplification. But Vives is chary of speculation for its own sake. If mathematics is cultivated only to gratify the mind, it "leads away from the things of life and estranges man from a perception of what conduces to the common weal." For that reason he returns to the past. His contemporaries are admonished to act on the dictum of Socrates "that everything should be referred to its practical use in life." This dictum is congenial to St. Augustine in his dual role as Platonizing philosopher and the elaborator of ethical precepts which conduce to the common weal of the heavenly city. Augustine anticipates Sprat in equating the light of the sun with the tedious obscurities of the liberal intelligence. It pales before Socrates' "more clear and certain invention." Socrates instructs us that whatever is, is not. But he is not aiming like "all before him . . . at natural speculation." The great abstractor is the practical man who first "reduced philosophy to the reformation of manners." His aim, Augustine says, is the "practice of morality." [10] Socrates supports him in this. But to read Augustine and Socrates on the insufficiency and worse of the physical world is to wonder.

Seventeenth-century science is Socratic as it is intentional.

---

10. *City of God*, VIII, iii; Vives, *De tradendis*, IV, v, p. 202.

The true practitioners of the Socratic method are not talkers but doers. They prefer productive inquiry "about the works of nature" to "exercising their wit and their imagination." The familiar defense of this exercise as an instrument to refine the intelligence does not hold much water to Sprat, who discovers a "greater excess in the subtlety of men's wits than in their thickness." To the new philosophers, "threads which are of too fine a spinning are more useless than those which are homespun and gross." The reasonable man asperses the reason. It is another instance of the paradox which has confronted us before. But not only is new science instrumental. So is literature, so is oratory, both of which, says the Dutch scholar Vossius, are "servants of the state." [11] In the *Dark Ages and the Age of Gold* (1973) I have written of the growing dichotomy between the active and contemplative personality and the ascendency of the former in the modern age. So in this context let me be brief. Cicero the rhetorician is like the moderns in his commitment to getting things done (*permovere*), but that perhaps is a function of his trade. Plato before him thinks that poets are useful as they compose admonitory or encomiastic speeches. The youthful student reads these speeches "that he may imitate" the paragons whom the poet is celebrating "and desire to become like them." Isocrates and Xenophon insist that the epic of Homer does literally make us better men. Lucretius in his famous poem presents the poet as a physician who, attempting to give wormwood to children, at first rims the cup "with the sweet and yellow liquid of honey." In assigning poetry a galvanic power the Renaissance is, however, to be distinguished from the classical past. Lucretius is tepid when put beside the flaming estheticians of the sixteenth century, who value rhythmical language as it corrects the vices of men (for example, Lombardus) and brings them forcibly to virtue (Varchi). It is in harnessing the mind, says Jonson after Scaliger, that the poet, who "is the nearest borderer upon the orator," chiefly excels. No classical poet is so strenuous in his poetics. I think these modern writers are admonishing themselves.

As late as the seventeenth century, the social and ecclesiastical

11. *On the Nature of the Art of Poetry*, 1647, Ch. VII; Sprat., *History*, pp. 6, 326.

establishment is understood to be ranged against useful activity. The aristocrat is recognized in the polemical literature of the age by his aversion to the practical arts. That is why he is identified with secular verse and the theatre, represented as an elegant diversion. I argue this case in the *War Against Poetry* (1970). In the second half of the seventeenth century a momentous change begins to occur. This change is attested in the revolutionary behavior of the sovereign. When Charles II confers his Letters Patent on the Royal Society, he affirms his desire "that the learned world may acknowledge us to be not only the Defender of the Faith but the patron and encourager of all sorts of useful knowledge." This new kind of sovereign, the definition of whose role and character occasions the Civil War and is resolved once and for all in the repudiating of James II, is denoted as earlier by the title *fidei defensor*. But now a second title describes him, is accorded him freely, and is felt as marching with the first. The King is the Patron of Experimental Knowledge, and "of this sort of knowledge" the Church of England "may justly be styled the Mother." Sprat, dedicating his history to King Charles, advises this more amenable ruler that "to increase the powers of all mankind . . . is greater glory than to enlarge empire."

The labor of abstraction achieves and masters the material world. The mathematician who formulates the logarithmic tables ("Napier's bones") is dedicated to essentiality, also to deriving a greater yield from his estate by manuring the land with salt. His consuming interest in rending the veil is supplemented by a more prosaic interest in military inventions, like the mirror he proposes for burning Spanish ships at a distance. Which comes first is a nice problem. The conjunction of the impulse to praxis and the pursuit of causal relations is illustrated in the writings of the sixteenth-century astronomer Leonard Digges, who translates Copernicus into English and affirms as his purpose "while life remaineth, not to be unfruitful to this commonwealth with study and practice." (Digges offers instructions on gelding livestock and bathing in the appropriate phases of the moon.) A half century later, Edmund Wingate is asserting his belief that arithmetic is supreme among the sciences—he calls it the Primum Mobile of mathematics—because it is efficient in resolving "all questions that concern equations of time, interest of money, and valuation of purchases, leases [and] annuities." To the astrologer John Dee, mathematics affords "both wax and honey." In "witness of the fruit received by arithmetic," he adduces the testimony of "all kind of merchants." [12] This corroborative testimony is dramatized in the good luck of Henry Briggs, whose chair of geometry in Gresham College, London, is endowed by the founder of the Royal Exchange. Sir Thomas Gresham is like a modern congressman, voting to increase the budget of the National Science Foundation. We know what occasions his vote and his interest. Perhaps we should take thought before assigning the same interest to his protegé.

To compute the capacities of barrels or to measure specific tracts of land is the kind of problem which the numerous geometrical treatises of the seventeenth century are likely to revolve. Ignatius Loyola commits his new and more militant order—militant as it wants to get something done—to the teaching of mathematics, not on its theoretical but on its practical side. In the course of study prescribed in the Jesuit schools emphasis falls chiefly on mechanics, "the paradise of mathematical science," says Leonardo, "because here we come to the fruits." With the reckon master in the commercial cities, Renaissance mathematics on its instrumental side begins. This practical man is avid of profit. He takes readily to a more compendious notation. Like Descartes repudiating the language of scholars, he writes out his instructions in his native tongue. The impulse that moves him is like that which moves Sir Thomas Gresham. I do not think the same impulse inspires Descartes in his radical abjuring of the physical world.

A prospect of "the wonders that may be performed by mechanical geometry" is vivid to Bishop Wilkins, who locates the fruits of what he calls "mathematical magic" in the laying out of drains or the digging of mines or the inventing of engines "whereby nature is in any way quickened or advanced in her defects." Wilkins typifies the ambiguous psychology of his time in

12. Dee in preface to Billingsley's *Euclid*, 1570; Wingate, *Arithmetique made easie*, 1630; and dedicating *Arithmotechnia*, 2nd edn., 1635; Digges, *Prognostication*, 1576; Napier, *New Logarithmes*, 1619.

paying homage to the past as he helps to inter it. In a threefold classification of humane studies he assigns the highest place to theology, which "alone may truly be styled liberal." The study of nature, all that "concerns the frame of this great universe," occupies the second rank. Technology, in this ordering, brings up the rear. It is an "artificial" study. But the formal ordering of priorities is misleading. Art imitates nature or repairs it, as in the work of the painter or the medical doctor. Or it helps "to overcome and advance nature, as in these mechanical disciplines" which are preferable to all others as "their end and power is more excellent." Technological labors are not "to be esteemed less noble because more practical, since our best and most divine knowledge is intended for action, and those may justly be counted barren studies which do not conduce to practice as their proper end." [13] Wilkins in his own time is eccentric in his reactionary devotion to Aristotle, who is honored more than Plato as the master of those who know. But the ground of the devotion is what counts. Plato, unlike Aristotle, disallows the application of mathematics to practical ends. His indignation is roused, as Plutarch remembers, at the ignoble trade of engineering which entails "the mere corruption and annihilation of the one good of geometry." Abstract thought, lending itself to mechanical studies, turns "its back upon the unembodied objects of pure intelligence to recur to sensation." As it asks help of matter, it is depraved.

Practical man in the seventeenth century and later is not so fastidious. The end is kinetic; as it is encompassed, any means to the end is approved. "But what is then the fee that must be given for this balm of Gilead, which silver and gold cannot pay for?" The Puritan preacher William Crashaw, the father of the poet, raises the question. In his character of homilist he answers, first, "even that which everyone may have, as well the beggar as the king, namely a humble and contrite heart." But then the preacher goes on to insist of this sovereign remedy that we "apply it. And this," he argues, "is the chief of all." [14] In the Renaissance, the commitment to praxis is conspicuous along the entire spectrum. Reuchlin

13. *Mathematical Magick,* 1648, pp. 1–3.   14. *Parable of Poison,* 1618, p. 57.

is right in postulating our temporal salvation as the common goal. The business or "chief" of preaching has always been kinetic. So far, perhaps, nothing surprising. With respect to the new philosophers and their satellites whose testimony I have mustered here, the insistence on application accords, we might say easily, with the nature of what they are doing. But note the *petitio principii*. What really are they doing, and why?

The "restitution and reinvesting of man" (Bacon's phrase) turns on the appeal to praxis. So does the reconstituting of language. But the modern emphasizing of praxis and the glorification of man is concurrent with a new and strident belittling of man and the depreciating of human endeavor as it pretends to substantial achievement, notably by Luther but also by the humanists who are his natural enemies. I am thinking, for example, of Reuchlin the indefatigable grammarian and his exalting of faith alone. The consensus opinion from the sixteenth century forward denies the efficiency of works. To this opinion the Calvinists, though they labor mightily, nonetheless adhere. What we can do of ourselves is not enabling. This conclusion is the burden of Elizabethan drama, in tragedy, in comedy also. It is not that the repentance of Faustus comes too late but that it does not signify. But the god from the machine, as personated by the omnipresent deity of the medieval drama and His wonder-working cohorts, is no longer any help to us either. A Tudor playwright like Lewis Wager, dramatizing the life and repentance of Mary Magdalene, makes short shrift of the intercessory power of the saints. He has abandoned, in this last-surviving exemplar of the miracle play, the staple resort of the medieval playwright. But the shrill commending of works is unabated. It is illogical—and we meet it everywhere in the scientific literature of the period. I believe we are to read it as fetishistic. Often in the propaganda of the Royal Society, the writer perceives his subject in terms of eating. Sprat says, talking is exercise and doing is meat. We need food to make us grow. The ancient poets and philosophers "may give an empty satisfaction but no benefit, and rather serve to swell than fill the soul." [15] Cowley indicts them as seeking willfully the intermitting of man's proper pursuit:

15. *History*, pp. 17, 113, 434.

> With the desserts of poetry they fed him,
> Instead of solid meats t'increase his force;
> Instead of vigorous exercise, they led him
> Into the pleasant labyrinths of ever-fresh discourse.

The persistent imagery is implicative. Food is material knowledge. But this knowledge is acquired in the sweat of our brows. Work and pray, Wilkins tells us, and things will come right. That is for the future. Knowledge for the present is not the occasion of pleasure but pain. Neither is it efficacious in conventional ways. It is a talisman. Sprat & Company are like the savage who eats his enemy's heart.

The familiar representations of St. George and the Dragon or Perseus and Andromeda tell only part of the story. The Dragon symbolizes our ancestral past, the undifferentiated state which the Jungians, drawing on the language of medieval alchemy, call the uroboros. The separation from this state is accomplished by the emergence of the ego or selfconsciousness. Its tilting weapon in the fight against the primordial dragon is Knowledge. That is the sense of Bacon's famous apophthegm. But the uroboros dragon is not simply vanquished and left for dead. The enemy is introjected and assimilated. The sun-hero, like Sprat, eats the heart of the dragon of darkness and takes into himself the essence of his adversary. Pound quotes a *sirvente* in which the Provençal poet laments the death of a friend. The hurt is mortal, "except in this wise, that they take his heart out and have it eaten by the Barons who live unhearted, then they would have hearts worth something."

The something of worth is, however, qualified as the slaying or eating engenders guilt, which must be expiated. Hence the frenetic summons to work. It engenders also in the victor the tendency or character of the victim. So we have it both ways. Man in the modern age is a Puritan and commits himself to labor. Concurrently, he is an Antinomian and denies the efficiency of labor. Sorel in his *Reflections on Violence* comes to mind. The victim does not die altogether but quickens, the past rising against and infecting the present and future. Perhaps this introjected past ensinews the present and future. The ensinewing or enfeebling, however you see it, is dramatized in the exalting of work, the great manifestation of which is the renascence of physical science.

The dragon fight and its ambiguous issue supply the clue to the inconsistency in the thought of the modern age, as to the preposterous claims of the new poetics. For works do not avail and no one knows it better than the man who is peddling nostrums or adjuring us to work for the night is coming. After all the scientific contempt for the cortex is not studied but real. The connection of science and material gain is ascertainable, it is important, but it is not an infallible connection. The "salvation of man" is a polysemous phrase—employing the vocabulary of medieval allegoresis—and means different things to different people. Sprat and Wilkins as scientists or promoters of science are first of all pragmatic or intentional. Ramus and Bacon are pragmatic and something more. Descartes in his dealings with the cosmos is not pragmatic at all. He is doing what he has to do and reading as he must. Like Democritus, he had rather find a single causal law than be king of Persia. The kingdoms of earth do not signify anyway, except as they arouse his distaste. The interest he evinces in a pansophical language is inspired less by intellectual than personal considerations. First comes the commitment to perceiving hidden relations. The practical or useful consequences of this anterior commitment—what follows from the calculus or analytic geometry—are a contingent phenomenon. I think that for Socrates, as partly for Augustine, the disputing of physicality is esthetically pleasing, necessary even. It is a psychological imperative.

The Scholastic philosopher is not noted for application. His detractors, like Bacon, are approved. Perhaps that is owing to his ignorance of technology or his disbelief in perfectibility, conjunctively in the kinetic power of knowledge. Or perhaps as he is remarkable for avoirdupois, like St. Thomas, he finds thinking more congenial than doing. I suppose that St. Thomas fails to put his mind to the invention of the geometric compass, not because he lacks the tools—they were not lacking to the Greeks—but because he lacks the impulse. In his treatise on the *Mechanical Technology of Greek and Roman Antiquity*, A. G. Drachmann discusses the practical labors of certain Greek and Alexandrian mathematicians who "strewed their inventions broadcast" in the centuries just before the birth of Christ but failed to find a fertile soil. He concludes: "I should prefer not to seek for the cause of the failure of an invention in the social conditions till I was quite sure that it was not to be found in the technical possibilities of the time." [16] The caution is salutary. Still the question remains: why does technology flourish in one period and not in another? what checks or what encourages the possibilities which make for its growth? In point of intellect, St. Thomas ranks with Galileo. That he does not do the same things or address himself to the same purposeful end, that this end does not even occur to him, is matter for a psychologist who is also a cultural historian to ponder.

Technology—the pack horses of science—is decisive for the entrepreneurial activity of Prince Henry the Navigator, whose captains push back the periphery of the known world. What inspirits to technological advance after so many incurious centuries? The problem has hardly been perceived, much less addressed, unless in the speculations of eccentric philosophers and poets. What passes for etiology is mostly circular argument, though the historian does not see this. Norman Cohn, in the classic account of millenarian movements in medieval and Reformation Europe, glosses his subject about as Marx would gloss it. Millennial fervor, mysticism also, is the effect of the cause which is economic dislocation. The answer to the question begets another question. The audience to which Richard Rolle and his fellow mystics in the fourteenth and fifteenth centuries are preaching has turned off the world. Is that altogether for economic reasons? I suppose that mysticism is like Lenin's "idea whose time has come." This analogy explains nothing but is useful as it acknowledges the tenuity of conventional explanations.

It is conventional to lay the new and growing interest in geography to the invention in 1440 of printing with movable type. Consequent on this invention, Ptolemy in Latin makes his first appearance (1462), then Strabo, and so on. But the Arabs were proficient in the study of geography from the eighth century forward. Quoting Charles Singer, the medical historian: "scientific instruments are at least as much the result as the cause of the appli-

16. P. 206.

cation of the scientific method." [17] Approved opinion suggests that the currency of the printed book inaugurates the vogue of the occult sciences in the early Renaissance. It is more plausible, it is less visionary to say that the two phenomena describe a relationship not causal but concurrent. In the middle of the fifteenth century the Ottoman Sultan Mehmet II, whose engineers have provided him with a great cannon, makes up his mind to move against Constantinople. The introduction of the cannon is decisive for warfare in western Europe. Only in the preceding century had a German friar named Schwartz constructed a tube from which balls were hurled by the igniting of gunpowder. Why did Schwartz do this? Bertrand Russell observes that "in Newton's theory of the solar system, the sun seems like a monarch whose behests the planets have to obey. In Einstein's world there is more individualism and less government than in Newton's." We are not distressed to suppose that the vision of the artist is a personal vision. It is harder to suppose that scientific perception is indebted to requirements or propensities of which the scientist himself is unaware. The Chinese have not made much progress in science, at least not until the other day. Temperamentally they have disliked, anyway they have rejected the idea of cause and effect. They have conceived of the universe not as mechanistic but organic, of events as correlative, interacting and depending, not isolable and confessing allegiance to law. "How could stable, wealthy China spin out so long a story of thoughtful keen observation and advanced technology, yet fail to nourish the roots which fed the flourishing tree of modern natural science? What was missing there that was present in Tuscany and Leiden and Cambridge?" [18] Whitehead says, in *Science and the Modern World:* "Having regard to the span of time, and to the population concerned, China forms the largest volume of civilization which the world has seen. There is no reason to doubt the intrinsic capacity of individual Chinamen for the pursuit of science. And yet Chinese science is practically negligible." That the concluding sentence is

17. *From Magic to Science*, p. 5.

18. Following Joseph Needham, *Science and Civilization in China*, II, 303; and review by Philip Morrison of Vol. v in *New York Review of Books*, 12/12/74.

out of date makes the observation more interesting rather than less.

The literature of Renaissance mathematics enforces the conviction that different ways of looking at the world are potential but apportioned to different periods of time. In the theory of numbers, significant progress is unrecorded in the West for more than a thousand years: from, roughly, the death of the Alexandrian mathematician Diophantus (c. 330 A.D.) to the beginning of the seventeenth century. The abstract way is mostly dormant through most of the Christian era. In the fifteenth century it flowers again. The first independent geometrical treatises of the late Renaissance resume the science of the classical period. That is true of baroque mathematics. When Nicholas of Cusa decides that the earth is a peripheral body, not fixed in the center of creation, he is following in the path marked out by Archimedes almost two thousand years before. John Napier draws directly on Archimedes, also on the writings of Euclid of Alexandria. From the commentary of Proclus *On the First Book of Euclid,* postclassical man reacquires much of the mathematical lore of antiquity. Cusa's contemporary, Johannes Mueller called Regiomontanus, who sponsors the revival of trigonometry, is aggressively contemptuous of the proximate past. It is ancient Alexandria to which he looks as his source. Why does he despise his immediate antecedents? Why should Juan Vives invoke Socrates?

The Renaissance means rebirth. But the present is always resuming the past. So you can say that all ages are contemporaneous, reenacting the same quarrels or reaffirming the same points of view. That is what Bruno is saying when, defending himself before the Inquisition, he quotes Ecclesiastes: "Nihil sub sole novum: quid est quod est? ipsum quod fuit." Pelagius is the contemporary of Milton, and Nestorius of the Nolan. Marsiglio of Padua is the contemporary of Thomas Hobbes. The betrayal of the Girondins by the Committee of Public Safety adumbrates that of the Mensheviks by the party of Lenin and Stalin. The great antagonists, Aquinas and Bonaventura, dying together in the time of the Council of Lyons, are Jefferson and Adams. Already Augustine in the *Confessions,* winding round and round "in my present memory the spirals of my errors," parodies the egocentric psychology of Descartes.

But these complementarities do not make the case for historical continuity, rather for the inconsequence of history. The "nuptial ring of rings" or "ring of recurrence" which Nietzsche celebrates in *Thus Spoke Zarathustra,* argues the permanent vitality in history of emotional affects or states of mind or states of being. It argues also their eclipsing. There is nothing new beneath the sun, still yesterday and today are not the same. Neither does yesterday usher in today. The right image for history is the helix. As in the volute of a Corinthian capital, the scrolls are wound up. They are homologs but separated by a horizontal plane. The enormous prestige of pseudo-Dionysius in Western Europe from the twelfth century through the Renaissance is indisputable fact. I attribute the fact to the revolutionary appeal of Platonic ideology in this period. Sometimes Platonic ideology is relatively torpid.

From the Romans we have inherited a solar calendar, marking the predictable succession of days and the changing but infallible course of the seasons and the anniversaries with which the historian is concerned. In the early Middle Ages learned clerks were charged also with annotating a lunar calendar, concerned not with predictable change but with those movable feasts whose recurrence, as it seems arbitrary, gives to formal history the appearance of a stunning *volte face.* The ecclesiastical historian, like the Venerable Bede, arranged his two calendars in parallel columns. A palimpsest would do better. The recurrence of historical and personal patterns is made conformable, in Yeats's essay A *Vision,* to the phases of the moon. Possibly the explanation will be felt as unconvincing. Like the myth of the Fall and the Tower of Babel, it is hardly contemptible if we are looking to account for the vagaries of things or the felt association that links them. Nietzsche sees in the mind's eye an eternal lane leading backward from the present moment. "Must not whatever *can* walk have walked on this lane before? Must not whatever *can* happen have happened, have been done, have passed by before?" So history repeats itself, but the repetition is not explicable in terms of that sequence we ordinarily affirm: billiard balls clicking, Newton's Third Law.

In this manner, Malory takes leave of his hero: "Yet som men say in many partys of Inglonde that kynge Arthur ys nat dede but had by the wyll of oure Lorde Jesu into another place, and men say that he shall com agayne and he shall wynne the Holy Crosse." History is definable not as the lengthened shadow of a man nor as the contention of abstract forces but as the emergence and thrusting back in the mind again of psychological configurations always potential in the capacious reticule which is human personality. This does not seem so different from saying that ontogeny recapitulates phylogeny, except that the recapitulating is serried.

The making of an individual personality is described by Jung in terms of entelechy, a synthesis of the self in which form-giving energy is actualized. A range of possibilities or a pantheon of gods is implicit. Synthesizing requires a given. We do not start from scratch—the idea of the *tabula rasa*—we put together "something already existent." Always there are two of us, one born only yesterday and himself alone, the other "grown-up—old, in fact . . . but close to nature, the earth, the sun, the moon, the weather, all living creatures, and above all close to the night." [19] The invoking of an archetype or primordial image which determines our bent looks like a fashionable redoing of Plato's doctrine of Ideas or Webster's "insculpt thesaurus." Impressive ideas, "although they come into being at a definite time . . . are and have always been timeless; they arise from that realm of creative psychic life out of which the ephemeral mind of the single human being grows." The Cartesian philosopher seems vindicated in the proposition: "Man does not make his ideas; we could say that man's ideas make him." But Jung differs from Descartes and his company; he stands with Aristotle and his in defining the collective unconscious, where the archetype lies hidden like a recessive gene, as "the repository of man's experience." He is a perplexing, perhaps a muddled philosopher, wanting to envisage an autonomous psyche, wanting to get free of earth's shadow, very much like the Platonizers of the Enlightenment, as when he disputes the principle: "Nihil est in intellectu,

19. Discussion of Jung draws on *Memories, Mysterium Coniunctionis*, "The Psychology of the Child Archetype," *Symbols of Transformation, Psychology and Alchemy*, "Freud and Jung: Contrasts," *Two Essays*.

quod non prius fuerit in sensu." But the bias of his work is in favor of the sensible world. "Individual consciousness is only the flower and fruit of a season, sprung from the perennial rhizome beneath the earth." Compare for the difference Coleridge, in the *Biographia Literaria*, presenting his version of the archetype—he calls it Imagination—"as a repetition in the finite mind of the external act of creation in the infinite I AM" (Ch. xiii). That is the Platonic thesis and whether it is true or false, God knows.

It does not help us to imagine the infant trailing clouds of glory or impulses to scientific achievement. It seems tenable to hypothesize, with Yeats in *Per Amica Silentia Lunae*, a "general cistern of form" or Great Memory, not replicating the infinite mind but made and modified by race and nationality and historical time. Our ideas, on this reading, are the shadow and sum of "the life, the joys and sorrows of our ancestors." Or they are, in Yeats's phrase, "but the line of foam at the shallow edge of a vast luminous sea."

We speak of a historical epoch as we recognize in its *dramatis personae* an aggregate or homogeneous cluster of these ideas. In the prism or diffraction grating which creates the spectrum of present possibilities, the spirit of the age is emblematized. This spirit, in any age, is more or less abstemious. As the light of the mind is decomposed by its agency, only a narrow band of color is emitted. Economy disallows a more total irradiating. In consequence of this decisive limitation, one part of the mind goes dead or it is enshadowed, concurrently another part quickens. In the Roman church of Santa Prassede—Browning's St. Praxed's where the Bishop orders his tomb—the medieval mosaic in the triumphal arch above the altar coexists uneasily with the pictorial art of the seventeenth century in the nave. The latter, though hardly top-drawer, is not despicable either. But what a declension. Not, of course, to the taste and psychology of the seventeenth century.

I think we are driven back on the proposition that there are, as by divine ordinance, two kinds of men, the abstracting kind to whom everything is possible except contentment in the visible world, and that more provincial kind to whom we are fallible creatures and not capable, unaided, of ascending to the ultimate height. That ascent depends at last on the arbitrary gift of grace.

There is much that a man can do and delight in, on this middle earth. But what he does is not understood as absolutely true or good or availing. His mundane endeavors only stain and do not pierce or resolve the white radiance of eternity. Resolution is, however, the prodigious achievement of physical science, now ascendant once more on the passing of the Middle Ages. The lynx-eyed man is the first of the two types I posit. He sets himself to distinguish between the cortex and the inner candor. But partly the suggestion of purposiveness is misleading. The arcane power is given which enables the scientist to look beyond the facade. Again, it is like the dispensing of grace.

Towards the end of an address to the British Association (1942), Einstein asserts that "the scientific method would not have led to anything, it would not even have been born at all, without a passionate striving for clear understanding." Is this why the scientific method was born? The explanation seems inadequate. Einstein, in an essay on Kepler (November 9, 1930), supposes "that the human mind has first to construct forms independently before we can find them in things." Afterwards comes the comparison "with observed fact." This means that the thesis of two cultures is not to the point as it is intentional or didactic. Paying tribute to the brilliance of Eddington, a great exponent in our century of *haute vulgarisation*, Einstein appends this proviso, that the scientist is mistaken if he thinks he can bring the layman to understand. To popularize is to be a fakir. The tribute is a little equivocal. "It is the duty of the scientist to remain obscure." [20] How like St. Jerome and the hermetic writers of the early Christian era! But duty is not the apposite word.

Men like Oppenheimer, Schrödinger, Louis de Broglie, a physicist and a student of medieval history, are sports in whom the rule is attested. It is seldom, says Lord Dunsany, "that the same man knows much of science, and about the things that were known before ever science came." By and large the myopic man, whom erroneous convention identifies with the humanist, is debarred from more than a copybook acquaintance with the laws of thermody-

20. Clark, *Einstein*, p. 621.

namics. His atavism is apparent and no doubt it is deplorable. To admonish him for failing to know what he does not know is, however, an exercise in forensics. His involvement with the surface is not willful but endemic. It is a function of his myopia.

Abruptly, Kepler sees it all. Kepler stands for the early seventeenth century as he accepts the symbology of mathematics, from which the delimiting case is excluded. Resort to the symbol is not only convenient. Kepler reads it as really denoting. "So it happens," he thinks, "that the conclusions of mathematics are most certain and indubitable." Numinous power attends on the symbolic mode of apprehending the truth. To say why, at this particular juncture in history, its hour should "come round at last" is venturesome. Jung has an answer ready, which covers all similar cases. "Life wants to create new forms, and therefore, when a dogma loses its vitality, it must perforce activate the archetype that has always helped man to express the mystery of the soul." There exists no proof that this is so. We ought not, however, to jeer at the metaphysician. The writing of history is still in its nonage. Maybe what Jung is trying for eludes him. Nonetheless, he makes the effort.

The outbreak of the First World War, according to Stefan Zweig, was independent of dogma, even of material need, *lebensraum*. The explanation lies in "surplus force, a tragic consequence of the internal dynamism that had accumulated in forty years of peace." In *The Valley of Shadows* (1909), a memoir of the Middle West on the eve of the American Civil War, the Scotch-Irish immigrant Francis Grierson records the impressions of his childhood: "In the late 'Fifties,' the people of Illinois were being prepared for the new era by a series of scenes and incidents which nothing but the term 'mystical' will fittingly describe." Things came about neither from conventional cause nor by preconceived method. "The appearance of *Uncle Tom's Cabin* was not a reason, but an illumination." The sack of Constantinople by the Christian crusaders does not rationalize but illuminates the decline of medieval Christendom. The appeal to the past illuminates the rise of scientific technology in the Renaissance. I think that is all we can say for certain.

Documenting the rise of the new technology, Lynn White, Jr., discovers no debt to classical antiquity. "It is hard to see what antiquity had to teach the technicians of the 14th and 15th centuries." Nor is the impulse to technological advance a utilitarian impulse. "Quite the contrary." Humanism rediscovers the mathematical texts of antiquity. But new mathematics is not born in the libraries of the *Cinquecento*. The mathematicians know where they come from. Modern scholarship suggests that the knowledge is not decisively enabling. What tells in this first dawn of modern science is not economic pressure nor the rediscovery of texts but art for art's sake, an unexpected way of glossing our salvation. Stillman Drake, in his account of the two schools of mechanics which flourished in sixteenth-century Italy, finds them often working independently. It is as if their discoveries arise by "spontaneous generation." They "appear to have scarcely been aware of one another's existence, though all the men concerned were working actively and publishing in a new and exciting field of study." Traditionally the historian of science, like Pierre Duhem, has detected a "grand continuity" or accreting of effort. "Viewed more closely, however, the simple notion of an orderly (if interrupted) transmission breaks down." [21] Maybe it is there, but the proof is still to seek.

The Christian Middle Ages are undistinguished in point of scientific achievement, and beget a race of men who are able to estimate such a thing as the medieval cathedral. Today in the ambulatory at Chartres the greatest number of worshippers congregate by choice before a contemporary shrine to the Virgin, encrusted with glittering paste. They see no disjunction between the gimcrack statue in its garish and sentimental setting and the glass and statues of the thirteenth century, except of course as they prefer the former. Everyone will have his own illustration. On the one hand the worship of St. Mary Meretrix, on the other the giant pylons that march beside the highway.

These pylons figure the abstracting temper, the renewal of which is coeval with a going back to antiquity as if the Middle Ages

21. Drake (and Drabkin), *Mechanics in Sixteenth-Century Italy*, pp. 13, 15; White, "The Flavor of Early Rensiassance Technology," pp. 45, 50.

had never been. The appropriate metaphor is of a great divide, separating the classic past from the modern or renascent age. The Graeco-Roman world is perceived as descending into the vast hollow called the Middle Ages, "a hollow in which many great, beautiful, and heroic things were done and created, but in which knowledge, as we understand it . . . had no place." To the nineteenth-century historian, whose vision is of a steady progress upward to the light,

> The revival of learning and the Renaissance are memorable as the first sturdy breasting by humanity of the hither slope of the great hollow which lies between us and the ancient world. The modern man, reformed and regenerated by knowledge, looks across it and recognizes on the opposite ridge, in the far-shining cities and stately porticoes, in the art, politics, and science of antiquity, many more ties of kinship and sympathy than in the mighty concave between, wherein dwell his Christian ancestry, in the dim light of scholasticism and theology.
>
> (J. C. Morison, 1887)

In this vision there is something bathetic and much that is eloquent and true. The humanist or natural philosopher is regenerate as he disinters the ancient world. Like his classical antecedents, he is an abstracter. Like them, he is often covetous of use. The crucial resemblance is that we feel him in his commitment to be involuntary or constrained. "It is the very error of the moon, She comes more nearer earth than she was wont." The Renaissance, hearkening to ancient imperatives, witnesses perhaps to a tide in the affairs of men that ebbs and flows back, an ungainsayable tide to be considered in terms of Freud's ugly and suggestive locution, "the return of the Ucs."

One can isolate this return, or flooding back from the collective Unconscious of long-dormant affinities and desires, in historical time. Michelangelo is idiosyncratic, a pallid word for him, also exemplary of the reemerging of the past, as he tells us that "sculpture is achieved by way of removing." To the man with an eye for the comelier truth which the bodice conceals or which lurks at the bottom of the well, that is the indicated definition of creative activ-

ity. The task of the sculptor—by analogy, that of the scientist and
the linguistic reformer—is "to chisel away the refuse of a piece of
marble." As he does so, says Galileo, he discovers the lovely figure
that "lies hidden within." Modern man is intent on this discovery,
or fining down. His impatience with the surface grows more exacerbated as the conviction grows that we can "comprehend what
each thing is in its essence" (Comenius).[22] I think in this connection of the powerful cursoriness with which Michelangelo touches
the face of awakening Day—a type of *humanum genus*—in the
monument to Giuliano of Nemours.

Because "the creative principle resides in mathematics," Einstein holds it true "that pure thought can grasp reality, as the ancients dreamed." But creation does not mean inventing. Einstein,
like Galileo, is chiselling away the refuse. To invent is to discover.
Sir John Beaumont, a spokesman in his minor poetry for the seventeenth century, infers this connection in applauding

> Strong figures drawn from deep invention's springs,
> Consisting less in words and more in things.[23]

Intellection is a parting of the veil. That is the understanding of the
linguistic reformers. James Harris is not contriving a new system.
He is leading forth what has been covert up to now. As a frontispiece for his "philosophical inquiry" (*Hermes*, 1765), Harris offers
the representation of a little angel or putto, removing the drapery
from a bust of the god. The angel, who is meant to symbolize the
Genius of Man, is revealing naked truth. On the bust, the characters of the Greek alphabet are inscribed. The winged woman who
records them is Memory. Only remembering is in question. Harris
agrees, Sprat also, that the physical world is prior to the intellect
that digests it. Knowledge "must be received before it can be
drawn forth." But ultimate priority belongs to disembodied Form,
which is "transcendent and superior to particulars." So we get the
stirring conclusion: it will be proper to invert the School axiom: *Nil*

22. *Continuatio*, Ch. 39; *Dialog on the Great World Systems*, pp. 116–17.
23. "Bosworth Field," 1629.

est in Intellectu, quod non prius fuit in Sensu. "We must now say—*Nil est in Sensu, quod non prius fuit in Intellectu.*[24]

Already in the seventeenth century, the propriety of inverting the axiom is assumed. Webster contrasts the intuited wisdom of God with "the creaturely, womanish, earthly, and serpentine wisdom" which is the meaner possession of "every mountebank empiric and quacksalver." In this second category are the Scholastics, the hole-in-corner investigators, the descriptive grammarians. "Holding the soul to be *tabula rasa* in which nothing is insculpt"— the death of Platonic Forms is a necessary consequence—they suppose "nothing in the intellect that hath not first some way or other been in the senses."[25] Webster supposes that the intellect is a kingdom sufficient to itself. In this kingdom are domiciled the "general forms" which go before the particulars. These forms, says Dr. Dee, who is introducing the first English translation of Euclid from the Greek (1570), "are constant, unchangeable, untransformable, and incorruptible." Unlike the protean truths of the empiric, they await the coming of the presenter in the fullness of time. On the title page of the translation, Time leads on his daughter Truth. The man who rests secure in the knowledge of a certain revelation is like that lucky Benjamin whom Moses describes. He dwells between the shoulders of the Lord.

The mathematical renascence of the seventeenth century is crucial for the achieving of this felicitous condition and that is partly how I should explain it, by analogy to Samuel Butler's discredited giraffe who grows a long neck to get at the nutriment he requires. Fermat and Descartes make the great advance in their discovery of analytic geometry (between 1630 and 1640), which turns the spatial figures of Euclid into numerical or algebraic equations. They are anticipated by Nicholas of Cusa, the exponent of learned ignorance. But though Cusa thinks we are incurably provisional in what we know, he allows of a symbolic approach to knowledge. But he does not look for his symbols in the manifold of finite

24. *Hermes*, 2nd edn., pp. 324–25n., 382, 391; Sprat, *History*, p. 97.

25. *Academiarum*, pp. 31, 69, 85.

and contradictory things. He finds them in the *hortus siccus* of mathematics. To make the inevitable and optimistic analogy to language: in this bloodless world "equivocal words, anomalous variations, and superfluous synonyms" find no admittance (Cave Beck).

The symbolic world of the conceptualizer may be a fabrication or figure. It is, however, true to itself. Kepler seeks to establish this truth by resort to induction. His method differs radically from Cusa's. Robert Small, in the standard treatment in English of his scientific achievement, sees in the *New Astronomy* (1609) "a more perfect example than perhaps ever was given of legitimate connection between theory and experiment, of experiment suggested by theory, and of theory submitted without prejudice to the test and decision of experiments." So we want to dissociate Kepler from the proleptic philosophers, for instance from the author of the *New Atlantis*. But the voyage to the moon, as related in the allegorical *Somnium* or *Astronomia Lunaris* (1634), while richly predictive in terms of scientific discovery, cries for consideration in other terms. Here Kepler is also the *vates* or seer, and the dream he dreams is of an enclosed garden, the "fiorita valle" where Dante breaks his arduous journey. The mother of the voyager finds herself transported, not on the wings of science but on the viewless wings of poetry, where poetry means wish fulfillment, "to any foreign shore I choose." The "marvellous region" to which she elects to flee with her son is Levania—Hebrew for moon—a place "fifty thousand German miles up in the air" and remote from the witchburnings of Kepler's native country of Weil der Stadt. From the festering quarrels soon to burst forth in the agony of the Thirty Years War, the celestial habitation is secure.

A recent editor of the *Somnium* wonders if, beneath Kepler's desire "to broaden understanding of the Copernican theory," there was not the hope of using that understanding to stave off the approaching holocaust. Kepler sharpens the question in a letter of 1623. Why not be done with "the cyclopian morals of this period . . . and secede to the moon?" Luckily for him, he finds an alternative. "If there is anything that can bind the heavenly mind of man to this dusty exile of our earthly home and can reconcile us with our fate so that one can enjoy living—then it is verily the enjoyment of . . . the mathematical sciences and astronomy." [26] As Kepler gives his suffrage to the world of abstract science, we can say that he has transcended the body or that he geometrizes in fulfillment of its needs. The key is the same key, though not always to "lucriferous inventions."

The abstracting writers of the early Christian period, as they are hunting this key, are auspicious of their greater successors in the Renaissance. They are all consulting the entrails. In between is the great hiatus when the search is broken off and the mind and soul are otherwise appeased. Proclus, the fifth-century Neoplatonist and mystic, is sequentially a writer on astronomy and spherical trigonometry. Euclid, though he is trained on Aristotelian logic, confesses the same debt as the mystic to Platonic ideology. From his cosmos, matter is excluded. Gregory of Nyssa, who prefers the ideal form to the colors in which it is dressed, is like his near contemporary Augustine or like the Roman Neoplatonist Victorinus Afer. As in the mystical fraternity of St. Francis, the embryonic scientist and the divinatory man come together. Victorinus is a mystic who survives into the Renaissance as the translator of Plotinus and Porphyry (1497). He is also a rationalizing theologian. Augustine is his pupil. Geometry is congenial to either as it is an impalpable study. The denial each enacts is of matter. The superseding of conventional language is a consequence of this denial. As matter is abraded, the attack on the word begins. It points to the picture of nobody. What follows, from Augustine, is indebted almost certainly to Plato and might be taken from the *Discourse on Method*. "There is one form given externally to all corporal substances according to which potters, carpenters, and others shape forms and figures of creatures." This form is "better in . . . the workman's draught than in the things produced." To reject the things produced is to dwell, like the mystic to whom language is irrelevant, in a world of shadows and inarticulate sounds. Augustine enters this world as he disputes the reality of sensible objects "that are to be seen or touched." [27] Cusa recapitulates his progress, in repu-

---

26. *Sommium*, ed. J. Lear, pp. 73–77.   27. *City of God*, VIII, vi; XI, xxix; XXII, xxv.

diating the discursive intelligence. Cusa and Augustine, in their compensatory reliance on the universal form, are prophetic of new science.

Comenius is scientific in his ultimate labor of reduction, the proposed *Janua Rerum* or key of all things. Partly his debt is to Bacon, as in the *Novum Organum* (1620), partly to Lull's *Ars generalis* (1287). How these two should be compatible is suggested by an illustration of the universe as Lull conceives it, in a Spanish translation of the *Ars Magna*. "Arbor Generalissima Scientiarum" reads the caption, surrounding a diagram of the heavenly spheres. Though the leaves are many, the root is one. In Comenius, as in the projector as a type, the scientist and mystic are the same. In the 1640s, Comenius visits England to find the sinews for the compilation of a vast encyclopedia of learning and the founding of a college dedicated to scientific research. The passage to the heavenly city is through the Gate of Language but language freed of its dependence on phenomena. When, says the author, "by the help of my *Janua Linguarum* youth had learned to distinguish things from outside, it should thence become accustomed to explore that which lieth within." [28] The yield of this interior comprehending is to be expressed—the apposite word—in a cento of useful knowledge. Expressing is, however, its own reward.

As the advocates of linguistic reform deprecate detail, they suggest their affiliation to the mystical communion. *De contemptu mundi:* under that rubric we want to consider them. Kircher, the mage and scientist, is following Ramón Lull in his attack on the multiplicity of tongues (*Polygraphia*), also in his revision of Lull's *Ars Magna Sciendi*. The thirteenth-century mystic is the great progenitor in the effort to create a comprehensive axiomatic system (*scientia generalis*) in which the repertory of scientific ideas can be digested. The anti-Scholastic (anti-particular) intention of the *Ars Magna* or *Ars Lulliana* (1265–74) is exemplified nicely in the hostile negatur with which Lull responds to a lecture delivered by Duns Scotus in Paris. The famous Schoolman is indignant at this affront from an unknown opponent. He answers ironically, after

---

28. *Continuatio*, Ch. 39; Lull, *Arte General para todos las sciencias*, 1586, facing p. 64.

the catechism. *Dominus quae pars?* What part is the Lord? But Lull does not reply in the formulaic manner. In his answer the gist of his philosophy is given: *Dominus non pars sed totum.* The Lord is not a part but the whole.[29] It is the sense of the Latin motto on the title page of the *Polygraphia*, also of the observation with which Kircher concludes his treatise on magnetism (1641). "God," says the latter-day mystic in his character of new philosopher, "is all Nature's magnet."

Not unexpectedly, the contemporaries of this medieval hater of finicking Averroism missed the point. Lull awaits the Renaissance to come into his own. Leibniz, elaborating the calculus, has a pattern before him in the *Ars Magna*. The odious fact with which each begins is that, in the empirical philosophy, "things themselves" (quoting Glanvill) "are lost in a crowd of names." [30] Lull proposes that a name or word be employed only as it represents a known thing. Resolving fundamental ideas to symbolic notation, he combines his symbols to fashion a set of theorems. They lie still beneath his hand. It is the anti-intellectual philosopher who works up conclusions that are "most certain and indubitable." A nonphilosopher like Walter Pater dismisses "metaphysical" questions as "unprofitable," not because the answers are evident but because the questions are incapable of resolution. So he gives himself up to the dark world of the solipsist, assailed by private and irrefrangible impressions which burn and are extinguished with his consciousness of them. Nature thunders in his opening ears and stuns him with the music or, it may be, with the cacophony of the spheres. How should he know? The scientist, however, thinks he knows.

The scientist resembles the linguistic reformer, also the enlightened churchman like the Cambridge Platonist John Smith, as he can see in the visible world "the prints and footsteps" and "the face and image" of the Creator, what Donne calls the "hieroglyphics of God." These hieroglyphics or lineaments, whatever the purblind vision of the sectary, are forever and essentially the same. Bruno says: "All in all and all in any given part, and I call this *natura*, the shadow, the footprint, of the deity." To see God in Na-

---

29. A. E. Waite, *Raymund Lully*, pp. 27–28.   30. *Vanity of Dogmatizing*, p. 151.

ture is not reserved to the modern age. From the foundation of the world God's nature has been revealed in "the things that are made" (Romans 1:20). Dante in his treatise *De Monarchia* detects the "certain footprint of the divine excellence." The difference in this particular between Dante and Bruno, between the thirteenth century and the Renaissance, is that the polysemous truth celebrated or countenanced by the past has become the single truth. More taking than the truth of the tangible world, it haunts the imagination of Renaissance man, though he must put out his eyes like the Abderite to perceive it. But the carnal beauty which language seeks to render, even to embody, is spurned. It is no more substantial than the music of the spheres. Bishop Wilkins in his *Discovery of a World in the Moon* (1638) supposes that we "would have no great loss in being deprived of this music, unless at some times we had the privilege to hear it." [31] That is only a debater's point. Heard harmonies, addressed to the sensual ear, are not so sweet as those that play to the spirit. The new philosopher, like the mystic, is attending to the inner voice.

By convention, the mystic is not associated with the scientific abstracter but with the poet. Each is presented as bemused with idealities. The poet, like the catatonic Shakespeare of Victorian paintings, listens hard for intimations of another world, not so gross as the corporeal world he inhabits. He resembles the mystic, for example Jacob Boehme, the inspired shoemaker of Görlitz. When Boehme lies dying he inquires hopefully of his son, "Do you hear that sweet harmonious music?" The son is willing but coarser grained and so the music of the spheres eludes him. In his skepticism, he is understood to figure forth the temperament of physical science. Unlike the mystic and poet, he does not have the advantage of consulting his inner ear. "Open the door," says Boehme, who is eager to disseminate the heavenly music, "that you may the better hear it." The good-natured maunderings of this seventeenth-century enthusiast represent, in the judgment of a modern historian of science, "the last original effort of the Renaissance against the scientific doom." But the opposition between the mystic and

31. Wilkins, p. 55; Donne, LXXX Sermons, 2, fol. 13; Smith, *Select Discourses*, 1660, pp. 440–41.

scientist is often more formal than real. The vocabularies are different. Plotinus, the type of the mystic, is merely occult: unscientific, in suggesting that the stars are "like letters forever being written in the sky." He proceeds, however, to define the art of the seer as "a reading of the written characters of Nature which reveal order and law." From this definition I think we gather his affinity to the scientist. The vision of the true mystic, says Hooper in his book on number symbolism, "was a revelation of order, and the depth of his penetration was in direct proportion to his comprehension of the precise coordination of all things in a Universal Harmony." [32] The mystic and the scientist are gifted with preternatural power. As that is so, each discovers his appropriate antagonist in the connoisseur of language, whose powers are not so charismatic.

Boehme the mystic, who hypothesizes a "dark world" as primary and poses against it an "outward world" as its "manifestation," is suggestive of Galileo or Descartes. The desire of this outward world "is after the essence of life" (*Signatura Rerum*). A searching out of the signature of things engrosses the philosopher of mechanism. In his opinion, the phenomenal fact or trembling veil (to run the two vocabularies together) is a sensory imposition. "By custom there is color," says Democritus, "by custom sweetness, by custom taste, but in truth there are only atoms and the void." The mystic and scientist evince the same contempt for the customary truth. The alternatives they offer are by no means the same. In the phrase of Marcus Aurelius: "Either Providence or atoms." But whether Providence or atoms is not so important as the positing of a substrate beneath the surface and the impassioned effort to apprehend it. The alchemist, in his quest for the philosopher's stone, is appealing to this substrate. But so is the chemist, who first enters the language in the middle of the seventeenth century and who, as he seeks to verify hidden relations, is sometimes called a Teutonicus, the word for Jacob Boehme. Nicholas of Cusa, who anticipates Copernicus as he believes in a heliocentric universe, believes also that the phenomenal world is a "showing forth

32. *Medieval Number Symbolism*, p. 136; Santillana, *Age of Adventure*, p. 207.

of the inner word" which is not declinable as to number or case. "What are genus and species to us?" asks Thomas à Kempis in his *Imitation of Christ.* To the devotional writer as to the mathematician, distinction pales before the underlying One. Each man is educated (like Erasmus a little later) by the mystical brotherhood of the Common Life at Deventer. The connection is perhaps fortuitous. It is, however, symbolic, as it proclaims a shared belief in the priority of endemic form. In the philosophy of Empedocles, says an early commentator, "the lower stands to the higher in the relation of mantle to core."

The old abhorrence of mantling or concealing is explicit in the art of ancient Greece. Pliny in his *Natural History* defines "the Greek thing": *Graeca res est nihil velare.* Michelangelo, who conceals nothing to the scandal of Pius IV, might write this saying above his lintel. To the Gothic sculptor Giovanni Pisano early in the fourteenth century, nakedness betokens truth exactly as it had to the Greek sculptor who represents Aphrodite Urania, the higher principle, as naked, and the lesser or terrestrial Aphrodite as clothed. The depicting of *Nuda Veritas* becomes, by the sixteenth century, a painterly convention. Botticelli illustrates. He is only one of many.

I describe this convention on its pictorial side in *Shakespeare's Poetics* (1962). Here, synoptic reference should be enough. Note, however, that the psychology on which the convention depends is asserted also in devotional writing. "If the soul were stripped of all her sheaths"—I am following as my principal authority the German mystic Johannes Eckhart—"God would be discovered all naked to her view and would give Himself to her, withholding nothing." Like the painter and sculptor, the mystic identifies the highest power with that "which is stripped of all things." The quotation comes from a work composed in the same years as Pisano's imitation of the Venus Pudica and the naked Hercules in his pulpit for the Cathedral at Pisa. Truth, which God embodies, is most nearly itself as it is "stripped from all 'clothing.' " When we read that "the men shall have their heads uncovered and the women theirs covered," we are meant to distinguish between the mantle and core.

"The 'women' are the inferior powers which are to be covered."
The men are "naked and uncovered" as their power is superior by
far.[33]

The mystic exalts nakedness as symbolic of pure essence. He
is hostile to whatever withholds it from view. His effort to apprehend the ultimate truth takes the form of a struggle to rise beyond
imagery. Like Satan in *Paradise Lost*, he strives to be free of our
common condition, he laments that he is

> now constrained
> Into a beast, and mixed with bestial slime,
> This essence to incarnate and imbrute,
> That to the height of deity aspired.
>   (IX. 164–67)

It is a function of this aspiring that when he meditates on God, he
should decline to avail himself of the conventional metaphors. Like
St. Paul in the first chapter of Romans, he knows nothing of the
avuncular deity with the flowing white beard. Like Plotinus, he
hungers after the ineffable which is the negation of predicates. God
is unique and simple, "without all mode and property." God is
without a name, He is "a superessential negation." But "the God
who is without a name is inexpressible." The highest state is
modeless or stripped not only as a testimony that it is most nearly
true (it "has nothing in common with anything"), but also as a
means of attaining to truth. That is how to read the Beatitude:
" 'Poor in spirit' means: as the eye is poor and devoid of color."
Descartes is bruited, also the logicians of Port-Royal. Human
beings lack that poverty which, as it embraces all things, is really
the sum of all wealth. "Every creature is something finite, limited,
distinct and particular, and thus it is no longer love." But God transcends distinction. (As we look to the future, we should understand
Him as symbolic of the Urform, the primary world of new science.)
God exists, says Jan Van Ruysbroeck, the Ecstatic Teacher, "in an

33. Discussion of Eckhart draws on Sermons: "Modicum et iam non videbitis," "Impletum
est Tempus Elisabeth," "Renovamini spiritu mentis vestrae," "Qui odit animam suam," "In-
travit Jesus in quoddam castellum," "Beati pauperes spiritu", *Book of Divine Consolation*.

absence of modes." To approach His undifferentiated condition, we must "discover in ourselves a bottomless not-knowing." We must put away definition to dwell "in eternal namelessness." The state of namelessness is "the state of void that is mere absence of images." It is approximated in the *Timaeus*, two thousand years later in the *Discourse on Method*.

Because imagery is singular, it makes against the plentitude with which the mystic desires to be filled. God is a pure Nought, the definition of the pseudo-Areopagite, as He is remote from partiality. Alternatively, God is a desert or silence, the definition or anti-definition of Nicholas of Cusa. Eckhart explores the silent desert. Oblivious of the different aspects of the Trinity, perhaps hostile to them, he immerses himself in "the abyss without mode and without form of the silent and waste divinity" from which the Three Persons, in their undivided condition, derive. To divide is to delimit. But "the hidden darkness of the modeless Good," in the phrase of Eckhart's disciple Johann Tauler, is hardly to be bodied forth. In that "ineffable darkness" we attain to the Unity in which distinction is transcended, I should say in which it is denied. Eckhart says: "What is neither here nor there and where there is a forgetting of all creatures, there is the fullness of all being."

The forgetting or obliterating of indigenous creatures is the goal of the new linguistics. James Harris, who tries his hand at the making of a universal grammar (1751), discovers a triple order of Forms in works of art. There is "one order, intelligible and previous to these works; a second order, sensible and concomitant; and a third again, intelligible and subsequent." The first order takes primacy. It is where Eckhart aspires to live. "After the first of these orders the Maker may be said to work; through the second, the works themselves exist and are what they are; and in the third they become recognized as mere objects of contemplation." With the extending of this hierarchy into the natural world, as by Bruno, subsequently by Leibniz and Spinoza, the tie to new science becomes apparent. "Natural substances . . . are but . . . copies or pictures" of antecedent exemplars or Forms. "The whole visible world exhibits nothing more than so many passing pictures of these immutable archetypes. Nay through these it attains even a sem-

blance of immortality, and continues throughout ages to be specifically One amid those infinite particular changes that befall it every
moment." This perception is the Ariadne's thread to which Leibniz
compares the universal language. Failing to grasp it the investigator, hurried "into the midst of sense . . . wanders at random
without any end, and is lost in a labyrinth"—Harris says: "of infinite particulars," and Eckhart: of "finite, limited, distinct and particular" things.[34] It might be Harris in his *Philosophical Inquiry* or
Bacon in the *Novum Organum* who discriminates among the varieties of knowledge, rejecting that which is sensible and even that
which is rational and "much higher" in favor of that most puissant
kind, the abstracting kind by which the soul identifies its Creator.
Eckhart, as he discriminates and chooses, necessarily turns his
back on "the multiplicity which is in this or that" and postulates as
"the ultimate goal" a "dark absence of modes [in which] all multiplicity disappears." Blessed Henry Suso, a good mystic and a bad
Dominican, reads the visible world as a procession of ephemeral
pictures. An illustration in the Berlin Library MS of Suso's Works
depicts the goal in the form of three concentric circles which represent the Godhead without beginning or end. As the soul encased in
a coffin dies into life, its sense of demarcation is annulled. It is
swallowed up once more in the abyss, "merged and lost," in the
language of the Dutch mystic Ruysbroeck, in its "superessence, in
an unknown darkness without mode." Now the soul has won its
way "back to the initial state" which is "void of all form or image."
The denigrators of the physical world from whom I have been
quoting are like the harbingers or forerunners in the poem by
George Herbert. They put the fatal chalk mark on the door.

And yet the abstracting temper of the mystic is not despairing
in its sloughing off of experience. It is optimistic and vital. The aus-
terity of the religious reformer in the beginnings of the Renaissance
is that of Meister Eckhart, fulfilled: "Three things prevent a man
from knowing God in any way. The first is time, the second corporality, the third multiplicity." The mystic, who pioneers in the
attempt to cancel the old demarcations, gives the lead to those who

34. *Hermes*, pp. 351, 377, 380–81, 383–88.

come later, in religion, in letters, in politics, in physical science. Cromwell, who intends the dissolution of the House of Commons (20 April 1653), is confronted with the mace, the symbol of parliamentary privilege. But Cromwell is indifferent to privilege, as to form. "What shall we do with this bauble," he says contemptuously. "Take it away." Luther, though finally he repudiates the mystical communion, is indebted permanently to the simplifying psychology it sponsors. "Except the Bible and St. Augustine, there is no book," he declares, commenting on the work of the fifteenth-century mystic called the Anonymous of Frankfurt, "which has taught me more of the meaning of God, Christ, man, and everything." Like Tauler, to whom he is also attracted, Luther puts little credence in outward manifestations. He is anticipating the end of the phenomenal world. "The angels are getting ready, putting on their armor and girding their swords about them" (*Table Talk*). Hence he promulgates the doctrine that man lives by faith alone. The Protestant playwright, who finds this doctrine agreeable, derides the agency of works in the achieving of salvation (R. Wever, *Lusty Juventus*, c. 1547–53). Catholicism, to a Protestant poet like Edmund Spenser, is identified scornfully with "all those needless works" (*Mother Hubbard's Tale*). The reformer of language, not less than the religious reformer, has no patience with the gathering of trophies. Like Eckhart, he has tasted the spirit and all mundane business seems insipid to him.

In the Renaissance, the absence of clothing or particularity—recurring to Eckhart's sermon, *Impletum est Tempus Elisabeth*—is felt to be estimable partly as it is expedient. That is the connection between new philosophy and praxis. More critically, nakedness is delightful for impersonal or esthetic reasons but not as it betokens carnality, rather the reverse. The absorption in what is denuded or abstracted explains the renewed vitality of mysticism in the same period that witnesses the emergence of Protestantism and its faithful counterpart, post-Tridentine Catholicism, together with a new and vigorous assertion of the claims of physical science and linguistic reform. The mystic, like Sebastian Franck in the early years of the sixteenth century, is efficient in his responses since "to the devout, all is an open book." He does not need to trouble him-

self with the tedious business of hermeneutics. He does not need
to be proficient even in the Scriptures themselves. "The Scriptures
are only the shell, cradle, sheath, lantern, court, letter, veil, and
surrounding of the Word of God." He abominates all that. The
man who is "born of the Spirit," says Zwingli, "is no longer solely
dependent on a book." [35] Francis Bacon is born of the Spirit. He
knows what he is looking at before he has seen it. The concept antedates the thing which is its exemplification. Bacon is not much
concerned with the thing. He does not have to be. Porphyry, the
pupil of Plotinus, is like that in asserting that we know "spermat-
ically" whatever is vegetative, but we know without analysis whatever is across that boundary from which no traveler returns.

The repudiating of analysis is attractive to the mystic simply as
it is attractive, also as it constitutes a shorter way to the truth.
Think of the extolling of Urquhart's mathematics as like a passage
through the Straits of Gibraltar in comparison to the overland journey "of seven thousand long miles." But the passage by land is
even more distressful to the mathematician as he is indifferent to
what he sees along the way. It is congenial to be assured that he
need not undertake the journey. The mystic rejoices in this assurance. The "Divine Intuition" on which Boehme is reflecting instructs him "that the inward, hidden spirit of the elements has
[already] revealed itself," for example in "the form of the fruit."
This fruit (or metal or mineral) is "only a mansion and counter-
stroke of the inward power," whose signature is apparent not as we
open but as we shut our eyes.

35. Zwingli and Franck quoted in Farrar, *History of Interpretation*, p. 341 and n.

CHAPTER FIVE

The Sorcerer's Apprentice

IN Germany in the sixteenth and seventeenth centuries, the mystical communion exhibits what is almost a kind of apostolic succession. The laying on of hands begins with Paracelsus, the equivocal scientist. His primacy descends to Boehme. Not only the Protestant is attracted to mysticism. Increasingly the Roman Catholic takes the point. The Jesuit Peter Canisius edits Johann Tauler. Looking back, there seems not much difference in first and last things between Protestantism and Catholicism, after the Council of Trent. The strategy of Catholicism as a political entity is always to absorb what it cannot subdue. It confers sainthood on the greatest of its mystics, on St. John of the Cross or Teresa of Avila. But it remains unsympathetic. For it perceives that to the mystic the concrete doctrines and forms of the Church are unimportant. But the business of the Church is to mediate between the unknown and the known, not to confess and exult in its own insufficiency. So it must dispute the dictum of the pseudo-Areopagite: "Unitive wisdom is unreasonable, insane and foolish." The mystic is subversive of the Church's pretension to speak in precisely qualified ways. As his abhorrence of reticulated form is so passionate, he helps to create in the years before the Reformation that Laodicean temper on which the success of the Reformation depends.

As the mystic scorns unitive wisdom because it is predicated on the exercise of the analytic intelligence, he is the antithesis of and the natural enemy to the Schoolman. And he is the ally of the physical scientist. The scientist insists on the possibility of knowing. But he also is hostile to the Schoolmen. Why should he attack them when their concern is, like his, with unitive wisdom? The answer is that the Schoolmen come to their conclusions through analysis. "In divine things," says Vives, expressing in a phrase the standard complaint of the Renaissance humanist, "they divide, singularize, particularize, completely, incompletely, as though they were dealing with an apple." That is just what they do. The scientist does not ignore particulars. But he sees them as a halfway house. *Universalia ante rem:* he is always wanting to associate this thing to that other. He is not willing to converse with and to dilate on the thing itself. He prefers the cosmic blue to the local green. The phrase encapsulates the meaning of a poem by Robert Frost and describes his own transition from a major poet to an inferior metaphysician.

> Why make so much of fragmentary blue
> In here and there a bird, or butterfly,
> Or flower, or wearing-stone, or open eye,
> When heaven presents in sheets the solid hue?

The scientist, like the mystic and the philosophical grammarian, is fatigued by all those items that follow in the prepositional phrase.

In the seventeenth century, the generalizing temper is reascendant. The scientist is one of the sons of Plato. He believes that "what we have here is an imperfect copy of what is in heaven. The woman you have is an imperfect copy of some woman in heaven or in someone else's bed." [1] The scientist goes from bed to bed, never pausing for long or lavishing much affection on this or that particular woman in his romantic quest for the perfect woman. Because he is not really concerned—despite his detractors, who have got him wrong—to peep and botanize on his mother's grave, he inaugurates the fashion, still current in our day, of ridiculing Scholastic discourse. The laborious method by which the Scholastic endeavors to find the truth is illustrated in the composition of Gratian's *Decretum.* This codifying of the canon law by an Italian legist

---

1. Frost in a letter to R. P. T. Coffin, February 24, 1938.

of the twelfth century pits one interpretation against another to arrive at the right reading, or synthesis. The subtitle of Gratian's book is a *Concordance of Discordant Canons.* As late as the time of the anti-Thomistic philosopher Pomponazzi, academic business is transacted in this way. Each lecturer in the University of Padua is assigned an antagonist or *concurrens* who speaks from a diametrically opposed point of view. Between these clashing views or endless jars, truth resides. Macaulay, whose psychology is that of the classical scientist, raises the question: "Who ever reasoned better for having been taught the difference between a syllogism and an enthymeme?" He sees no need to stay for an answer.

Discrimination between the scientist and the discredited seer is not so apposite as the perception of sameness. Liberal historians like Macaulay or Henry Charles Lea read history as the repudiating of the past by the future, so they miss the ambiguous compound which is the present. Living for a long time with the contradictions and unexpected complementarities on which the proposition depends, I do not see it as eccentric. I do see that it needs qualification. Bacon as scientist looks mostly to a grand instauration or beginning, Webster to a restoration of what was. Bacon is honored, Webster is ridiculed, as by the astronomer Seth Ward, for "his canting discourse about the language of nature" and "his large encomiums upon Jacob Boehme." He dwells in the warm ether where "the highly illuminated fraternity of the Rosy Cross" utters its sibylline truths. Like the Rosicrucians he supposes that God "hath set all these [natural] things as so many significant and lively characters, or hieroglyphics, of His invisible power." The universe is a "great unsealed book" but not composed of "creaturely-invented letters," rather of "legible characters that are only written and impressed by the finger of the Almighty." [2] The finger of God, the footprint of God: language like this is disgusting to the scientific intelligence.

But consider the interpenetrating in Webster's psychology of superstition and scientific acuteness. Reflecting on the state of modern medicine, he quotes with approval the sonorities of Para-

2. Webster, *Academiarum,* pp. 19, 26, 28; Ward, *Vindiciae,* A4, F4v.

celsus and Robert Fludd. But the esoteric language in which his vision is couched only translates Bacon's vision to a different tongue. Medical science as reinvigorated by William Harvey deserves to be praised. It has "grown to a mighty height of exactness in vulgar anatomy and dissection." Now there follows, but in the jargon of the "skyrer" Edward Kelley, the Baconian reservation: "yet is it defective as to that vive and mystical anatomy that discovers the true schematism or signature of that invisible Archeus or spiritus mechanicus, that is the true opifex and dispositor of all the salutary and morbific lineaments." [3] It is not surprising that Seth Ward is bemused.

Most of us would agree, perhaps without taking thought, that "there are not two ways in the whole world more opposite than those of the Lord Verulam and Dr. Fludd, the one founded upon experiment, the other upon mystical ideal reasons." Webster pursues either indifferently. "Even now he was for [that], now he is for this, and all this in the twinkling of an eye." But this and that are more closely kin than appears to a superficial inspection. Bacon the experimenter is disclosed in a different light in the recollections of his amanuensis William Rawley. "I have been induced to think," says Rawley, "that if there were a beam of knowledge derived from God upon any man in these modern times, it was upon him. For though he was a great reader of books, yet he had not his knowledge from books but from some grounds and notions within himself." Bacon on his more familiar side is earnest in asserting, as in laying out the plan for the *Great Instauration*, that "all depends on keeping the eye steadily fixed upon the facts of nature and so receiving their images simply as they are." Sometimes "a dream of our own imagination" supervenes. By the dream, Bacon lives and is remembered.

Webster resembles Bacon as he sees with the mind's eye, also as he requires the testimony of the senses. His attack on metaphysics because "it brings no better instrument for the discovery of truth than the operations of the intellect" is incomprehensible to

3. *Academiarum*, p. 74.

the lucid but shallow mind of his academic opponent. "Why!" Ward inquires, "hath Mr. Webster any better instrument than this? Is it sense, or is it revelation?" [4] In fact, it is both. To establish the role of air in the calcination of metals, the medical doctor Jean Rey is put to analysis (1630). The heart of his achievement is, however, synthetic. Two methods are potential, to assay by the balance or else by the reason. "The latter is only employed by the judicious, the former can be practiced by the veriest clown." So the question the old crone addresses to Thales of Miletus is answered: "How canst thou know what is doing in the heavens when thou seest not what is at thy feet?"

The schism between new science and revealed religion, preached in our schools at least from the time of Darwin and Huxley, is only an apparent schism. Webster, the scientific promoter and the champion of social and political reform, who dedicates his *Examination of Academies* to the Parliamentary Major-General Lambert, is also a writer of revelatory books bearing titles like the *Saints Guide* on religion. In this he is reminiscent of John Napier, whom we ought to remember not only as the inventor of logarithms but as the author of a "plain discovery of the whole Revelation of St. John." The conjunction is important. Science also is revelatory and Webster is its hierophant. The clergyman and linguist Jeremy Collier the Elder and his correspondent Hartlib are cut from the same cloth. "Mr. Roger Williams of Providence in New England" is addressed and admired by Thomas Urquhart of Cromarty. Williams the evangelist feels the same esteem for his pansophical friend. Each man in different ways is sealed of the new dispensation. Neither the projector nor the religious enthusiast has much traffic with conventional discourse. The theologian William Perkins is like Descartes as he pins his faith to the underlying truth, and so identifies concern with the nuances of language as involvement with secondary business. Perkins demands that the austere rules he has set down for speaking—no more windlasses or assays of bias, no more circumstantiation—"as well be practiced in

4. *Vindiciae*, E4.

writing as in speaking." [5] The distinction of the classical scientist between testing by the balance and the reason is implicit.

A generation ago in a series of influential papers, R. F. Jones set forth the received reading of the scientific distrust of language. It is plausible, and easy to support with quotations from the literature of the seventeenth century. "The distrust of language felt by the early Baconians" is seen as arising from "the difference between the ways of acquiring knowledge adopted by the old and new sciences." Old science—in this context, superstition—means books. "But with the advent of Bacon willingness to experiment and observe was proposed as the prime characteristic of a scientist." [6] On the contrary, the scientist and mage at their highest pitch are superior to experiment and disdainful of the physical world. Each cocks his ear to catch those revelations which take their rise from anterior notions within himself. Kepler the physicist is partly a mage, the emulator of the Neoplatonists Pappus and Proclus. Like his master Tycho Brahé, he is adept in casting nativities. What Kepler is looking for is the pre-existent harmony imparted by God at the creation of the world. In his researches he moves easily from demonstrating a theorem on star-polygons to a discussion of amulets and conjurations. But his mysticism and his scientism, like Cusa's and Newton's, are equally a consequence of his attention to the voices of silence. Descartes, like St. Teresa, sees visions. The result, in her case, is the *Interior Castle* (1577). Under this title, the Cartesian psychology and cosmos are comprehended. Illumination is critical to the thinking of William Gilbert. In his devotion to the inductive method, Gilbert presents the popular image of the scientist. He is also a mystic who supposes that the earth, to avoid being brought to confusion, "turns herself about by magnetic and primary virtue."

Among the well-developed types one encounters in the literature of the Renaissance is the serious projector who is incidentally a crank. But the description is inexact as it evokes the idea of a steady progression, here and there intermitted, "From Magic to

5. *Direction for the Government of the Tongue*, p. 17; Urquhart, *Logopandecteison*, G3.

6. *Studies in the History of English Thought and Literature from Bacon to Pope*, p. 144.

Science" (Charles Singer). Pietro Bongo, a credentialed mathematician of the late sixteenth century, is also a celebrant of the chastity he associates to the number seven. The medieval Cistercian von Heisterbach explains: "Seven is the number of virginity, since no number below the number of ten can be generated from it." [7] Campanella, who is undeflected in the pursuit of scientific truth by years of imprisonment, schemes with no sense of an awkward transition to make a bombing plane out of peacock feathers to blow up the heretics in England. The "Natural History in Ten Centuries" on which Bacon is working at the time of his death considers whether the heart of an ape, "a merry and bold beast," worn near the heart of a man, is a source of comfort and courage. Bacon thinks it is. He is not appealing to sense but revelation. His biographer Rossi documents the connection between them. Thomas Harriot, whose name is linked by his contemporaries with a necromantic School of Night, dedicates a work on algebraic equations to Henry Percy, the Wizard Earl of Northumberland. [8] Harriot is more talented than his patron. So the common chord tends to get muffled. The greatest German algebraist of the sixteenth century, Michael Stifel, is drawn at first to mathematics by a study of the mystic numbers in Daniel and the Book of Revelation. Stifel looks into the seeds of time by manipulating numbers and words. The facile correspondence of sense and nonsense in his writings demolishes, at least for me, the opposition between new science and old superstition. Also one wants to see, what is not often said, that in the Renaissance superstition is not old but new, in the sense that its vitality is enormously augmented. Trevor-Roper, who reads the witchcraze as a recrudescence of the distempered past, is like Santillana, for whom mysticism is the protest of the past against the scientific present. It is the present, not the past, that is obsessed and oracular.

The merging in a single personality of the scientist and the illuminated man is not peculiar to the formative years of new science—the years of the *Fabrica* and the *De Revolutionibus*—

---

7. *Dialogue of Miracles*, Bk. I, Prologue; Bongo, *Numerorum Mysteria*, 1591.

8. *Artis Analyticae Praxis*, 1631.

when the dark perhaps still trenches on the light. Charles Hotham, who participates in the work of the Royal Society, is concurrently the translator and disciple of Jacob Boehme. At the death of Sir Isaac Newton there are found among his papers (on the authority of William Law) large abstracts out of Boehme's work, "written with his own hand." Leibniz, who writes with enthusiasm of the *lingua adamica*, finds that term in the mystics and notably in Boehme. Among his friends is George Dalgarno, who is instructed by intuition "that from all antiquity there must have been some vestigia of that primitive and divine, or purely rational sematology, taught by Almighty God or invented by Adam before the Fall." No one believes any more in the language of Adam. The *characteristica realis* is still current, as in the formulations of symbolic logic. Each emerges, however, from a single matrix.

Discussing the relation of magic and science in the sixteenth and seventeenth centuries, Keith Thomas describes them as advancing together, then moving apart as the superiority of the empirical method is established.[9] But that is not why they move apart nor are they in the beginning rival cosmologies. Each partakes of the "beam of knowledge derived from God." Empiricism is vindicated only as the Platonic impulse is exhausted or temporarily quiescent. The cultivating of alchemy, astrology, cabalistic speculation rises not coincidentally but sequentially with the rise of new science. The magus is unlucky in his ways and means. He aims, however, like the scientist, to read in the Book of Nature "all that is therein contained." I am quoting Webster.[10] Galileo uses almost the same words. Neither Webster nor Galileo is looking at nature with the eye of a naturalist. "De quoi s'agit il?" says Marshal Foch, and returns to his maps.

The quest for a scientific shortcut or Northwest Passage parallels the search for wealth through the transmutation of metals, the search for truth in the lines and indentations of the hand. At the beginning of the fifteenth century the science of chiromancy enters Europe from the East. That it is a bogus science is not so important as the comprehensive power to which it lays claim. The future is a

9. *Religion and the Decline of Magic*, pp. 641–45.   10. *Academiarum*, p. 28.

code, it is like the double helix, and gives up its secrets to the charismatic man. In the same period astrology, against which Dante and Aquinas had raised their voices but in vain, gains ground on astronomy. Dante puts the diviners and astrologers, who arrogate to themselves the providential wisdom, in the Fourth Bolgia of the *Inferno*. "Who is more guilty than he who makes the divine judgment subject to his will?" In the sixteenth century, the guilt is dissipated and the astrologer enters on his majority.

Copernicus is for the closet and the future. The popular craze is for stone or metal talismans on which the signs of the zodiac are engraved. In the inscription, celestial power and protection are understood to reside. Medicine relies increasingly on this power. Exactly as it becomes a more scientific study, it is infiltrated by the occult. The essence of each disease is detected in the constellation beneath which the afflicted man is born. Sidereal influence is the explanation of whooping cough, first observed as an epidemic in 1414. The leech consults the lunar periods or the hours of day and night as he wants to determine the state of the bodily humors. Blood rises in the daytime, it descends in the body with the setting of the sun. Bad blood is bilious blood, so the bile subsides earlier to avoid mixing with it. At the third hour the physician is on the qui vive.

Agrippa, like Paracelsus, is a considerable physician, and a notorious wizard who composes three books of occult philosophy. Hocus-pocus is the business of twenty-one chapters. Others might have been written by a member of the Royal Society, which is not always disinclined to hocus-pocus. Agrippa's English translator suggests a connection. Here is lore "to defend kingdoms . . . to increase riches, to procure the favor of men, to expel diseases, to preserve health, to prolong life, to renew youth, to foretell future events, to see and know things done many miles off." [11] These desiderata are vivid to the Royal Society. The "experiment with the two dogs," as registered by Birch in his history, has for its object the annulling of mortality. To one of the victims "a quantity of nox vomica in butter" is administered, to the other "a quantity of the

11. J. F., Preface to *Occult Philosophy*, 1651.

grand duke's oil of tobacco." The Fellows want to ascertain the re-
storative effect of serpentinestone and water on the two dogs. Their
curiosity is frustrated by the "poisons not working during the sitting of the Society." [12] The humanitarian, who recoils at these vigorous investigations, is reassured by the saying of the Stoic philosopher that "nothing is harmful to the part which is helpful to the
whole."

Attention to comprehensiveness is the hallmark of Jansenist
logic. It has its complement in the Powder of Sympathy, a universal panacea, which inflames the imagination of Sir Kenelm Dighy,
the follower of Hobbes and Descartes, or in Sir Edward Somerset's
"portable engine in way of a tobacco-tongs, whereby a man may
get over a wall or get up again being come down." The promoter of
the pansophical language tutors his contemporaries in the art of
writing with "a knotted silk string so that every knot shall signify,"
or of construing holes in the bottom of a sieve. He is gratifying the
old hermetic desire to keep what one knows to oneself, also the
more modern desire to achieve a comprehensive language, as in
contriving a seal by which "any letter, though written but in English, may be read and understood in eight several languages and
in English itself to clean contrary and different sense." The contrary senses are not only obscure to anyone except the correspondent but are "not to be read or understood by him neither," if
the letter is opened before it falls into his hands. [13]

In these conspiratorial devisings, ingenuity is more apparent
than use. That is not always true. The search for the Philosopher's
Stone, the great fad of the fifteenth century, is informed through-
and-through by utilitarian considerations, writ large. The fad is a
long while in petering out. The characteristic success story in the
subterranean literature of the seventeenth century is likely to tell
us "how at the Hague a mass of lead was in a moment of time
changed into gold by the infusion of a small particle of our
Stone." [14] The renewed currency of alchemical research, for it is a

12. *History*, 1756, IV, 41.   13. *A Century of Names*, B1v-C2r.

14. Waite, *Hermetic Museum*, II, 271.

renewal, is explicable in terms of Reuchlin's dictum that science and the Cabala "both lead back ultimately to the salvation of man." Alchemy flourishes when Neoplatonism is in the ascendant and the mind turns irresistibly to thoughts of an ending and a better beginning, for example in the twelfth century, the age of Joachim of Flora, whose followers await the advent of the Last Days. The reemergence of Ramón Lull from the dark backward is a function of the God-given power he possesses to locate the "right and true composition of both elixirs and universal medicine" by which the quintessence is achieved. "My beloved son," says the mystic, "to make thy Luna deaf of sound and heavy of weight. . . . Take vitriol and dissolve thereof a strong water, and dissolve therein salt armoniac." [15] It is Sir Epicure Mammon on the verge of success, except that chicane and selfinterest are touched with a lunatic zeal.

The attempt of the sorcerer to take order with experience is in the event unsuccessful. Nostradamus survives only in the Sunday supplement. The physical scientist is the better maker. But the validating of the scientific attempt after the fact is not so much to the purpose here as the uncanny nature of the attempt itself. If it is true that the scientist is the pupil of his vaticinatory colleagues, why is it true? The distrust or disusing of physicality, under which term language is emphatically to be included, is common to the early Christian centuries and to the period of scientific revolution, beginning with Cusa. Each period is one of intense dislocation. So the reaction to what is happening on this side of the grave is mournful or apathetic. Dislocation begets not only the preferring of the inner world but a hysterical reading of the world outside the self. This reading is manifest in an absorption with violence and temporal doom, in the conviction that life is a Dance of Death, more dramatically in the conviction that the end of the world is at hand. It is manifest, finally, in the positing of alternatives. The exaggerated Platonism of the first five centuries of the Christian era, like its resumption in the formulae of new science and linguistics, is an alternative.

15. *Philosphical and Chymical Experiments*, 1657, Ch. VII.

In the waning years of Roman rule, despair is epidemic. St. Jerome in the fourth century concludes his translation and amplification of the chronicle of Eusebius with the terrible battle of Adrianople against the Goths. But the dismal story is seamless. As it begins, "barbaric hordes range through our lands and everything is uncertain." In his melodramatic recension, Jerome is looking to put things right. It is apropos that he should make for himself a hell of heaven, where "heaven" is the random spinning of particles in Brownian motion. Eusebius is superficially more hopeful. He finishes his chronicle on an upbeat, with the Peace and Victory of the Church under Constantine. But the language he uses and the vision it communicates are more telling than the event. "Destruction . . . had overtaken the whole brood of God's enemies and at one stroke had blotted them out from human sight." The wicked man is cast down, who had been exalted like the cedars of Lebanon. "And I passed by, and lo, he was not." The vision is apocalyptic, like that of the religious and social evangels in the Renaissance. Sprat is not so hectic but he too has seen the Pisgah-sight.

"Come then, pick up once more . . . Josephus's *Histories* and go through the tragic story of what then happened" when the Romans waded in the blood of the Jewish nation. The history of Eusebius is a continual brooding on the horror "fulfilled in my time." I think of Thomas Muenzer, crying for blood and rejoicing in the carnage which sustains him. Of course he is a hero to Engels and the rest. The confuting of heretics, like the wicked Jews, is agreeable. So is the death of the virtuous Christians, who "found fulfillment in fire." The gloating account of a woman immersed in boiling pitch elicits the comment: "Such was the battle won by this splendid girl." Jesuit art of the Counterreformation—for example, the blood-curdling frescoes in the Roman church of Santo Stefano Rotondo—resumes this same attention to gruesome detail. From the marble tombs of the Renaissance as from the Purgatorial mountain which the early Fathers are ascending, death looks gigantically down. Origen of Alexandria rids himself of the books he has cherished, he denies himself food and sleep, he goes without shoes in the cold. "Such a longing for martyrdom possessed the soul of

Origen." [16] Like Donne in *Biathanatos* or the living man dressed in his shroud, he covets the end.

Living in the world and time is supportable as it is understood to be transient, also as the world is made over in the image of the disaffected man. Gregory of Tours contemplates a savage landscape imagined as by Dürer or Hieronymous Bosch. In his Eight Books of Miracles he is obsessed with wonderworking as a palliative to his misery, also with such questions as how "a fly might be a demon." The Frankish history harps on the same string. Beginning the second book, Gregory resolves to mingle "the miraculous doings of the saints and the slaughter of the nations." If life is no good, death to life is good. Everywhere, liberal culture is on the wane "or rather perishing." He hears his contemporaries cry: "Woe to our day." So he decides, "on account of those who are losing hope of the approaching end of the world"—it is an extraordinary phrase— "to collect the total of past years from chronicles and histories and set forth clearly how many years there are from the beginning." [17]

When the world is turned upside down, whatever is sensory— this time, this place—is rejected. The cult of flagellation argues hatred of the word made flesh. It burgeons with the impulse to monasticism, which means many things, often beneficent, but in this context retreat from the world. Lea in his history of the Inquisition dates the first apparition of the Flagellants as an order or mock-order in the mid-thirteenth century. Not until the Renaissance, however, does the monastic word "discipline" come to be identified with a physical scourge. [18] The identification is right in its time. In the Renaissance, "the three ages are complete." Michael Servetus, announcing the end of the world, has seen the apocalyptic horsemen and the opening of the vials of the wrath of God. The millenarianism to which this tormented revolutionary makes his last-ditch appeal signifies the forsaking of hope in earthly order. The Utopian societies sponsored by Renaissance writers like More

16. Eusebius, *History of the Church*, pp. 112, 240, 243, 245–46, 381.

17. *Book in Honor of the Martyrs*, Ch. 103; preface and beginning of *History of the Franks*.

18. As by Henry Peacham, *Compleat Gentleman*, 1622; James Wadsworth, *English-Spanish Pilgrim*, 1629.

and Campanella are located in the sun or moon or the land of Cockaigne. The myth of the Golden Age, although it invokes the past, is primarily an eschatological myth—see the polemics of seventeenth-century science—and it quickens in the imagination of late medieval Europe as the impulse to mysticism quickens. Richard Rolle, the English mystic, is seeking a way out. So are the peasant revolutionaries whose preaching is coeval with his. The mystic appeals to Abraham's bosom, the revolutionary to the kingdom of heaven on earth. The difference between them, to apply the terminology of the old philosophy, is not "essential" but "accidental." Each begins with the Everlasting No.

In the fifteenth and early sixteenth centuries, we attest the presence among us of the once and future king. Frederick Barbarossa is resurrected as the Emperor of the Last Days. His mission, like Jack Cade's, is to revenge our discontents on the powers that be. The communism of Hus or Muenzer or John Ball is supposed to be enacted in historical time. Its ground note is, however, the deprecating of temporality. The emotional content with which the Third Rome or Third Reich is charged is not positive but negative. That is the connection between the abstracting temperament of the Renaissance and the chiliasm of the early Church. Let us "hasten and run," cries St. Cyprian in the third century, "so that we can see our home country and greet our fathers." It is what Plotinus will say. Augustine echoes Plotinus: " 'Let us fly to our bright country; there is the father, and there is all.' " The flight is defined as becoming "like to God." The more the soul "looks after things mutable and temporal, the more unlike is it to that essence that is immutable and eternal." [19] I see no need to fish for parallels in the *Discourse on Method*.

Outside the walls of Hippo, the Vandals are sitting down to their siege. As their victory is felt to be imminent the glories of our blood and state, "being but a breath and a light smoke," are put away. It is not fit in "these declining times" for men, who "are but pilgrims in this world," to lust after "temporalities." Here is not so good as there, "that royal and imperial city of angels above . . .

19. *City of God*, IX, xvi.

where the will of Almighty God is their only law," not the vagaries of barbarian kings. Despising "the fumes of vain words," the wise man—he is by definition an ascetic—endures with patience the calamities that fall on the children of God. For calamity does not matter "in respect of this short and transitory life." Goodness is equated with deprivation. The kingdom is spiritualized and deferred. The doctrine of the two cities is promulgated. In this world "the predestinate and the reprobate" dwell side by side. But the general judgment is coming.[20]

The early centuries are Platonic and millenarian as they accept the doctrine of the two cities. The same description holds for the twelfth-century renascence. Bernard of Clairvaux, in his Platonic impatience, modifies the canonical or Augustinian description of the three ages which comprise the life of the universe. The primitive age before the Law and the more hopeful age beneath it are compressed to a single age, anticipating the millennium or perfected life under Grace. Joachim of Flora imagines the Rule of the Father, or Night, as giving way to a Reign of the Son, or Dawning Age, at last to the Age of Noon. The middle period is elucidated by Charles Singer, concluding his survey of *The Dark Ages and the Dawn of Science:* "The early morning twilight is over, the dawn is upon us and it was the risen sun that Harvey and Galileo saluted, and in the light of which Francis Bacon and Descartes did their prophesying." The time of Noon or crowning age is abstracting, always to the millenial temperament. Its president is the Holy Spirit. It is supposed by the Calabrian mystic to await the year 1260. The Renaissance, though it is necessarily more patient, is not less convinced that the millenium is at hand. It is therefore not less exclusive in its response to ephemeral or secondary business. "We are at the threshold," says Cromwell to the Barebones Parliament (1653), "and therefore it becomes us to lift up our heads and encourage ourselves in the Lord." Luther, speaking for revealed religion, expresses the "firm belief" that "the last day is already breaking." Sprat, speaking for new science, breathes the same assurance, "so near is mankind to its happiness." Is there no dif-

20. *City of God,* I, i, viii, xxxiv; II, xix; IV, iii; V, xvii, xxiii.

ference between Luther and Sprat? or, a more likely illustration, between Boehme and his contemporary Joannes Sturmius, who is eminent in the continued fraction expansion of π, and arranges prophetic verses on the twenty-one throws of the dice?

I am not venturing a cheap shot at the occasional credulity of the scientist. Everyone rides his hobby horse. In another context, emphasis might fall as easily on making distinctions rather than connections. Luther in his Table Talk is pathological, Sprat in the *History* is merely vulgar. The point is that the scientific renaissance of the sixteenth and seventeenth centuries, like that of the pseudo-sciences, is an exorcistic rite.

The scientist, as he is the devotee of perfect coherence, is the colleague of the arithmologist, the linguistic reformer, and the maker of the more simplified allegorical poem. Like them, he conceives the world under the aspect of a blueprint. The number mysticism which dominates in the early Christian and late classical period and which flickers with a crazy light in the pages of Philo and Origen, Augustine and Bishop Isidore, and the Neoplatonic philosophers, signalizes the great disorder by which these centuries are recognized, also the violent order which attempts to redress it. The venerating of form becomes idolatrous as the walls are beginning to crumble. Number is the annulling of decay. It means the imperious insistence on order which physicality in its infinite permutations disturbs. It is the impalpable bedrock on which classical science is founded.

The scientist continues and fulfills the preoccupation of the mystics and millenarians and their successors in the modern period with the making of unassailable systems. He is the numerologist, par excellence, and his ruminations, not less than those of St. Augustine, are intended to banish the void. He does not acknowledge that the pattern of existence (which may be a contradiction) is "Epicurus' dream of innumerable worlds" in which whimsy determines "the casual coming together of atoms, and so by their parting dissolves them." He affirms as dogmatically as the more primitive numerologist that "nature has some cause, knowledge some form, and life some direction and sum." [21] To find out this direc-

21. *City of God*, IX, v; XI, xxv.

tion he fabricates a model, which is the scientific control. The model, like the *hortus inclusus* of symbolic logic, is an ideal construction. It is elaborated for the purpose of discovering the nature of reality. It is intended to objectify. In numerological or paratactic constructions the irreducible particular is, however, forbidden. Partly, that is for defensive reasons. The analytic intelligence, as it is unconcerned with the promoting of a comprehensive scheme, imposes no such ban. It may be figured as working empirically (like William Harvey or Vesalius but not like Francis Bacon), and with no special goal in view. It assays or it engages in a labor analogous to titration. In the year of Shakespeare's death, Harvey communicates to the Royal College of Physicians the first fruits of his emergent theory on the circulation of the blood. Special pleading is no part of his intention. Shakespeare in beginning his plays is ignorant of their endings. He is also indifferent to them. To the man obsessed with form, this indifference is a luxury he cannot afford.

Often we feel, reading in the literature of the Middle Ages, that the search for form, though unsuccessful, is conducted without anxiety. Hugh of St. Victor, dilating on the "Names of the Sacred Books," is fantastic, also laconic. So is the influential encyclopedist Raban the Moor (*De Numero, De Universo*). So is Jacobus de Voragine, the author of the *Golden Legend* or Readings in the Lives of the Saints. And sometimes the writer brings us up short. Dante, like Augustine, seems urgent or selfindulgent, as in making a gratuitous acrostic of the representative penitents in *Purgatorio* XII, or in locating Eden at the exact center of a southern hemisphere of water and Jerusalem at the center of a northern hemisphere of land. The geographical opposites confirm, perhaps they establish the antipodal opposites of first felicity and first sin against redemption from sin and felicity renewed. Our sense is strong that the proposition depends on the writer's ipse dixit. Complementarity is obvious but not the reason that engenders it when Guido del Duca the Ghibelline, lamenting the moral fall of Tuscany and Romagna, devotes to each account the same number of lines and orders each account in three parts. In *Purgatorio* XXXII, seven flames are made to shine on the soldiery of the celestial kingdom, seven nymphs encircle Beatrice and carry seven lights in their hands, the holy chariot puts forth seven heads. Of course these details are explicable allegorically. The chariot, for example, presents ecclesiastical corruption. But though the fact or supposed fact—the Church bemonstered with the Seven Deadly Sins—tallies with the number, the correspondence strikes us as curiously insistent. Dante does not possess the modern faculty of apprehending beneath phenomena a clearly articulated pattern. He finds a substitute for this necessary pattern—necessary, as art must always pretend to form—in willful analogizing or in the superstitious exploiting of number. He has got to assimilate the errant fact somehow. If the favor of integrity is not imparted from within, it will have to be traced on the surface. In the kind of art he sponsors, arbitrary parallels function as the cohesive agent.

Dante is, with Shakespeare, the most visual, hence temporal, of the greater writers. It is a real man, not a wraith, not a symbol, who follows Virgil through the night of the dead and up the penitential mountain, "con questa vera carne." But already in Dante the finding out of an ordering principle in the work is a matter of overmastering importance. The compulsiveness is modern. The principle itself—as Dante, like Spenser in his psychology, is of the Middle Ages and so not endowed with the more penetrating eye of modern man—is located in the extrarational virtue imputed to number. After nine revolutions of the heavens, dating from the birth of the poet, the Lady who is the heroine of the *Vita Nuova* first enters his life. Her mortal sickness terminates on the 9th of June, 1290—on the ninth day of the ninth month and at the beginning of that decade "in which the perfect number [10] was nine times multiplied within that century in which she was born." Here Dante reckons "according to the division of time in Syria . . . seeing that Tismim, which with us is October, is there the first month." Having fabricated the connection himself, he proceeds without irony to ask "why this number was so closely allied" to the woman. The reason is that "the revolving heavens are nine . . . [and] together have influence over the earth." At the birth of Beatrice "all these nine heavens were at perfect unity with each other as to their influence." Three is the efficient of nine. And "the Great Efficient of Miracles" is Himself Three Persons in One. It follows, by an act of will to which reason is satisfied to pander, that "this lady was accompanied by the number nine to the end that men might clearly perceive her to be a nine, that is, a miracle, whose only root is the Holy Trinity."

The educing of form is God's business. The power is of God which brings "form for the nests" (*Paradiso* XVIII). He is in character, conferring gratuities. He does not need to confer them. This generous power, aloof from ulteriority, belongs also to the artist, in fact it describes him as he collaborates in the endeavor to "fill the cradles right" (Yeats in "Under Ben Bulben"). Obsession with form is, however, morbid as it reflects a *horror vacui*. To assert the control which might otherwise elude him, Dante, as the Middle Ages reach their term, builds the *Divine Comedy* of duads and triads. His choice of *terza rima* is an odd choice prosodically for a long discursive poem, as odd as the Spenserian stanza. The interlocking form to which he commits himself, like the triune scheme he employs in dividing his poem into parts—33 cantos in each of the 3—or the studied antitheses on which Milton constructs *L'Allegro* and *Il Penseroso*, or the arbitrary correspondences of the *Faerie Queene*—these describe a kind of architecture whose function is not philosophical but placatory. Dante and Spenser are more taken than Milton with sensuous experience. The fascination in their work with compulsive design, which is the negation of such experience, is rooted in their intense response to the drossy and mutable world whose transmutation is the subject of their verse: the world of Guelph and Ghibelline or the exiled Colin Clout. Arbitrary construction, whether rhetorical or ritualistic—as in the *tableaux vivants* or the allegorical pageant—replaces real turbulence with an appearance of order, which is often apprehensible in diagrammatic ways and is thereby the more airless and evidently controlled.

In the nineteenth century the unhappy poet John Davidson, who dies at last by his own hand, seeks to elaborate "a new cosmogony" in which this order does really exist. Having survived for fifty years in a world unfitted for him "and having known both the Heaven and the Hell thereof," he resolves "to destroy this unfit world and make it over again in my own image, because that cannot be transcended." The regenerative instrument is to be "a new poetry," which means explicitly "a new habitation for the imagination of man." To the building of this better habitation, Dante in his new poetry addresses himself. The Thomistic scheme which informs the *Divine Comedy*, like the Neoplatonism of the *Faerie Queene*, promises access to "the king's highway that leads to the eternal dangerless kingdom" (*City of God*, x, xxxii). The poet, as he possesses these alternatives to experience, is enabled to conduct others and not least himself to that equable city which Cacciaguida evokes in the *Paradiso*, a city that never was yet.

The "new cosmogony" which the troubled psyche announces is perfectly symmetrical, therefore irrational. It entails no necessary correspondence with things as they are. Its collocations are spurious. This does not mean that they must fall to pieces as they are touched. The more arbitrary the structure, the more hectically will it stipulate its own coherence. Spenser's poetry, as illuminated by what I believe to be the valid insights of scholars like Hieatt and Fowler, is only the most obvious illustration. The 24 units of the *Epithalamion* match the units or hours of the marriage day which is the subject of the poem. The first 16 stanzas, which celebrate the waking day, conclude with one refrain: "The woods shall to me answer"; the remaining stanzas, given over to the night, with another: "The woods no more shall answer." The division signalizes with mathematical nicety the hours of daylight and darkness at the summer solstice in Spenser's latitude on the day the poem is written to commemorate. More than this, the longer lines, pentameter or hexameter, total exactly 365. So the greater round of the year is reflected. This passion for exactitude is remarkable in other poems. I want to avoid a plethora of illustration, so I shall ask the reader to see for himself. The interior music which is Spenser's principal achievement depends on the invoking of an endlessly reticulated pattern of conventional emblems or syntactic units or numbers or names. The iteration is hopeful, for it pretends to describe and so to master the world outside the poem. The poet, as he mutters the formulae of which his model (he would say, his microcosm) is built, thinks to bind and metamorphose the greater world, as by charms and conjurations. An addiction to number is crucial to the incantation he is performing. He is innocent of the modern doctrine of expressive form. Design does not betoken a unity he perceives in his material but compensates for his myopia in failing to perceive it. The failure is potentially mortal in the context of the late sixteenth century. It is redressed by a levying on number whose function is unifying or contagious.

If, like Sidney or Jonson in most of their poetry, the better maker rejects numerology as childish (medieval), he is inclined as an alternative to give primacy to rhetoric, which he carries to the final power. Subordination is displaced by equal predication. The compulsive rhythm seems not to manifest logical exigency so much as an obscure need to propitiate a distressing response to the world without the self. The paratactic style allows the writer to force the response into rigid and highly artificial patterns. In these patterns, the odd is made even. Milton displays a bewildering array of subordinating devices. But his syntax is so complex and idiosyncratic as to yield an effect more beholden to sound than to logic. The hypotactic style, as it seeks to mirror things as they are, will depend, conversely, on the essentially mimetic use of modifying elements, relative clauses, phrases in apposition or else subordinated to one another: the style of Shakespeare. Milton is the parodist of the hypotactic style.

The medieval maker, unlike the new scientist or philosophical grammarian, is formal in our modern sense only ostensibly. Medieval allegory is defined, like the lucubrations of Philo Judaeus on the Ten Commandments, by an infinite-progression scheme. Ideally, it is coexistent with the end of the world. It can go on forever for it is not responsive to an awareness of mandatory fact. The author's fiat is controlling, perhaps his loss of interest, perhaps his death. This kind of writer, like a free-falling body, continues until he is checked. How should he not? In his world there are no laws but only injunctions. The *Faerie Queene*, as it is unfinished, is the right representative of the medieval poem, also as it asserts design by hunting numerical guidons. In each book one canto and always the same canto is devoted to instruction. In each book one canto records the adventures of Arthur which, with one exception, occupy in every book the same position. I do not suppose that the exception proves the rule, though I am at a loss to explain it. Freud would say it is no accident. In the eighth canto Arthur intervenes.

That is not because the narrative requires his presence but because the number eight, in medieval arithmology, signifies regeneration. The appearance of Arthur at this moment in the poem is no more necessary (rational) than the octagonal pillars in the Knights' Hall at Mt. St. Michel. Anarchy is the mirror image of despotism, and formlessness of coercive form. So to most readers the *Faerie Queene* appears formless.

The sequence of 12s with which Spenser likes to work suggests the same point. The *Shepherd's Calendar* is divided in 12 eclogues, so made proportionable to the 12 months of the year. These in turn stand for the 12 ages of man, whose progress from youth to age might with equal logic be depicted in 3 ages or 7. What we are confronting here is not logic so much as a wistful allegiance to the coercive power predicated of the duodecad, which symbolizes a unified cycle and even creates it, as the sign is identified with the cause. "Are there not," the Lord inquires, "twelve hours in the day? If any man walk in the day he stumbleth not, because he seeth the light of this world" (John 11:9). Spenser, who designs his epic poem in 12 books, walks in the light of day and hopes not to stumble. As he conceives his story, Book XII is the real beginning, also the conclusion. The snake bites its tail and completes a perfect circle, as in the hieroglyphic by which the alchemist symbolizes transmutation. The governing intention is not so much artistic as a banning of chaos. This intention is evident when, in the twelfth book, Gloriana, the Faerie Queene, is made to celebrate her annual feast in the course of 12 days: "Upon which 12 several days the occasions of the 12 several adventures happened, which, being undertaken by 12 several knights, are in these 12 books severally handled and discoursed." The 12 virtues which the 12 knights embody are summed in Magnificence, the quintessential (or duodenal) virtue, whose embodiment is Arthur. To exorcise the horror and suspicion of a vacuum, and to honor the Stagyrite who posits Glory as the end and prime achievement of Magnificence, Spenser sees to it that design dominates absolutely in the auguring of Arthur's union with Gloriana. This union is the apogee of the poem. All lines converge, symmetry is accomplished, not the symmetry of a tree but that of an equation, and the narra-

tive scheme and the ethical scheme, like Antipholus E. and Antipholus S., discover their interesting connection.

The medieval maker, whether he is harried, whether he is
equable, is necessarily brazen. In contrast to his more scrupulous
successor in the modern period, he postulates *a priori* connections.
To a random series of similar effects, he assigns a meaningful or
causal relation. It is a tenet of medieval natural history that the
newborn cubs of the lionness seem dead for three days and that on
the third day the lion comes and with his breath endows them with
life. This supposed fact begets, on the insistence of glossarians like
Honorius of Autun, an analogy to the death and resurrection of
Our Lord. The practice of Honorius, whose twelfth-century encyclopedia supplies the preacher with a collection of sermons for
the principal holy days, is to symbolize an event in the biography
of Jesus not only by discovering a parallel in the Old Testament but
by stipulating analogies in the animal kingdom. Arbitrary parallels
are equally conspicuous in the construction of the medieval cathedral. The head of the church has got to point to the east because
that is the quarter in which the sun rises. On the western portal
the Last Judgment must be depicted, by analogy to the going down
of the sun. The north is cold and dark and the south warm and
light and therefore, as at Chartres, the heroes of the Old Testament must stand in the north porch and those of the New Testament in the south.

Alternatively, form is imposed by the elaborating of a sacred
chronology. Since the divinity of Jesus is attested by the Adoration
of the Magi, and in His Baptism when a voice from Heaven salutes
Him as God, and in the miracle He works at the Marriage of Cana,
the Middle Ages, reading backwards, assert the identity of these
three feasts, which are supposed to have taken place on the same
day of the year. The medieval insistence on numerical complementarities is still alive, in furtive ways, in the seventeenth century.
The death of Cromwell occurs predictably on September 3, 1658:
the anniversary of the day he had arrived at Drogheda, and beaten
the Scots at Dunbar, and opened his first Parliament as Protector.
The biographer Aubrey, taking a hint from the mathematician John
Pell, points to the recurrence of the number six in the career of

Alexander the Great.[22] The recurrence suggests that the career is of a piece.

Flux is denied and history made to exhibit more than a linear progress. Where God created Adam, there the Annunciation is held to have occurred. The Cross of Golgotha is raised in the center of the earth, which is the center of the universe. Around it revolve the sun and the planets. Beneath it, Adam is buried. The blood of the crucified Jesus, running into the earth and washing the bones, redeems us from original sin. Nearby stands the altar where Abraham makes ready the death of his son. Isaac is real, he is also analogous. He must carry the wood against his own immolation even as the Savior bears His own Cross. But the complement, as Augustine picks at it, is more extensive. "Who is the ram for sacrifice, caught by the horns in a bush, but He who was fastened to the Cross as an offering for us?" The coming on of this offering is predicted long before. The cradle in which the infant Jesus is sleeping is already the altar on which He is slain. "Ponitur in praesepio, id est corpus Christi super altare": quoting the glossarian Walafrid Strabo.[23] The Cross on which Jesus hangs is made of the Tree of the Knowledge of Good and Evil. He dies on a Friday, the day on which the Incarnation is accomplished, and the Creation of the world, and the imparting to Adam of the breath of life; and at the third hour, in which Adam is first guilty of sin. The forgiveness of this sin turns partly on the mercy associated with the Virgin, as opposed to the folly presented by the mother of us all. Mary is the second Eve. That is the significance, in medieval painting and sculpture, of the apple she holds in her hand.

Dedication to typology is no doubt a *pis aller*. Medieval man believes in the Resurrection and the Life, so he has his eye on last things. The anonymous maker of a play from the Chester cycle is adjuring us:

> For now you know the time is come
> That signs and shadows be all done;

22. Aubrey, *Day-Fatality*, 1696, in *Miscellanies*, 1890.

23. Strabo glossing Luke, Ch. 2; Augustine, *Contra Faustum*, Bk. XII, para. 25.

Therefore make haste that we may soon
All figures clean reject.

The High Middle Ages are, however, to be distinguished from the early centuries as from that late and turbulent period which ushers in the Renaissance. The beginning and the ending, when the moon is a crescent moon, are marked by the collapsing of nerve. As dramatic change impends, when the Roman world is dying or the modern world is struggling to be born, the cultivating of arbitrary formulations intensifies. I see it as an expedient to avert the threat of chaos.

The master spirit in the twelfth and thirteenth centuries is committed, like Jacopo Torriti, to parting the veil. And obviously the veil detains him. Who would not agree who has looked at the apse mosaic of Santa Maria Maggiore? It is tempting to say of Torriti that contemplation suffices, as of "this majestical roof fretted with golden fire." Obeisance to analogy or number does not inhibit his ardent attending on the effect. In the "Coronation of the Virgin," numerology participates. But the great mosaic is not a paradigm. It is a celebration in stone of all those intractable (secondary) details which engage and enrapture the senses. The remoter past is indifferent to detail. Its allegiance is given to Plato and his epigones: Porphyry, Proclus, Plotinus. Its cultivating of numerology is more assiduous as its craving for form or the simulacrum of form is more desperate, concurrently as the sustenance it derives from this middle earth is so much more thin. History is a place of skulls. So Augustine declines to consult it. He creates his own history. Recalling that the ark is fifty cubits in breadth, he decrees a parallel to the descent of the Holy Ghost on the fiftieth day after the Resurrection. As the vessel which rides out the Flood and which figures the human body is enlarged, so in the time of Pentecost are the hearts of the disciples. But the ark is also thirty cubits in height, a decorous measurement, for "Christ is our height, who in His thirtieth year gave His sanction to the doctrine of the gospel." Noah, who preserves the seed of man, as he counts his family discovers himself the eighth in number; Christ, in whom "the hope of our resurrection has appeared," rises on the eighth day from the dead. The Deluge, continuing for forty days and forty nights, prefigures or corroborates the sacrament of baptism by which our sins against the Ten Commandments in all four quarters of the world are remitted. What is the connection? Augustine answers smoothly: "4 times 10 is 40." [24]

Failing to detect the shape beneath the surface—the great and saving achievement of Renaissance science—the observer has no choice but to predicate fetishistic qualities of the surface. Each number of the decad is invested with cosmic or moral or theological attributes. For the decad is the perfect sum. It contains within itself, says Philo Judaeus, "every variety of number," both even and odd and the various fractions.[25] Philo is establishing the integrity of the Decalogue. Mystic arithmetic governs in making for the integrity of the *City of God*. Ten books of the twenty-two are devoted to refutation (the Commandments are ten), twelve books to affirmative argument and exposition (the Apostles are twelve). The efficiency of the sacred hieroglyphic is in binding together, but by a species of reticulation the eye cannot discern, what would otherwise be loose and discrete. The cause of this preternatural power derives, on the word of St. Isidore, "from this, that in the beginning God made twenty-two works." A close perusal of Scripture is indicated, but that is the métier of these hunters after form. "For on the first day," says Isidore, God "made seven, that is. . . ." But let us take his word. The configuration is of substantial importance in its own right. The numerologist, as he has got his feet on the ladder, does not pause to consider it, or not now. "On the second day," God made "the firmament alone. On the third day, four things: the seas, seeds, sowing, and planting. On the fourth. . . ." And Isidore continues, until he gets to the requisite number.[26]

From the enumeration certain consequences follow. It is necessary that there be "twenty-two generations from Adam to Jacob,

24. *Contra Faustum*, Bk. XII, paras. 14–25. (The eighth day is "the day after the seventh, or Sabbath day.")

25. *Concerning the Ten Commandments*, III, 140–41.

26. *Etymologies*, Bk. XVI, Ch. xxvi, para. 10.

from whose seed sprang all the people of Israel, and twenty-two books of the Old Testament as far as Esther, and twenty-two letters of the alphabet out of which the doctrine of the divine law is composed." Agrippa at the other end of the great divide is predicted. This fanatical excursus on number begins with a particular question. Isidore, who wants to know first of all why the peck is comprised in forty-four pounds, perceives that this measure is equivalent to twenty-two sextarii. After that there is no stopping him and especially since, in building his sacred edifice, he allows himself the saving dispensation of counting only "as far as Esther."

The congeries of number which the Neoplatonist or the exegete of the Iron Age identifies with significant form is not sequential but tyrannical. We are willed to believe that the river flowing out of Eden, as it rises in four heads, betokens the cardinal virtues, or that the number of the Apostles is verified by the twelve stones taken from Jordan. Irenaeus, the first of the great Catholic theologians, assures himself that there can be only four gospels. That is because there are four quarters of the world and four winds and four cherubic forms. Irenaeus wants to know where we are. Modern man asserts that the hieroglyphics which are his most considerable achievement are the translation or representation of immanent law. The book of Nature, says Galileo, is written in mathematical characters. It is possible that Augustine would make the same assertion. Only in terms of the evidence he adduces, the assertion fails to prove out. The difference is qualitative (unless one is willing to describe the language of modern mathematics as a solipsistic exercise) between the calculations of the scientific philosopher and those of the alchemist, who represents the transmutation of matter by inscribing on the figure of a dragon or salamander the mystic letters "all is one" (ἐν τὸ πάν), and attaching crucial importance to the presence in those three words of exactly seven letters. In his mind is the saying of Deuteronomy: "The Lord shall cause thine enemies that rise up against thee to be smitten before thy face: they shall come out against thee one way, and flee before thee seven ways" (28:7). As Lactantius is aware of the power of the heptad, he seeks to invoke it by composing his *Divine Institutes* in seven books. The same purpose inspires Macrobius in his division of the *Saturnalia*. "Of the perfection of seven" Augustine "could say much," and in fact he goes on at some length. Martianus Capella is more copious than Augustine. It is he who fixes the number of the liberal arts as seven. For him the controlling text is in Proverbs (9:1): "Wisdom hath builded herself an house, she hath hewn out seven pillars." Analogy dictates that there will be seven virtues and seven deadly sins and—as Yeats remembers—seven topers of Ephesus. Not reason but desperation attaches this mysterious faculty to number. No alternative offers. "Take number from all things," says Isidore of Seville, "and all things perish." [27]

Everything I have read, more persuasively what I have seen, suggests that man in the High Middle Ages is not so pestered as this. The perception of organic form continues to elude him, as it eludes his predecessors. So he is put to employing the same crazy surrogates. In his eclecticism he continues to honor the paradigmatic teaching of Platonic philosophy. Mostly, however, his allegiance goes to "solider Aristotle." His genius and temper are plastic. He does not desire to retreat into a non-physical world. The figures at Chartres stand where they do in deference to sacred mathematics. But they stand forever. The blind shade that speaks to Dante on the terrace of Envy "looks" expectant. How can this be? If anyone wants to know, says the poet triumphantly, it was lifting up its chin in the manner of the blind. This shade or nonperson "is a citizen of the one true city," gladdening thereby the heart of Augustine. Nonetheless we see it peering, with its sightless orbs. In the Abruzzi not far from Rome is the city of L'Aquila, founded in the thirteenth century by the aggregating of 99 autonomous districts. Necessarily, the number breeds. The 99 *rioni* have their complement in 99 castles, 99 squares, 99 fountains, 99 churches. In the Fontane delle Canelle, 99 stone heads eject water. A bell in the old tower of the Law Courts tolls at evening 99 times. But go to L'Aquila and see what the thirteenth century constructed, while it was manipulating number.

Earlier in the century the Fourth Crusade, lured by Venetian greed, breaks off its attempt to redeem the Holy Sepulchre and

27. *Etymologies*, III, iv, 13; *City of God*, XI, xxxi.

sacks the Christian city of Constantinople. The fate of the Eastern Empire, though long deferred, is written. Pope Innocent resolves to extirpate his fellow Christians, the Albigenses of southern France. The resolution is suicidal, medieval Christendom turning on itself and rending itself. It needs a great man to kill a great thing. Innocent III is this man, the first pope to brand and isolate the Jews of Rome who, in more tolerant times, had produced a pope themselves. Tolerance argues assurance. Antisemitism testifies to the draining away of assurance. Like the virulent Jewbaiting of the late nineteenth century as the nations of Europe prepare for Armageddon, it is the hysteric protest of a menaced psyche. The founding of the papal Inquisition in these years is a corollary phenomenon. So is the baleful eminence of the ascetic healer Fulk of Neuilly, who leads his pauper army to destruction and initiates the madness of the Children's Crusades. The story of the Wandering Jew, the emblem of eternal expiation and always, when we hear it, the presage of trouble to come, is first bruited. The Middle Ages, at the apogee, are making ready their own extinction.

In the waning Middle Ages the remoter past is reincarnate. A fascination with number returns with it. This fascination becomes progressively more acute from the fourteenth century onward. The architectural unity of the *Divine Comedy* depends on the imputing of sovereign power to an arithmological constellation. To choose one compendious example: in the sacred heptad, by the common consent of many centuries, the contagious virtue attributed to number is understood to be extraordinarily potent. So Dante builds the Mount of Purgatory of seven ledges. By ascending them he arrives on the heights of theology. In witnessing so insistently to this belief in the efficacy of number, Dante reaches back a thousand years and beyond. No one, says Philo Judaeus, can be innocent of the fact that "those infants who are born at the end of the seventh month are likely to live, but those who have taken a longer time, so as to have abided eight months in the womb, are for the most part abortive births." [28] In this translunary sphere where number is regnant, the sorcerer and the mystic are lodged. The

28. *Questions and Solutions*, IV, 323.

new scientist and the philosophical grammarian escape confine-
ment there. Their incantations are fruitful in the event.

New philosophy, fleeing the world, creates a better alternative. The Jesuit churches of the Counterreformation, made in the
same decades and in the same spirit, create their own interior cosmos. The fantastic *trompe l'œil* of the Gesù, the mother church
where St. Ignatius lies expecting the Resurrection and the Life,
enacts the rhetorical question: "O grave, where is thy victory?"
The vaulted hall displaces the colonnades of the post-classical basilica. Unity is more than integrity. The aisleless nave, bordered with
chapels, proclaims a catholic religion. This means that the whole
man in his quirkiness finds no admittance. Neither does the unfil-
tered light of day.

> Churches are best for prayer that have least light:
> To see God only, I go out of sight—

Donne, concluding "A Hymn to Christ." In the fifth-century basilica of Santa Sabina, there are as many windows as bays. The seventeenth century walls up the windows. Inevitably, there are exceptions; the greatest is Borromini. But the masters of the baroque, if
they repudiate the brazen world, reconstitute a purged and golden
world within. The interior gloom is irradiated, not by life but by
art. Churches like San Silvestro in Capite, Santa Maria in Via,
Santa Croce in Gerusalemme transport us to a world where the
boughs hang heavy in a perfect sky.

Bernini, evoking his ecstatic St. Teresa for the Cornaro chapel
of Santa Maria della Vittoria, is resuming with a different eye the
labor of the first seven days of Creation. You can say that the fantasy world of baroque affirms the corporality which radical Protestantism condemns, even as the flourishing of mosaic in the
hundred years of the Iconoclasm answers to the spoliation of the
Greek emperors of Constantinople. But the corporality has been
miraculously changed. Bernini's St. Teresa is participating in a theatrical performance. Spectators appraise this performance from
their boxes. What they see is not less true than the world outside
the theatre. Only is is a rival experience. However cunning the

representation of nature, still nature is felt as inimical, its unruly presence as intrusive. The *hortus inclusus* of the medieval basilica—I think of the Roman church of Santi Quattro Coronati—is alive and open to the air. The equilibrium which the church as an entity confesses is not analogous to the frozen form of the artificer or the mathematician, rather to that of the equable man. The harmony of Santa Maria in Cosmedin at the foot of the Aventine Hill is not frozen but dynamic, its restfulness is not ordered but earned.

To man in the modern age, this harmony and repose, which suggest a mode of coming to terms with experience, no longer suffice. The physical world is not his satisfaction and his problem, but a world of intangibles. What a rotten word "intellectual" is. Modern man is displaced or vagrant. But his restless hands are still busy incessantly at their appointed task of creating form. The static and isotropic universe is the work of these hands. "Flesh and blood cannot inherit the kingdom of God; neither doth corruption inherit incorruption." The scientific and religious reformer is appealing from this puddled time to an enclosed garden or universe of discourse where the intransigent fact is denied.

The increasing poignance of the appeal accounts for the arbitrary aspect of much late medieval art. If one were to bisect Jan van Eyck's famous portrait of Giovanni Arnolfini and his wife (National Gallery, London), beginning with the chandelier which depends from the top of the painting—precisely in the center between the wedded couple—and proceeding through the mirror just below it, in which the image of the chandelier is repeated, the resulting line would coincide with that of the floorboard which divides the balance of the painting into perfect halves. If you look at this explicit division, you see on the left a man whose left hand is extended to grasp the right hand of the woman who stands on the right. In the right background her leather slippers are evident, in the left foreground the clogs he has discarded. As they form opposing triangles, they complement the parallel triangles formed by the bent arms of the man and woman. In the convex mirror between them their back view is reflected, and the front view of two analogous persons who stand before them and out of the painting. But the mirror reflects also, and so accentuates a further complementarity, the unshuttered window to the left of the husband and the canopied bed to the right of the wife. For the marriage of Arnolfini, the world, which is always running away, has been conjured.

This is like and unlike the religious art of the Middle Ages. The likeness is in the petrified character of the Arnolfini portrait. The difference—employing for comparison the Carolingian mosaic in the Roman basilica of San Marco—the Byzantine Christ who is not a man but the Alpha and Omega, pendant on a gold ground—is that the art of van Eyck six hundred years later is by intention naturalistic. This intention is alien to the medieval maker. The twelve sheep we see coming from the two sacred cities—they are always the same cities—in the abbey church of Sant'Elia near Monte Soratte are like nothing in nature. The Virgin and the female martyrs who are paying her homage, two on one side, two on the other, in the apse of San Sebastiano on the Palatine Hill, are not women but the apotheosis of woman. In these tenth-century frescoes, the generic figures exist in isolation. They give no hostages to time. Hieratic immobility describes them. The immobility is, however, not compulsive or defensive. It is the emanation of a school. Imagine the Pantocrator in the stylized mosaics created for Pope Paschal I, acknowledging tradition in every gesture and detail, frozen for eternity against the sky of Heaven—and endowed with the lineaments of a real human being. That is what we get in van Eyck. He is not emulating experience but seeking to coerce it.

Resort to mathematical structure is more evident and possibly more necessary in a crowded canvas like Jan and Hubert van Eyck's "Adoration of the Mystical Lamb" (St. Bavon Cathedral, Ghent). In the massive polyptique, attention is focussed and also dispersed. The problem, to find out order in a marshalling of the powers of Heaven and earth, seems to be resolved by the application of calipers. The order which results from the meticulous arrangement of Prophets and Sybils, militant men and contemplative men, male and female, present and past is more willful than natural. That does not argue a lesser kind of art. Van der Weyden's "Last Judgment" (The Hospital, Beaune) is in the arrangement of the figures obviously in fee to arithmetic or geometric design. It is also among the great paintings of the world. But the pattern it manifests communicates a sense of imposition as against a sense of revelation. A "modern" painter like Rubens does not impose. He seems to assert that the form which determines the shape of the painting rises irresistibly from the materials themselves. In the allegory entitled "Peace and War" (National Gallery, London), no pains are spared to suggest the appearance of order. The weight is equally distributed among Venus and her attendant revellers and the sanguinary party of Mars. But though the adherents of Peace dominate on one side of the painting and those of War on the other, they intermingle freely. There are no arbitrary lines of demarcation to which one is forced to advert. The scene is formal and yet fluid. The orderly arrangement to which the eye attests confesses no debt to the will of the painter. In form, it is not artistic (capricious) but natural (involuntary).

Oderisi, the miniaturist and illuminator of manuscripts in Dante's time, is in his art as mechanical as the brothers van Eyck. So Dante, whose "sweet new style" is new as it is realistic, puts him in Purgatory. One might say that Oderisi is Byzantine and let it go at that. But Giotto and Cavallini in the same time are already elaborating a more natural-seeming art. Compare, with the ancient mosaics in the nave of Santa Maria Maggiore—emblematic scenes from the life of Abraham, Moses, Jacob, and Joshua—the humanizing of Scripture achieved by Torriti in the apse. Assurance is briefly the possession of Giotto and his followers. Then the new departure is queried. *Nunc semper stans.* Leonardo says: "After the time of Giotto the art of painting declined again because everyone imitated the pictures that were already done." Why this abashed reluctance to put oneself forward? What the imitative man or faithful acolyte requires is implicit in Augustine's phrase, defining the perfect stasis which is God: "now ever standing still."

The world of the scientist is the same in all directions. Geometric space is isotropic. The American astronomer Edwin Powell Hubble explains what this means. "There must be no favored location in the universe, no center, no boundary; all must see the universe alike." The God of St. Bonaventura is looking at isotropic space. Menacing its homogeneity is the distressing achievement of a painter like Masaccio, a revolutionary figure in the early fifteenth century as he naturalizes and so profanes the icon. "Masaccio showed by his perfect works how those who take for their standard anything but nature—mistress of all masters—weary themselves in vain" (Leonardo). As he gives his figures life and form and roundness of relief, as he plants them firmly on the ground—I am echoing Vasari's praise of the stories in fresco from the life of St. Catherine of Alexandria (San Clemente, Rome)—he does not release us from destruction but immerses us in the destructive element. The executioner who turns the wheel on which the saint is tormented really bends to his work. But Catherine and her Wheel define the perfect icon. To the man with his feet to the fire, the indigenous thing is a profanation. In Masaccio's Trinity fresco (Santa Maria Novella, Florence), the donors of the painting are included in the total composition. They appear to be the vital ones, looking at a picture in a frame. Masaccio, unforgivably, is opening a window on the world.

Number allows of the appearance of form where realistic technique—for example, perspective—is unavailable. It is the necessary and conventional recourse of the artist throughout the Middle Ages. The felt priority of number, which communicates the sense of deliberately arrested form, is neither necessary nor conventional. The artist is acknowledging in the world he inhabits the loss of equilibrium, concurrently his attempt to repossess it. I think we detect him screwing down his refractory material as to a mechanical chase, not only in the art of the later Middle Ages but in the panoramic drama of the fifteenth century and the early Renaissance. In a morality like the *Castle of Perseverance*, the Bad Angel is known by the presence of the Good. The dyspeptic Backbiter, who finds out the worser reason, is verified by the more hopeful Shrift. The Seven Deadly Sins are not merely paralleled, they are identified by the Seven Moral Virtues, as the Four Daughters of God are identified by the World, the Flesh, and the Devil, to whom Covetousness is allied. But why, in either party, are there just four opponents—or Four Rivers of Paradise, or Four Stars over Eden, or Four Evangelists who by their teaching must irrigate the world? The numerologist has an answer, which the idly curious will find in Hugh of St. Victor. The authors of the chronicle of *Gorboduc* are still telling it over in the Age of Elizabeth. But the Chorus to the play, as it is composed of four dukes and "four ancient and sage men of Britain," is more paradigmatic than wise. The King is a King in that he has his Queen, and the Older Son (with his Parasite) in that he is paired with a Younger (who has got to be accompanied in the same way). These central protagonists will each require a counsellor, just as in *Tamburlaine* the composition of the hero's party (Techelles, Usumcasane, Theridamas) will entail, on the adverse side, an identical composition (the Kings of Fez, Morocco, and Argier, whom Bajazeth leads to war). That the victor in this contest may be recognized, Tamburlaine in victory must confer on his three chieftains just those crowns which their three opposing numbers had worn. This is not art, in the modern acceptance of the word. It is magic.

The ritual, which is intended to impose cohesiveness, is appropriately a recapitulation of the fifteenth-century morality play, in which the triad of Mind, Will, and Understanding is transformed to that other triad of Maintenance, Lechery, and Perjury as by folding back a piece of paper. In determining the form of the whole, numerological complementarity is decisive, not the kinetic power of an idea working upon and giving shape to the material. Character has no influence in this kind of art and is mostly without substantial content. The important thing is position. Marlowe's Zenocrate impinges on the play only as she is balanced by her rival Zabina. There is in her death no compelling sense of meaning. It is an unassimilated fact, not explicable in terms of the antecedent action nor consequential in terms of what is to come. The vagrant fact is placed and related to the whole as the dying queen is surrounded by three physicians, three chieftains, the three sons of the hero. "Number itself," says the author of the *Didascalion*, "teaches us the nature of the going out and the return of the soul." [29]

Doctor Faustus is, in necessary ways, not really more formal than this. Recognition in terms of theme is absent: "ambition that o'erleaps itself and falls on the other." In the juxtaposing of the Good and Evil Angel or of the impious Mephistopheles and the

29. *Didascalion*, II, 4.

pious Old Man, the medieval pretense of significant form remains apparent. Comic characters go by pairs: Robin Ostler and Rafe, Wagner and the Clown, Wagner and the Horse-Courser. The two virtuous scholars are complemented by Valdes and Cornelius. Pope and Cardinal reappear as German Emperor and Knight or as the Duke of Vanholt and his Duchess. Historians of the theatre will tell you that this insistent pairing is required by the conventional practice of doubling opposite roles. I think Marlowe and his predecessors find the practice congenial for reasons independent of theatrical exigency. As Marlowe applies the last stroke to his canvas, Faustus is discovered swallowed up in Hell. That is not in consequence of his thriftless commitment but, like the death of Tamburlaine or Barabas, only of the need to put period to the play.

The arbitrary nature of the construction is naked to the eye and replicated often in sixteenth-century verse. In the poetry of the Elizabethan miscellanies from the middle of the century almost until the end, the metronomic beat and the phrasal seesaw—depending on the inflexible position of the cesura—resolve the inimical line against which the poet is contending to a pair of identical units. The resolving is like mortification, perhaps to be laid to anxiety or a vicious taste, hardly to ineptitude. For the same imposed structure governs in the blason and contra-blason, as written for example by Sidney and Donne; and in the sonnets of Shakespeare, whose basic strategy is the formal antithesis ("Mine eye and heart are at a mortal war"); and in the masque and anti-masque, whose chief practitioner is Jonson. Every poet is an opportunist, making what he can of his donnée, liking it especially as it negates or affirms what he has just been affirming or negating. More than opportunism is implicit in the figure poetry which sixteenth-century Hellenism recreates from its reading in the Greek bucolic poets and in the Greek Anthology—poems shaped like lozenges, spheres, spires, rhomboids. This highly mechanical art which, finding life intransigent, turns to the manipulating of ciphers is attractive to the classicizing poet of the sixteenth and seventeenth centuries. Thomas Watson contrives an arithmetical, antisyllabical poem in the shape of a pillar with a double acrostic.[30] George Her-

30. *Hecatompathia*, 1582, LXXXI.

bert's typographical verses, like "The Altar" and "Easter Wings," are more famous and more interesting. I see them as illustrating the exaggerated dependence on rhetoric by the kind of temperament which repudiates, as too little amenable to rule, the various nature of conventional experience, "all that worldlings prize . . . contracted to a rose . . . [that] biteth in the close."

Gertrude Stein says, in her *Lectures in America:* "I really do not know that anything has ever been more exciting than diagramming sentences." The virtue of this elegant but airless exercise is that "one is completely possessing something and incidentally one's self." The promulgator of scientific law aspires to complete possession. So does the artist, who endeavors like the God of the Creation to disappear into his handiwork while still exerting though not confessing absolute control. He is or he wants to be the "unseen good old man" behind the arras. His aspiration is dramatized in the early Renaissance by the extensive deploying of selfregarding rhetorical devices whose function is to impose authority but at a remove. Spenser in the *Faerie Queene* applies the yoke by omitting conjunctions:

> Faint, weary, sore, emboilèd, grievèd, brent,
> With heat, toil, wounds, arms, smart, and inward fire.
>
> (I.xi.28)

Gascoigne introduces consecutive verses with the same word or words. He is making or reciting a litany. The poetaster William Warner utilizes what the text books call the echo sound: "Yea, such an one, as such was none, save only she was such." To say that this is bad poetry is true but insufficient. More than poetry is in the cards.

The assiduous cultivating of aggressively coercive rhetorical devices—I have hardly scratched the surface in touching on them here—is complemented initially by renewed attention to the intricate (or cohesive) possibilities of rhyme, as in much of the poetry of the *Old Arcadia*. Rhyme is the invention, not of the Goths, but of an age which is trying to reassert its authority. The fascination with measured or quantitative verse begins as men see their chance to carry the stabilizing process still further. (Perhaps poetry is like music or mathematics.) The movement called Euphuism is a bizarre manifestation of this process. It represents a defensive and indignant withdrawal from the anarchic world of the past. The job of Italian criticism in the sixteenth century is to bring the world to heel. J. C. Scaliger is to Italy what Ramus is to France and like Ramus deserves oblivion, except as he reminds us of the pitfalls to which the wayward or frightened intelligence is prone. Scaliger affirms the isotropic universe as he educes different arrangements from the paralleling of words that are generically and homophonically alike. As an example:

Et canis		venantur		servat
	in sylvis		& omnis	
Et lupis		nutritur		vastat

The disconcerting presence of unpredictable fact is dissipated. In the woods, the dog (or wolf) may hunt (or be nourished) and all things may keep (or destroy), as the disposer pleases.[31] In what Scaliger calls *versus concordantes*, only an innocuous paradigm confronts him. It is totally responsive to his will.

The Renaissance means loosening and freedom; on another side, the goal is to bind. Proteus verse, the rearranging of words without altering the sense or metre, invests the disposer with the mesmeric faculties of Prospero. The mathematician Joannes Sturmius, as he wills an end of the Thirty Years War, composes a book devoted solely to variations on the following prayer: "Dent his mox regionibus ut sancti veniat pax" ("May the saints grant that peace may presently come to these countries"). Sturmius is not addressing himself to conventional supplication. He is enchanting the conspirators who trouble his equanimity. For the line is a chronogram of the year 1640, if the appropriate letters are evaluated in accordance with the Roman abbreviations for number. So D (500), M (1000), and C (100) will, if added to I (recurring five times) and to X and V (recurring two and three times respectively), yield the prodigious figure of 1640. Nothing aberrant will intervene. For twenty-three pages the words (or counters) are transposed, and still the same date emerges.[32] Experience is not so tractable. The war has eight years to run.

31. *Poetices*, 1562.   32. *Precatio Pro Pace*, 1640.

In just this period Caravaggio, like a nova, astonishes the world. Caravaggio sinks the type—the constant image of the Regina Coeli—in a realistic representation, the Madonna of Loreto. For most of us, the Renaissance is crystallized and defined in this infinitely personal work. It is hard to suppose that as the work is personal, it is the occasion of scandal. That is the heart of the critique elaborated by new science and the occult. The mathematician Jacques Bernouilli, taking a single line in honor of the Virgin, shows us how it may be varied, as the maker dictates, more than forty thousand times. The indigenous thing is an insult. Bernouilli also is a man of the Renaissance.

Fixating on number or position characterizes the palindrome, verse which reads the same, letter by letter, whether read from the end or the beginning. To discover an antithetical meaning by reading the poem backwards, the definition of *versus recurrentes*, is metaphysically the same sort of enterprise. The point is to manipulation, not only of words but facts, nor least when the facts are disagreeable. The pseudo-science called *gematria*, which the Renaissance recovers from the early Christian centuries, stipulates for every letter a numerical equivalent. To speak of proper names is partly a contradiction, for names and phrases are only numbers, hence divested of eccentricity. This is the world of modern linguistics, anyway in hope. Quoting Archibald Hill in his analysis of "The Windhover": "The trouble is that no good poem is a sequence of prose equivalents." [33] Number allows of perfect equivalence. It is also predictive, where prediction is imposition, for the numerologist is calling the tune. The Hebrew word for "issues of death," occurring in the Psalms, is represented arbitrarily by the number 93. In the logic of *gematria*, there are just so many different ways to die. The mysterious number which denotes the Beast of Revelations is 666. Pietro Bongo sees the number as figuring Martin Luther ("perfidi Heresiarche"). The correspondence depends on the equating of letters with numbers. The mathematician works out his equation—Latinizing the surname but not the given name—by adding up the sequence M (30) A (1) R (80) T (100) I (9) N (40) L (20) V (200) T (100) E (5) R (80) A (1). But Bongo's friend

33. Quoted D. H. Stewart, "Linguistic Limits," p. 8.

Michael Stifel identifies the Beast with Pope Leo X, and his letters and numbers also tally. Stifel is a Protestant.[34]

A seventeenth-century scientist like Johann Faulhaber gets our approbation as he meditates on the powers of consecutive numbers and arrives at a computation of their sum. We are embarrassed as he uses number to create a calendar predicting or rather fettering the future. Spenser's preoccupation with number is satisfying to him, I suppose in deeply personal ways. That is why he does not address it in his critical comments. I think we agree that it yields in the work only a superficial cohesiveness. Milton is more modern in that, like the new philosophers on their successful side, he sees exterior design as obedient to the bare bones within. But the superiority of Milton to Spenser or of the scientist Kepler to the astrologer Simon Forman ought not to obscure their basic affinity. The difference in locating the cohesive principle—on the one hand numerology, on the other expressive form—defines the bounds of the Renaissance and the later Middle Ages. But the line of demarcation is not so striking or important (when one attempts to assess the characteristic features of that longer span of time which is at once medieval and modern and in which the modern world is born) as the fascination with order which is common to both periods and which serves to associate more than to divide them. The difference between the man of the late sixteenth century and of the centuries just before is one of degree. Each proclaims his adhesion to the renascent age in his insistence on discerning or asserting the presence of a paradigm wherever he looks, "as if a magic lantern threw the nerves in patterns on a screen."

As we condescend to the compulsive logic of the late Middle Ages and the Renaissance, we are provincial or purblind. We fail to grasp the subterranean link that connects the earlier time to the immediate and hypothetically more respectable past, in which the isotropic universe of linguistics and symbolic logic is already emergent, "moving its slow thighs." The reality of our world is not announced by fiat but is understood to be conformable to fact. To what extent does the acknowledging of the fact turn on personal

34. Stifel, *Arithmetica integra*, 1544; Bongo, *Numerorum Mysteria*, p. 626; Revelation 13:18.

predilection? New science opposes to "spiritual raptures and revelations" a true acquaintance "with the tempers of men's bodies, the composition of their blood, and the power of fancy." [35] New historicism arrives at its conclusions by counting peers and commoners. It repudiates haughtily the quasi-mystical divining of a pattern in history by visionary writers like Motley and Prescott, or Holinshed and Hall. We are modern or enlightened, like the new historian and the new philosopher, as we concede that the ameliorating of our desperate condition, figured in the first total war that decimates Europe in the early decades of the seventeenth century, is not to be managed by assertion. Newton's *Principia* works. That cannot be said of the same writer's speculations on the Book of Daniel and the Apocalypse of St. John. The past is superstitious as it searches for the *lingua adamica,* the thread which will guide us from the Minotaur's cave. The modern grammarian—Chomsky, Nicole, James Harris in the eighteenth century, bedfellows in last things—differs from the pansophical writer of the earlier time, whom we all agree to be hunting a will-o-the-wisp, as he conducts his inquiry into the nature of language in accordance with principles more nearly scientific and therefore more generally approved. He does not pronounce but attempts to discover. Perhaps what he discovers is what he knows already. Or suppose that his discoveries are incumbent on him. Is it tenable to assert that prolepsis, compulsiveness wane with the beginning of the modern age? I think the reverse is true.

Teilhard de Chardin is vaticinatory and notably modern as he sees us "impelled by the necessity to build the unity of the World." Already he glimpses the future and prescribes it: "we shall end by perceiving that the great object unconsciously pursued by science is nothing else than the discovery of God." [36] Sir Francis Bacon is in popular hagiography the patron saint to experimental science. As the modern age begins, Bacon is chastizing his slumbrous predecessors who, like the denizens of Plato's cave, organize the world in terms of merely sensuous impressions. Their ignorance follows of "the abstract notions derived from these impressions." Now igno-

---

35. Sprat, *History,* p. 359.   36. *Building the Earth,* p. 58.

rance or lethargy is disallowed. "Now is it time . . . to awake and rising above the earth, to wing . . . through the clear air of philosophy and sciences"—let us say, after Teilhard, as far as the Theosphere. Why is it time?

Charles Singer, in his absorbing account of science under the Roman Empire, stigmatizes Seneca for falling into the trap which had caught so many before him, the projecting of philosophy on the natural world. "Some moral significance," Seneca tells us, "should be attached to all studies and all discussion. Whether we seek into the secrets of nature or treat of divine things, the soul must be delivered from its errors and from time to time reassured." Subsequently the historian of science turns impatiently to Pliny the Elder. His uncritical account of phenomena is wanting. "It is based on no theory, it is supported by no doctrine, it is founded on no experiment." [37] To put the two passages together is perhaps to understand how the power of new science transcends the experimental method to which it appeals. Not only truth but reassurance is the fruit of the scientific cosmos.

Language, natural phenomena witness in their essence to a unifying principle which no diversity can efface (Campanella). That is the doctrine or faith of our fathers. It is the possession before them of Ionic Greece and dormant for centuries thereafter. The Renaissance "dawns" as the vitality of the ancient doctrine is renewed. Its function is assuaging, to direct the eye of the mind from things to language or, what is more pallid than language, to symbology. The process is one of increasing attenuation and depends on the detesting of physical fact. The *vates* or new philosopher—Descartes as white magician, Newton in his dual role of cosmologist and Scriptural exegete—prefers to matter of fact a paraphrase or perfect translation which "must always be called the same" (*Timaeus*). This magisterial person, in science, in language, is waving his wand above the void.

37. *From Magic to Science*, pp. 15, 23.

CHAPTER SIX

A Rage for Order

AS the spectre of formlessness emerges from its long incubation, attention to form becomes obsessive. The obsession is manifold or polysemous, like the richest productions of medieval allegory, in that the writer or philosopher who reflects it in his work may desire on one side to pull things apart. He is a man at sixes and sevens, now devoutly committed to ordering, and now delighting in the representation of spectacular carnage (as in the *Arcadia* and the *Faerie Queene*) which cannot really be justified as exemplary. The High Middle Ages maintain a precarious equilibrium between these rival impulses. In the later centuries, the equilibrium begins to break. The waxing of violence follows sequentially, also a growing reliance on arrested form, which is the warder.

The exacerbated concern for form in this transitional era tallies with, as it expresses, a loathing for the discrete stuff which is our daily portion. The modern systematizer contemns the bread and wine as a carnal representation. "It smells of mortality." He is Misanthropos who builds an abstract scheme independent of time and place, and spills his seed on the ground. Or he is, like King Lear and in fanatic ways, the punctilious man, also the nihilist or anarch who would "Strike flat the thick rotundity o' the world." Hamlet is peculiar in his willingness to acknowledge the contrary impulses which beset him. The conventional and more timorous response, which seems to me to be dramatized in much of the artistic achievement of the Renaissance and the later Middle Ages, is to evade or beat down what Banquo calls "the cursèd thoughts that nature Gives way to in repose." The evasion is accomplished by creating a ritual which reduces the danger inherent in a divided response to experience by hedging round and devitalizing experience. New science and linguistics enact this ritual. The distaste for eccentricity or the fortuitous event each communicates in its dealings with phenomenal fact is satisfied or possibly diverted by the appeal to a deterministic universe.

In the incorporeal art of the morality play, which is by and large a creation of the fifteenth century, the devitalizing process is already far advanced. The *Pride of Life,* about 1400, is insistently catholic. The playwight, like an emaciated version of Henry Fielding, the premier novelist of the Englightenment, describes "not men but manners, not an individual but a species." The new allegory perfected by Milton and the Augustans carries further the denying of integrity to physical phenomena, which entail a fractionating or disordering of the controlled existence the ritual is intended to evoke. Fixed notations replace the more ample and therefore confusing terminology of mimetic fiction. Imagery is microcosmic and compendious. The concept or abstract idea dominates in the icon which, unlike organic metaphor, functions only as a vehicle or sign. The variety and chaos of a world of myriad details are repudiated for a more lethargic and hence more submissive and predictable world. The new allegorical hero, who is demonic or determined man, personifies eternal form. His actions are wholly predictable as they are defined by the demon which shakes him. Decoding is not so easy in the more tangled art of the past. What do Paolo and Francesca have to teach us?

The drift from mimetic characterization toward the world of transparent personification, which is possession, meets with occasional resistance. In the *Faerie Queene,* the man is not always immersed in the type. He is, however, enthralled as surely by the context in which the poet has placed him. As he inhabits a world of spirits more puissant than himself, the actions in which he participates are fated actions. Quoting Shakespeare in the *Comedy of Errors:*

This is the fairy land. Oh, spite of spites!
We talk of goblins, owls, and sprites.

If we obey them not, this will ensue—
They'll suck our breath, or pinch us black and blue.

But to the abstracting temperament, nature in its entirety is fairy land, a machine constituted of interrelated parts, each of which is governed absolutely by law.

This is the universe hypothesized by Plato. The Gnostics of the early Christian era, as they people the world with demons and assign to letters of the alphabet numerical values endowed with magical potency, employ a coarser vocabulary. But its import is the same. Man is no longer an integer. As he forfeits volition, he cannot respond to the capricious tendering of grace. So Tertullian—he principally among the Church Fathers—perceiving that possession is disfranchisement, contends against this heretical sect. He thinks man is autonomous. St. Augustine, who is more fundamentally a Platonist than theurgic professors like Porphyry, thinks otherwise, and once again it is he who adumbrates the modern point of view. Augustine attacks the proliferating of demons not because they inhibit free will but because they signify an intermediate agency, operating unconscionably between man and his Master—"as if God and man had no other means of commerce." The only intermediary Augustine will tolerate is the Son of God in whom God is dilated. By analogy to "the sun's and moon's beams [which are] reflected upon the earth without contamination of the light," he insists that there must be no "corporal matter in the doctrine of beatitude." I think it comes down to much the same thing, the denial of free agency by the interposition of demons or the assertion that an all-powerful God impinges on man as on a piece of litmus paper, "not by any corporal creature unto him, nor reverberating the air between the ear and the speaker, nor by any spiritual creature, or apparition, as in dreams or otherwise." [1] In either case man's role is attenuated, more radically by Augustine. He envisages an essentially bloodless world.

The conclusive attenuating of free agency is, however, the work of the Renaissance. Augustine proclaims the omnipotence of grace and concurrently the bondage of the will. In the battle

1. *City of God,* VIII; IX, i, xvi; XI, ii.

against the Pelagians, which is the crown of his life, he arrives at last at the doctrine of total predestination. Still the Renaissance remains unsatisfied. For while it demands a deterministic reading of things, it rejects the role of grace, which after Augustine is the central idea of medieval psychology, as anarchic and unpredictable. In the person of the Epicurean Edmund in *King Lear,* it repudiates this expression of divine whimsy and supplants it with mechanical law. The systematizer, in his role of artist, denies his characters real lineaments or divests them of autonomy as he wants to secure their freedom from the hateful dance of particles in flux. Determinism or demonic possession confers this freedom. But it precludes the possibility of tragedy, or of comedy of the higher kind (Ibsen, Chekhov, J. M. Synge), which are based, if not on free will, at least on the conceding of dimension to their protagonists and of dignity to the particular fact. Mimetic art is, however, empty of meaning to the kind of temperament which demands a less dramatic existence than mimesis is able to afford.

The vogue of the *Corpus Hermeticum* in the Renaissance is traceable to the demand for a less dramatic, which means a more orderly existence. The promoters of new science are expressing the same demand or felt need. Reading cursorily in Ficino and the others, we are apt to miss the forest for the trees, the levying on the occult. Dr. Dee's most recent biographer shows how the acceptance of Hermeticism, as it argues our capacity not only to understand but to manipulate nature, "marks the dawn of the scientific age." [2] The prime source of Ficino's magic in his *De Vita* is Hermes Trismegistus. Ficino believes in the possibility of calling down the assistance of benevolent demons. To these planetary demons, Hermes assigns control of the terrestrial world. The ambition of Ficino is to put them in his pocket. As this ambition is realized, man becomes the master of his fate. Gnosticism is squeezed for its quotient of use. But the pessimistic view of man's stature and capacity we associate with it is discarded. Events are determined. Man is, however, the Primum Motor, anyway in hope.

2. P. J. French, *John Dee,* p. 87.

Frequently in the Renaissance, the preferring of cabalistic speculation to "science with the teeth" is tinged with millenarian zeal. But the expectation of paradise, in which the babel of tongues will have ceased, is centered in the present or immediate future. Augustine, the greatest of the early millenarians, defers the hope of a perfect communion to the ending of the world. In this, he differs sharply from the modern syncretizers. Like them he laments, among the miseries of the human condition, first of all the confounding of tongues. The great western Babylon endeavors to impose her tongue on all the lands she has subdued, "to procure a fuller society." But Augustine repudiates this ambitious endeavor. He is mindful of concupiscence, what Shakespeare calls "the imposition hereditary ours." The Cartesian saying is almost parodied in him: "If I err, I am." [3] His error proves his being. He writes the *City of God* in response to pagan criticism of Christianity, after Alaric's sack of Rome (August 28, 410). Given this cataclysmic event, it seems logical to assert that the God of the Christians does not avail. Augustine answers adroitly: He does not! in all temporal ways. The opening books of his great polemic, as they are pretty much special pleading, are tedious. But they are crucial. They establish the proposition that nothing mundane avails. Augustine's grammar is Christ.

A thousand years later, the coming together of Platonism and millenarianism begets the expectation of a temporal kingdom or Fifth Monarchy. Economics has supervened: the tie that binds. What is mundane avails absolutely. The Antinomianism of the seventeenth century allows us to get clear of our concupiscent past. The heretical sectarians of the sixteenth century who go to the fire believing that "offenses committed in body did not matter if spirits were pure" are canonized and approved by the next generation. The clearing of the past (the imposition of Genesis) is, however, only a beginning. In the seventeenth century, hope in another world is no longer felt as sufficient. Fear of the void, the other face of the coin on which Bacon's hopeful features are stamped, requires that we set our lands in order in human time. Dante, who

---

3. *City of God*, XIX, vii; XI, xxvi.

wishes good success to the imperial undertaking of the great western Babylon, proclaims this order in the *Commedia*. The mischief of Nimrod is repaired as by Amphion, who insures that the fact and word will come together at last: "si che dal fatto il dir non sia diverso" (*Inferno* XXXII). But Dante is more wistful than practically expectant. The good emperor Henry is dead. He must hope till hope creates "from its own wreck the thing it contemplates." After his time, the emotional weather changes.

Philip Melanchthon, Luther's second in command, finds his avocation in introducing and popularizing the new mathematics. In the preface he contributes to Stifel's *Arithmetica integra* (1544), not less than in his religious pronouncements, Melanchthon is legislating man's fate. His devotion to astrology and his belief in prodigious births are not inconsequent facts but complementary. The stars are fraught with secret influence to which the learned man is privy. I do not think it inconsequent that in 1596 Kepler should announce his discovery of the relations underlying the construction of the universe (*Mysterium Cosmographicum*), and England rejoice at the Queen's emergence from her sixty-third or Grand Climacteric Year, made ominous by the multiplication of the sacred numbers 7 and 9. In the scientist as in the mage, preoccupation with form attests to consciousness of the void. *Timor fecit deos.* A single metaphor describes the activity of Paracelsus the mage and Maurolycus of Messina, the sixteenth-century geometer, Ward and William Lilly in the following century. Each is a great stickler, the man with the baton whose business is to marshall the crowd. Lilly the astrologer divines disaster in the stars. "Our summer and harvest are past, our winter is not ended." This gloomy prognostication makes him disconsolate. But "truth is truth and a spade is a spade." [4] The truth is that nothing happens without cause.

Brutus in Shakespeare's tragedy is exorcizing demons. He craves a piece of work that will make sick men whole. That is how I would explicate the European witchcraze. Robbins, in his *Encyclopedia of Witchcraft and Demonology*, estimates that 200,000 persons at a minimum were executed for the practice of "arts

4. *England's Merlin*, 1644, A3–4.

inhibited and out of warrant" in the period 1484–c. 1700. The toll of
victims rises steeply in the later years of this period. Pirenne
makes the connection between the prevalence of witches and the
advent of modern times.[5] In sixteenth-century Venice, only 5 persons were sentenced to die of more than 1500 brought before the
Inquisition. As our sickness waxes, the perilous antidote commends itself more strongly. Our fathers in the beginning of the
enlightened age are like rats that ravin down their proper bane.
Not the medieval but the modern imagination concocts the horrors
of the Witches' Sabbath. Breughel the Elder, depicting the black
assizes where Satan receives the adulation of the damned, has
found a new subject with which to harrow his contemporaries. Jean
Bodin, the type of the enlightened man, requires the burning of
witches as he must believe that everything has its cause. Calami-
tous events are diabolic, hence rationalizable. That is what Bodin is
saying. He cannot accept the empery of fortune, whether for good
or ill.

The witchcraze is not the work of an ignorant peasantry but
engendered by the same psychology that sponsors the scientific
cosmos. Glanvill illustrates in his attack on the modern Sadducees
or skeptics, in whose skepticism the role of fortune is enlarged.
"And those that dare not bluntly say, There is no God, content
themselves, for a fair step and introduction, to deny there are
spirits or witches." [6] This author is indifferent to gossip, as to
arguments from religious faith. He casts his tract in the form of a
logical discourse, gravid with the weight of "reasonable evidence"
and more persuasive as the appeal is to reason. That the evidence
does not persuade us any more is neither here nor there. What
matters is its purport. In the existence of witches, the existence of
God is confirmed. But God is a surrogate or stand-in. An impersonal and less dramatic deity is already advancing from the wings.

The rejection of randomness is the clue to the personality of
the Milanese physician Cardano. It is tenable to present him as the
originator of probability theory (*Liber de Ludo Alea*). In his autobiography, we get a caricature of the theory. But Cardano is not

5. *History of Europe*, II, 266.   6. *A Blow at Modern Sadducism*, 1668, Blv.

aware of the difference. On the night of his nativity, "Mars was casting an evil influence . . . and its aspect was square to the moon." Cardano "could easily have been a monster" except for the fortunate conjunction of Mars and Virgo, "over which Mercury is the ruler." The conjunction insures that Cardano does not deviate from the human form. It fails to protect him from a maim in the genitals so that for a decade, the best years of his life, he is unable to lie with women.[7] The preoccupation with causal relationships makes strange bedfellows, like Campanella and the Pope who collaborate in the practice of astrology. Campanella is a modern man as he attempts not only to decipher but to confine the heavens. In more than linear ways he is the contemporary of Galileo who, so far as I know, has no commerce with judicial astrology.

Against the general belief that the "diversity of languages . . . [arose] from the building of Babel and . . . the interposition of the divine being," Sprat pits his more orderly idea that this diversity was "brought about by natural means." The Creation is a machine from the operation of which "chance or luxury or [arbitrary] compulsion" are excluded. Sprat considers it "enough for the honor of . . . [God's] government that he guides the whole Creation in its wonted course of causes and effects." The analogy is to the restoration of process on the overthrow of the Protectorate: "it makes as much for the reputation of a prince's wisdom that he can rule his subjects peaceably by his known and standing laws, as that he is often forced to make use of extraordinary justice to punish or reward." The ecclesiastic does not dispute the existence (in posse) of prodigies or those sudden reversals of use and wont which depend on the whim of the Creator. But his embarrassment and uneasiness are evident. Given his psychology, encapsulated in the saying: "The universal disposition of this age is bent upon a rational religion," it is only a question of time before the indulgence of prodigious activity will wither.[8] What of irenicism, the kowtowing to power? The deterministic universe admits it surreptitiously, under color of law.

7. *Autobiography*, completed 1575, Ch. II.   8. *History*, pp. 360, 374.

Belief in the wonted course of causes and effects is not so likely to give scandal when applied to the operations of physical science, and in this latter case Sprat affirms it without reservation. In the governing principle, the faith of classical science is embodied: "If the same kinds and proportions of ingredients be used and the same circumstances be punctually observed, the effect without all question will be the same." Sprat is aware of the demurral, entered occasionally by the experimental philosophers themselves, that is is impertinent to assert a constant law since contingency is always decisive: the conditions which obtain at the moment, even the nature of the experimenter as he bends to the work. "In natural science," says Heisenberg, "we are not interested in the universe as a whole, including ourselves, but we direct our attention to some part of the universe and make that the object of our studies," then we extrapolate. But if you assert an isotropic universe, "pretty much alike everywhere and in all directions," extrapolating raises no problems.[9] On November 24, 1639, a transit of Venus, not hitherto observed, occurs exactly at the time and in the manner predicted. The youthful astronomer Jeremiah Horrocks (1617–41) is elated at this witnessing to his powers of prediction, but not surprised.

In his generalizing from particular fact, the classical scientist supposes that he is speaking to the nature of Truth. The kind of speaking that denotes him is from the chair. For example, Newton: "Hypotheses, whether metaphysical or physical . . . have no place in experimental philosophy." The scientific historian Cajori, pointing to hypotheses Newton did in fact adduce, insists that to lift the ringing statement from its context is to misconstrue it. But the illustrations he brings forward show forcibly, at least for me, the impatience of this greatest of classical scientists with the equivocal case. I take as characteristic the lordly avowal of Descartes: "There is no phenomenon in nature which has not been dealt with in this treatise." Of problems solved or investigated, Cardano leaves

9. E. P. Hubble, quoted in Clark, *Einstein*, p. 213; Heisenberg, *Physics & Philosophy*, p. 52; Sprat, *History*, pp. 243–44.

"something like forty thousand, and of minutiae two hundred thousand." Alciati calls him the Man of Discoveries, where discovery means the precipitating out of the truth.[10]

In his preface to the second edition of the *Principia*, the Cambridge astronomer Roger Cotes recognizes and defines the experimental philosophers as they "frame no hypotheses, nor receive them into . . . [science] otherwise than as questions whose truth may be disputed." The scientist undertakes to eliminate these questions by resort to the laboratory. He has already made up his mind that the laboratory holds all the answers. Newton, describing an eternal structure of nature which depends neither on a particular time nor space, is "possessed with the idea that the fundamental concepts and postulates of physics . . . could be deduced from experience" (Einstein). His design, as he proclaims it in beginning the treatise on *Optics* (1704), "is not to explain the properties of light by hypotheses but to propose and prove them by reason and experiments." The proof is not always in the pudding. To make sense of the orderly wheeling of the planets, Newton still requires the intervention of the Deity. But this summoning of a merely supposititious power is abhorrent to the lawgiver as his art is perfected. "M. Laplace," says Napoleon, on being presented with a copy of the *Mécanique Céleste*, "they tell me you have written this large book on the system of the universe, and have never even mentioned its Creator." Laplace answers triumphantly: "J n'avais pas besoin de cette hypothèse-la."

Physics is a logical system of thought whose basis cannot be distilled from experience. The act of seeing affects what we see. As we measure momentum, we cannot simultaneously ascertain position. "There is no objectively existing situation" (Max Born).[11] Portia says, in the *Merchant of Venice:* "Nothing is good, I see, without respect." For "respect," read "context." What I perceive turns not only on the angle of vision but also on what I am: Glanvill's

10. Cardano concluding his *Autobiography*; Descartes, *Principles of Philosophy*, 1644; Cajori, *History of Mathematics*, pp. 671–76; Newton concluding 2nd edn. of *Principia*, 1713.

11. "Physics and Metaphysics," p. 234.

tendentious point in the *Vanity of Dogmatizing*. Hence the doggerel couplet in commendation of Glanvill's book:

> Our firmest science (when all's done)
> Is nought but bold opinion.

"Perhaps it will appear in the end," says David Hume, "that the
necessary connection depends on the inference, instead of the inference depending on the necessary connection." [12] The classical
scientist dismisses the possibility or disdains its implications as
scholastic. Sprat is willing to confess that "many experiments are
obnoxious [liable] to failing, either by reason of some circumstances
which are scarce discernible till the work be over, or from the
diversity of materials." But the "instability and casualty of experiments" does not persuade him to a belief in any "irregularity of Nature." If we were required to conclude—as by experiments on
blackbody radiation—that God plays dice (F. S. C. Northrop),
then, says Sprat, we would have reason to despair. In fact, "uncertainty . . . arises only from some [mechanical] defect." [13]
    On this proposition the Marxist and the deterministic philoso-
pher like Pomponazzi take their stand. Neither is willing, constitu-
tionally, to accept the wry conclusion that experimental data do not
lead necessarily to the theoretical concepts, that we never know
the object, that we only speculate about it (Heisenberg). That is
why the Marxist, as he is faithful to his conceptualizing forebears in
the Renaissance, attacks the Copenhagen interpretation of quantum theory as "agnostic" (Blochinzev). It is a splendid word in this
context and notably precise. The determinist brings the integer
within the bailiwick of law. To make against the subversive content
of the indeterminacy principle, he hypothesizes "hidden parameters" which experiment does not reveal but which account in a
causal way for the result of the experiment. What looks to be flux is
an imposition.
    Modern or lynx-eyed man confronts the spectre of caprice in

12. *Treatise of Human Nature*, 1738, Bk. i, Pt. iii, Sect. vi.   13. *History*, pp. 243–44.

things with his sense of homologous relations. We are not to see him as averting but as straining his eyes. He is not put to denying the existence of evil. Milton's vision of the fallen angels is horrific but pervaded by design. It is a modern vision. Dante is medieval as he might descend forever the narrowing cone of Malebolge or ascend forever the Purgatorial Mountain. Why just seven ledges? Why not twelve or twenty-four? But Dante is also formal in our sense, and therefore saving. The *contrapasso*, as dramatized in the torments inflicted on the damned, is esthetically pleasing. It makes a coherence. Quoting *Inferno* x: "His words and the nature of his suffering had already told me his name." The unendurable perception is not of pain but whimsicality.

But to back off a little. There is a kind of mind that can live in a universe whose parameters are open to change (the lexical contradiction being understood and accepted), where, abruptly, the sun for sorrow does not show his head, or stands still in the heavens, rises or might rise in the west. This is not the mind of Pyrrho, who is pleased to know nothing, but the mind of the greater mystics, *homines Deiformi*, made in the comprehensive image of God. The autonomy of the modern age, its successful repudiating of the past, depends first of all on an invoking of the Law of the Excluded Middle. A proposition is valid, or the contradiction of it is valid. No third possibility exists. The Sun never alters in his rising and going down. "If he does," says Heraclitus, "the Erinyes, ministers of justice, will find him out." The mystic is ignorant of immutable law and willing to suppose a myriad of possibilities. St. Bonaventura, the most affective devotional writer produced by the Order of St. Francis, is also a consummate scholar who attempts, like St. Thomas, to synthesize theology and philosophy. He does not diminish, he enlarges the mind. St. Thomas, the prince of intellectual writers, is a poet and mystic who does not diminish the spirit. But the point is to Bonaventura, who concludes his *Itinerarium Mentis in Deum*, the golden book of Franciscan mysticism, with the injunction: "Ask grace, not learning; desire, not understanding; the sigh of prayer, not industry in study . . . mist, not clarity." Out of the mist a more catholic order looms.

In this second half of the twentieth century, a time of breaking and recovering, the saying from Matthew takes on its original vigor: "The Stone which the builders rejected, the same is become the head of the corner" (21:42). Walter Hilton in the fourteenth century chooses "rather to sleep for a while in the shade of the Faith than to wake in the dim light of the intellect." His sleep is not stupor but fruitful of wild surmises. He is not voicing the conventional aspersing of rationality, rather an awareness of its limitation. There are more and stranger things in heaven and earth than are dreamt of in the philosophy of the succeeding age. He is eccentric as he gives these things welcome. Boehme is like this, in bidding us acknowledge that "we have been locked up, and led blindfold, and it is the wise of this world who have shut and locked us up in their art and their rationality, so that we have had to see with their eyes." What the lynx-eyed men are willing us to see is a universe which pays allegiance to the army of unalterable law.

In all questions touching the physical world, this law is sovereign. Increasingly it claims dominion over metaphysical questions. Already Adam Smith's method is Newton's, applied to psychology and morals. It is "to attain, by generalization, certain simple truths from which it will be possible to reconstruct, synthetically, the world of experience." [14] In the same year as Grierson publishes his monumental edition of Donne, the type of the speculative intelligence, Einstein, Freud, and others join forces to create a scientific organization "quite indifferent to metaphysical speculation and . . . transcendental doctrines." They require "a strictly empirical and positivistic point of view." But by degrees they perceive that the natural sciences must "take on themselves a philosophical character" as they consider "the question of man's place in the world." So physics, psychology, and biology come together. "And finally, the anthropological sciences, especially history and sociology, find themselves brought into closer and closer connection with biological concepts." [15] The former relate to the latter as so many footnotes to the primary text.

14. Halévy, paraphrasing the *Wealth of Nations*, in *Growth of Philosophic Radicalism*, p. 100.

15. Clark describes this meeting in *Einstein*, p. 154.

The astronomer Cotes approximates, however crudely, this intimate connection in presenting the coercive system elaborated by Newton as "the safest protection against the attacks of atheists." God's "infinite wisdom and goodness" are manifest in the *Principia,* "and nowhere more surely than from this quiver can one draw forth missiles against the band of godless men." Skepticism is out, so is the openended universe. Donne says in a sermon: "the best men are but problematical, only the Holy Ghost is dogmatical." [16] New philosophy controverts this proposition.

Hatred of atheism, a term almost unknown to the Middle Ages, becomes conspicuous with the Renaissance. It is the real protest of the benighted or equable past against the scientific doom. Atheism, in the fifteenth century and later, does not mean what it means to Roger Cotes and his successors, the repudiating of divine intelligence, neither do we want to make the conventional modern equation with unknowing. Atheism means determinism, the insistence on order which constrains us from the cradle to the grave. Bacon is an atheist, he is like Galileo, as he declines to believe "that an army of infinite small portions or seeds unplaced should have produced this order and beauty without a divine marshal—and offers to say how the order was contrived and to fix it once and for all. [17] The marshal need not of course be anthropomorphic.

Cardinal Bellarmine, as the representative of the Holy Office, suggests that Galileo, the champion of a heliocentric universe, will be prudent as he contents himself "with speaking *ex suppositione* and not with certainty." In the year of Shakespeare's death, and Cervantes', the issue between the hypothesizer and the dogmatist is joined. Galileo differs from these others in that he is the connoisseur of certainties. He is unwilling merely to conjecture that the Sun and not the Earth is at the center and therefore immovable, or that the Earth moves with a diurnal motion. His habit is declarative. The sentence of the Church that this authoritative person "ab-

16. *Sermons,* ed. Simpson and Potter, VI, 301.

17. Bacon is quoted in D. C. Allen, *Doubt's Boundless Sea* (p. 5), a record of "the trepidation of the orthodox" in the Renaissance.

stain altogether from teaching or defending . . . and even from discussing" what he asserts to be true is mean and blind absolutely. The ugly story suggests, however, the dubiety that characterizes the oldfashioned intelligence. The Jesuits are vindictive and deceitful; Pope Urban, perhaps, is only confused. If "God is all-powerful," he inquires, "why should we try to necessitate Him?" [18] Here he parts company with his associate Campanella. It is curious that Bishop Wilkins, putting off the singing robes of classical science, should speak from just this position. "To be very solicitous about any particular success, what is it but to limit and confine the power of God?" The quotation comes from Wilkins' *Discourse on Providence* (1649), a term not yet in fee, or not wholly, to the Law of the Excluded Middle. [19]

In Galileo's *Dialogue on the Great World Systems* (1629), the foolish Simplicio, who is set up to be knocked down, disputes the master's rationalization of the ebbing and flowing of the sea. He wants the countenancing of alternative possibilities. His position is that "God, by His infinite power and wisdom, might confer upon the element of water the reciprocal motion [as of tides] in any other way than by making the containing vessel [earth] to move." The conclusion is a red flag to new philosophy. Simplicio says: "it would be an extravagant boldness for anyone to go about to limit and confine the Divine power and wisdom to some one particular conjecture of his own." But the endeavor to confine is the copestone of the arch that gives on a more predictable future.

"It is certain that many things which now seem miraculous would not be so, if once we come to be fully acquainted with their compositions and operations." Sprat, who desires this plenary acquaintance, supposes that "the highest pitch of human reason" is attained as we follow the connected links in the great chain of Nature, "till all their secrets are open to our minds." [20] St. Thomas, reacting skeptically to the metaphor of an inextricable chain, entertains without perturbation the idea of an emerging universe, providential but not static, in which alternative explanations are admit-

18. Following Santillana, *Galileo*, pp. 99, 121–22, 239.

19. P. 107.   20. *History*, p. 214.

ted. In "the abyss of the Eternal Ordinance," who knows what is potential? (*Paradiso* XXI) Commenting on the Ptolemaic hypotheses, St. Thomas agrees that they offer the most persuasive account of things. Then he adds: "we must not say that they are thereby proved to be facts, because perhaps it would be possible to explain the apparent movements of the stars by some other method which men have not yet thought out." The receptivity to "some other method" is the cardinal sin to new philosophy, as it senses and shies from the possibility of randomness. How St. Thomas can live with himself is a secret that perishes with him.

Astrology incurs the anger of the Schoolman, also of Renaissance thinkers and reformers like Pico (1495) and his unexpected confederate Savonarola (1497), in each of whom the rage for order is high. Pico attacks astrology, partly as he dislikes the analogical habit which presents the planets as rejoiced or dejected, partly as he thinks that God may "ordain things otherwise than the usual revolution of the heavens would effect." But Pico's divergence from Aquinas tells more than his affinity. He is groping by fits and starts for a predictable cosmos, for which he finds hints in numerology and magic. So long as magic has no traffic with demons, it is "the absolute consummation of natural philosophy." [21] Giovanni Baptista Della Porta, the author of a treatise on white or natural magic, clarifies for us this implausible definition. The white magician performs "strange works, such as the vulgar sort call miracles." Rightly read, they are "nothing else but the works of Nature." Della Porta sees law as overmastering but as operating through angels or demons, "inferior things [who] serve their superiors" and are responsive finally to God. Campanella affirms this sequence in proposing that the rise and fall of religions, even the fate of Christianity, is written in the heavens, "sunt que nobiliores rerum inferiorum causae," the nobler causes of inferior things.[22] So astrology prepares the triumph of new philosophy. But the triumph is conclusive only as the intermediate thing becomes supererogatory. Cal-

21. *Disputationes adversus astrologiam divinatricem*, 1495; *Oratio de hominis dignitate*, 1489.

22. Campanella, *Atheismus Triumphatus*, 1631, p. 111; Della Porta, *Magiae naturalis*, 1589.

vin, in his condemnation of astrology (1549), is shrewder and more elegant than many of his scientific contemporaries, who dabble in arcane business. He sees the latter as getting in the way. Dante says: "Where God governs without an intermediary, natural law is suspended" (*Paradiso* xxx). Calvin, dispensing with intermediaries, holds fast to natural law. Like Augustine on the Gnostics, he requires that the divine ordinance be administered directly. The universe he inhabits is determined through and through.

Pomponazzi will not believe in the substantiality of angels because it cannot be proved by mathematics. He is an atheist and an intolerable prig. Pomponazzi's astrology is our necessity. Melodramatic atheists like Cyril Tourneur's hero-villain D'Amville, perhaps like Christopher Marlowe, are off the point. Their function is only to scandalize. Campanella is censured as atheistical in his time because he asserts (like Bishop Sprat) that the supposed dominion of chance is only "in respect of man's ignorance of the whole." [23] That is what Einstein asserts to the last. Taking issue with a young colleague who thinks that causality "can be neither confirmed nor disproved by experience," he proposes that chance itself is amenable to law. Were we to know a coin's velocity, its mass, its moment of inertia, every causative factor in the instant we toss it in the air, we should know for certain on which face it would fall. "Everything is determined, the beginning as well as the end, by forces over which we have no control. It is determined for the insect as well as for the star. Human beings, vegetables, or cosmic dust, we all dance to a mysterious tune, intoned in the distance by an invisible piper." [24] The piper whose existence the naked eye cannot perceive but whose eerie music compels us is only another metaphor which betokens the footprint of God. "Animals and plants are living effects of Nature; this Nature is none other than God in things." [25] Bruno, defining it, is sanguine. But inexorably the primal thing erodes the freedom he sees in prospect as we parse the heavenly grammar or recognize the footprint of God. This is the price of our escape from contingency.

23. *Atheismus*, pp. 16–31.

24. Clark, *Einstein*, pp. 112–13, 346–47.   25. Third dialog of *Lo Spaccio*.

Witnessing to God's footprint or the army of unalterable law is, however, an act of faith. Increasingly it separates Einstein from his more skeptical contemporaries in physics, as the skepticism of St. Thomas returns in the guise of the uncertainty principle. Contemporary physics is driven by experiment to acknowledge at the bottom of all phenomena the empery of chance. After all we are free, though the freedom which confronts us may be more than we can bear. The basic laws of nature are inimical to law. As they are fundamentally statistical and indeterminate, they give the lie to the deterministic universe. On a large scale they appear to affirm it: "but this was only because they involved such a vast number of events. They had the monumental stability of an enormous life insurance company though, like it, they rested on individual uncertainty." [26] The pronouncements of the insurance company are illustrative, like figures of speech. Fulke Greville, a dour Elizabethan almost solipsistic in his pessimism, thinks that "wit serves but to resemble." He means that it does not define. We are necessarily content when "there" turns out to be "here." Robert Frost, presenting poetry as metaphor, "saying one thing and meaning another, saying one thing in terms of another," goes on uncharacteristically to try for a general statement. "So also is philosophy—and science, too, for that matter, if it will take the soft impeachment from a friend." The overtures of this friend have not been received with much favor, or not until the other day. The probabilistic universe fills Einstein with incredulity. An "inner voice" tells him that it is not the real thing. "Quantum mechanics is certainly imposing. . . . but does not really bring us any closer to the secret of the Old One. I, at any rate, am convinced that He does not throw dice." [27]

If chance governs in the subatomic world, perhaps it governs in the greater world also? Dante and Virgil are prophetic of our own time as they honor the goddess Fortuna, with whom our puny wisdom cannot strive (*Inferno* VII). Bruno is of the Renaissance as he expels her from the heavens. Nonetheless, he makes out an in-

---

26. B. Schonland, *The Atomists*, p. 188.

27. Clark, p. 340; Frost, *The Constant Symbol*.

teresting case. Fortune is blind and therefore impartial. "I who throw all into the same urn of mutation and motion am the same to all." [28] To the man who can accommodate to it, the unpredictable character of the mutable goddess is beneficent. Rightly understood, she is saying: "Be not therefore anxious for the morrow." (Matthew 6:34)

The anxiety of post-Renaissance man is expressed in his adherence to unchanging principles. He will send you to the fire if you call them in question. In validating a statement he has recourse to rules, as of the calculus. He does not open the rules themselves to verification or dispute. He generalizes or makes statements, but only about the signs he is employing. "Every science," says Montaigne, "has its principles presupposed, by which human judgment is everywhere limited. If you drive against the barrier where the principal error lies, they have presently this sentence in their mouths: 'that there is no disputing with persons who deny principles.' " Niels Bohr is denying first principles, he is shaking the modern world to its foundations in hypothesizing an atom from which the resident electrons take leave evidently as they please. "I find the idea quite intolerable that an electron exposed to radiation should choose *of its own free will* not only its moment to jump off, but also its direction." Were this idea to gain acceptance, says the scientist on his esthetic or compulsive side, "I would rather be a cobbler, or even an employee in a gaming house," where God does presumably throw dice. The writer might be Leibniz or Cardano, to whom indeterminacy is a personal affront. Already the Renaissance mathematician, four centuries before Einstein, is saying: "I hold that nothing happens by chance in nature." What atheism really signifies in the Renaissance is made clear, paradoxically, by an academic hack writing in the 1930s who decries the relativity theory as it "produces all events out of the compulsion of its godless subjection to laws." [29]

So long as one conceives of the creation under the aspect of potentiality, the need persists to invoke an extrarational agency, like the demons of Gnosticism or the intelligences, in Donne's

28. Second dialog of *Lo Spaccio*.   29. Clark, *Einstein*, pp. 211, 525.

poem, who guide the spheres. If, however, one postulates a comprehensive design ("the freeborn Sun . . . impaled within a Zodiac"), angelology withers, the willful deity familiar to us from our reading of Horace ("dextra rubente") disappears from the cosmos. Here is the connection to linguistic reform. As the deterministic psychology strengthens, eccentricities in language are made conformable to law.

Under the hegemony of law "If any thing shall occur that is confused," the teacher of language feels competent to stipulate "how it ought to be reduced into order." That is, according to Cyprian Kinner, the ninth and ultimate step in the ascent to education, first glossed in the Renaissance as the universal panacea.[30] "Young years," an Elizabethan preceptor supposes, are "pliable to what you will." [31] So a rational course of instruction, beginning early in life, can refashion the world. The stakes are high. In the middle years of Elizabeth's reign, William Bullokar, attempting to formulate a systematic grammar, reaches towards the goal of the universal comprehensibility which the later seventeenth century believes itself to have achieved. Bullokar's grammar conduces "to no small commodity of our English nation." It tutors us in our own and foreign tongues, and affords also an "easy and speedy pathway to all strangers" by rationalizing the eccentricities of English.[32] The impulse to be done with eccentricity is characteristic of the modern age and hardly exhausted yet. I quote from a quarterly on orthographic reform published in the 1970s: "hwot thu wurld neds most iz an 'ezi-tu-lurn' vurzhun ov inglish." Bernard Shaw as a playwright lives by the word. In the preface to *Pygmalion*, he proposes to break it down. ("The reformer England needs today is an energetic phonetic enthusiast.") His affiliation to the present is apparent.

Dante, in his unfinished Latin treatise on the vernaculars of Italy, seems to anticipate the Renaissance and later as he endorses the beguiling notion of the one simple tongue or language of grace

30. *Summary Delineation*, B4.   31. Francis Clement, *The Petie School*, 1587, Clv.

32. *Grammar at Large*, written 1580 but never published, as described on t.p. of Bullokar's *Booke at large*, 1580.

which the Hebrew nation preserves even after the fall of the Tower of Confusion. But the experiencing of the *Commedia*—I mean by the poet himself—makes for a profoundly different point of view. At the end, Dante compounds for harmonious confusion. The leaves are many and the roots are many. Nimrod's task is impossible of fulfillment but not because it is impious, rather because human choice renews and changes with the turning of the spheres. "The usage of mortals is like a leaf on a branch; it goes and another comes" (*Paradiso* XXVI). For the subsequent time, this conclusion—it is not dispiriting, only acceptive or ecumenical—has no meaning, or what it means is perceived as undressed and uncomely, like the stone which the builders rejected. Spenser in his final cantos speaks for the future—he speaks for the Port-Royalists, for Coleridge, and the philosophical grammarians of the twentieth century—as he decides that mutability is the handmaid of law.

Language first exhibits a self-conscious awareness of the presence of law just at the period when new science is beginning to proclaim it. The achievements of Kepler coincide with the publication of the first significant spelling book in English.[33] Elizabethan spelling is a various thing. Shakespeare in this respect is careless of consistency, even in signing his name. To his contemporaries, "Shakespeare" is impartially Shakeschafte or Shagspere or Chacsper. Christopher Marlowe appears to them as Morley and Marlye and sometimes as Merlin. At least seventy-three different spellings designate the man whom posterity calls Sir Walter Ralegh. Now these whimsicalities are construed as figuring disorder. In sixteenth-century France the grammarian Louis Meigret endeavors to establish phonetic principles, not only to the end that language may be spoken well but that it may be written as spoken. Each letter or character must describe a perfect equivalence with the vowel or consonant it is supposed to represent.[34] Gabriel Harvey the Areopagite, who is as true as the needle to the pole of the time, entertains high hopes of the interconnecting of orthographic and prosodic reform. Harvey identifies prosody with the pronunciation

33. Edmund Coote, *The English Schoole-Master*, 1596.
34. *Le Tretté de la Grammere Françoeze*, 1550.

of the word or syllable in verse. "There is no one more regular and justifiable direction either for the assured and infallible certainty of our English artificial prosody particularly, or generally to bring our language into art and to frame a grammar or rhetoric thereof, than first of all to agree upon one and the same orthography." [35] The Irish poet Richard Stanyhurst attempts to determine pronunciation by joining to his classical measure (1582) an invariant orthography in which the quantities of syllables are signified by the spelling of the words. The result is not uniformly preposterous. But it is the impulse—to come to the one infallible agreement—that takes the eye.

The rule of law enjoins an end to the superfluity of letters. So the orthographic reformer—for example, Thomas Whythorne—announces his intention to "write words as they be sounded in speech." He is happiest as "the writing and pronunciation do both agree," unhappy as "divers superfluous letters" make against this concurrence. There are, says the epistolary writer James Howell, "some critical authors who bear no good will to C, calling it the mongrel androgynous letter, nor male nor female but rather a spirit or monster." Since "by her impostures she trencheth upon the right of s, k, q, assuming their sounds," the law-abiding grammarian will desire her exclusion from our English Abcee or hornbook. Possibly the alternative characters he elaborates remain too protean. The later seventeenth century approximates more nearly the perfection of ratio. Francis Lodwick devises an alphabet in which no character will communicate more than one sound nor will any sound be expressible by more than one character.[36] He is working at the behest of the Royal Society. New science is like Briareus and has its hands on all the ropes.

Mostly, the energy of the scientist goes to the constraining of physical fact. Newton's youthful interest in phonetics is, however, worth remarking. John Ray, the scientific classifier, is also a diligent collector of "English Words Not Generally Used." He is fol-

35. Harvey to Spenser, Letter iv, 1580.

36. Lodwick, *Essay towards an Universal Alaphabet*, 1686; Howell, *New Grammar*, 1662, pp. 18–20, 83; Whythorne's unpublished autobiography, ed. Osborn.

lowing, as he acknowledges, in the track of Bishop Wilkins. His contemporary, the mathematician John Wallis, invents the sign for infinity, and is deeply solicitous of reducing English to grammatical rule. Ramus, "that glorious star of arts and sciences," proposes new letters for "reducing . . . [his] mother tongue the French into a more easy and true character." [37] Literature, as often, emulates science. In the alphabet according to Jean-Antoine de Baïf, the influential poet and academician, letters not met before are made to do duty, while supposedly gratuitous letters like Q and W, X and Y, are put away as the relics of an arbitrary convention. Baïf resolves the opposition of spelling to sound by giving precedence to the latter. His governing principle is to employ "l'ęgzakte ékriture konform' w parlér . . . létre pōr son ō voeięl ō konsonant." [38] As the equivalence is established, the confusion of Babel is understood to be redeemed.

To make the written and spoken word jump together, the Cambridge humanist Sir Thomas Smith (1513–77) creates a phonetic alphabet in which the number of conventional vowels is doubled and Roman, Old English, and Greek characters are utilized as superior representations of the sound the writer wishes to convey (1542). Smith exemplifies vividly the character of the reformer as ardent and apparently random projector, also the common intention informing his various projects. The intention is to bring the vagrant instance to heel. Smith, the first Regius professor of Civil Law at Cambridge, is also a mathematician and natural philosopher and—sequentially, I think—an astrologer and alchemist, who endeavors to turn iron into copper. (The ready and easy way is always in prospect.) He belongs to the purifying party in religion, he renders the Psalms in English verse. He is an imperialist, who promotes the colonizing of Ireland (subduing the rough rugheaded kerns). He is a political preceptor who takes order with government, as in the constitutional treatise *De Republica Anglorum* (1565). Accepting the argument first sponsored by Erasmus that

37. Ramus is described by the French teacher and phonetic reformer John Eliot, in preface to his *Ortho-Epia Gallica*, 1593.

38. *Etrénes de poézie francoeze an vers mezurés*, 1574; M. Augé-Chiquet, *Baïf*, p. 339.

the pronunciation of Greek taught in Western Europe is a bastard-ized version of classical Greek, Smith and his friend Sir John Cheke attempt in their lectures at Cambridge to popularize a re-formed pronunciation which acknowledges order, but not injunc-tively. "Recta" is the word.[39]

Not to pile up citations: let a single title, the "unreasonable Writing of Our English Tongue," suggest the rationale of these many essays in linguistic reform produced by the sixteenth and seventeenth centuries.[40] In our mortal life, nothing weighs more than speech which comforts reason and augments it: paraphrasing Bullokar in his translation of Aesop (1585). This writer believes that in speech "Consent at the beginning wrought, by God's gift in mankind." With the building of the Tower of Babel, consent or harmony is forfeit. But modern man can retrieve it. The present alphabet is, however, an inadequate instrument. "Concord is none." Bullokar's nostrum is to denote the double value accorded a letter by the addition of diacritical marks. His more nearly predict-able phonetics (taking the wish for the fact) looks bizarre to eyes that have grown accustomed to the disjunction between spelling and sound. Still he hopes of his uncouth figures (which I am simpli-fying here) that

> Ye may soon fynd by lite bed, they doo no far way rang.
> From the old uzed ortography graet gayn iz in the chang.

The moral he discovers in Aesop is in the nature of a personal tes-tament. "Variance maketh strong men to be weak." [41]

Variance or heterogeneity is the "rogue male" which the devo-tee of order pursues relentlessly. The racker of orthography, as a pedantic character in Shakespeare describes him, speaks "dout . . . when he should say dou*b*t; det, when he should pronounce de*b*t . . . neighbor *vocatur* nebor; neigh abbreviated ne. This," the lawgiver asserts, "is abhominable—which he would call abom-inable." To make an end of "cacography" in language, he demands

---

39. *De Recta et Emendata Linguae Graecae Pronuntiatione*, 1542, pub. 1568.

40. John Hart, 1551.   41. *Aesop*, A3; *Booke at Large*, C1, R3.

that the speaking voice be made subservient to "exact propositions"
on the model of physical science.[42] If we accept the analogy to
science, we need not assume dejectedly that a name or vector
which points to the fact is "introduced simply by means of descriptive phrases" or takes its rise from arbitrary convention. "A name is
a fixed point in a turning world." [43] Instability lives in the surface.
"Underneath are the everlasting arms."

Laying bare the chief primitives of which Latin is composed,
Comenius discerns simultaneously and just under the surface "a
seed-plot of all arts and tongues containing a ready way to learn the
Latin and English." From his psychology, skepticism is debarred.
The foundation he endows or reconstitutes affords its inmates immediate access to the entry-door or gate of language. This gate is
already unlocked.[44] Bentham, as the lure of quantification becomes
irresistible, identifies the gate—like so many hopeful men in the
centuries before him—with the general principles of mathematics.
These principles, "it is taken for granted," will be universally
recognized as opening on the universal grammar and, incidentally,
the Chrestomathic Day School on which Bentham has set his
heart.[45] They are enabling as they hold for every case. Bentham is
the great quantifier but he also deprecates detail as it blurs and
complicates "general principles." Complication, Bentham thinks, is
"the nursery of fraud." Of course he and his cogeners fall to quar-
reling with language, which is always exfoliating, so escaping. This
odious personality survives to the present as he gives memorable
expression to the chief shibboleths which describe the modern age.
His attack on literary discourse, "the herbage of this jungle" he
desires to level, recapitulates the more general attack of Renaissance humanism on language. As the seventeenth century commences, Samuel Daniel is dismayed that we must now "contend

42. Robert Robinson, *The Art of Pronunciation*, 1617; Alexander Gil, *Logonomia Anglica*, 1619.

43. P. Ziff, *Semantic Analysis*, p. 104.

44. *Janua Linguarum Reserata*, 1650.

45. "Hints towards the composition of an Elementary Treatise on Universal Grammar," *Works*, 1853, Vol. VIII.

for words themselves." He is satiric in discovering "a great per-
verseness amongst them." He does not find them "so far gone from
the quiet freedom of nature that they must thus be brought back
again by force." In any case, he assumes that the commonwealth of
letters is best and healthiest when governed least: *in pessima republica plurimae leges.*[46] It is an archaic assumption.

The dictatorial role to which the humanist aspires is congenial
for chauvinistic reasons, as in the attack on what are called inkhorn
terms. The poet and critical legislator Gascoigne, as he is more stu-
dious "to make our native language commendable in itself than gay
with the feathers of strange birds," had rather be faulted "in keeping the old English words (*quamvis jam obsoleta*) than in borrowing of other languages such epithets and adjectives as smell of the
inkhorn." Dante is only counselling prudence when, in the *De
Vulgari Eloquentia* (Ch. vii), he suggests that discriminating
writers will want to use the sieve. Gascoigne, in his hostility to
polysyllabic diction, is counselling exclusion. Macbeth, who surmises that his bloody hand would "the multitudinous seas incar-
nadine," is more than pusillanimous, a word not to be used. "The
more monosyllables that you use, the truer Englishman you shall
seem." [47]

The indulging of Latinity, which is the making of Shakespeare's blank verse, counts among the vices of style. It is "for
defense of my country language" that Renaissance poets render
Virgil in English. The rhetoricians look askance, not only at language "fetched from the Latin inkhorn," but at all excursions into
foreign speech.[48] There are exceptions to this rule. In the more
catholic opinion of the antiquary Richard Carew, we are like provident bees as we borrow from others: we "gather the honey of their
good properties and leave the dregs to themselves." [49] But the

46. Daniel, *A Defense of Rhyme*, ?1603; Bentham, "Fragments on Universal Grammar,"
Works, viii, 355.

47. Preface to *The Posies*, 1575; *Certayne Notes of Instruction*, 1575.

48. Puttenham, *Arte of English Poesie*, 1589, Bk. ii, Ch. ix; Thomas Phaer in his trans. of
Virgil, 1558.

49. *Epistle on the Excellency of the English Tongue*, c. 1595–96 (in Camden's *Remains*, edn.
of 1614).

conventional opinion does not support catholicity. These verses of George Herbert's honor the convention:

> Let foreign nations of their language boast,
> What fine variety each tongue affords;
> I like our language, as our men and coast;
> Who cannot dress it well, want wit, not words.

In France, however, the pox is known as the English disease. "So far as possible use French words, especially old native ones." That is Ronsard's advice.[50] Something depends on the customary speech of the tribe.

"I love Rome but London better, I favor Italy but England more, I honor the Latin but I worship the English." Richard Mulcaster, the famous headmaster of the Merchant Taylors' School, as he is patriotic makes a virtue of provincialism, as he is bookish an apophthegm upon it. "But why not all in English?" he inquires.[51] To this position Edmund Spenser, Mulcaster's dutiful pupil, adheres. So he returns to what he takes to be the language of Chaucer. In choosing "old and unwonted words," Spenser stirs the loyalist sympathies of his contemporaries, who make it a point of praise "that he hath labored to restore as to their rightful heritage such good and natural English words as have been long time out of use and almost clean disherited." If on the other hand he discovers holes in the mother tongue, he declines to patch them "with pieces and rags of other languages." He fears lest our English tongue become "a gallimaufray or hodgepodge." [52]

The earlier sixteenth century is not so troubled by the spectre of formlessness and hence neither so intense nor exclusive. In this period, the importing into English of alien words is generally approved. The poet fulfills his proper function as he drinks of

> the well of fruitfulness
> Which Virgil clarified and also Tullius
> With Latin pure, sweet, and delicious.[53]

50. *Abbregé de l'art poëtique françois*, 1565.

51. *First Part of the Elementarie*, 1582, K3, Hhlv, Hhiiiv.

52. "E. K.," Epistle Dedicatory to *The Shepherds' Calendar*, 1579.

53. Stephen Hawes, *The Passetyme of Pleasure*, 1509, ll. 1160–63.

But the impulse to purity grows on the age. Pluralism is anathema to the hag-ridden man. Already Skelton wavers between the plain and aureate styles. The poets of the *Court of Venus*, notably Wyatt, later of *Tottel's Miscellany*, seem consciously to archaize. Against the high incidence of Romance vocabulary in the earliest Tudor verse, they oppose—as if fulfilling a meditated program— the undiluted strain of native English. Chauvinism does not sufficiently rationalize this retreat to the past. The rejection of Spenser makes that clear. Spenser is hopefully Saxon but in idiosyncratic, therefore unacceptable ways. "In affecting the Ancients [he] writ no language" (Jonson). Not parochialism but a zeal for perspicuous language impels Sir John Cheke to insist on a homogeneous vocabulary, "unmixed and unmangled with borrowing of other tongues." [54] As he is faithful to this insistence in his version of the Gospel of St. Matthew, he replaces Latin *proselyte* with *freshman*, and *centurion* with *hundreder*. Matthew is not an *apostle* but a *from-sent*, Jesus is not *crucified* but *crossed*. Cheke thinks he sees a bond between aureate diction and the anarchic state of language. So he hurls his inkhorn at the devil.

The almost religious irritability of the linguistic reformers turns on the perceiving or asserting of this bond. "Strange terms" and "dark words" are subversive of transparency. [55] Smith, agitating his basic pronunciation of Greek, is put to silence by Stephen Gardiner, the Roman Catholic Chancellor of Cambridge. It is an adumbrating, as in a teapot, of the altercation between Pope Urban the agnostic and Galileo the determinist. Cheke, who is more contentious, engages the Chancellor in a series of Latin epistles, published out of harm's way in Basle. [56] When the new orthography is calumniated, as by Guillaume des Autels, Meigret rejoins in the *Defenses . . . contre les censures ę calomnies de Guillaume*. But this rejoinder provokes a *Réplique . . . aux furieuses Defenses*, and in turn a *Response . . . a la dezesperée Réplique*. What is crucial to these serio-comic polemics is not the pedagogue's familiar distrust of license but the provincialism he associates with it.

---

54. Letter of July 16, 1557, to Sir Thomas Hoby, appended to *The Courtier*, 1561.

55. Puttenham, III, iv. 56. *Joannis Cheki Angli De Pronunciatione Graecae*, 1555.

Hobbes illuminates the root concern of the reformers. The prime target is not the harmless antiquarian, rifling the pages of his thesaurus, but the language of the Schools or of the "strong lines" poets, who are stigmatized as "dark and troublesome" in their rendering of truth. The practitioners of aureate diction, as they "stand wholly upon dark words," are only attempting to impose on simple folk who "cannot but wonder at their talk and think surely they speak by some revelation." It does not occur to the humanist or linguistic reformer that to render the truth one must imitate its labyrinthine ways. On the contrary, says Bullokar: "truth washeth all away and maketh everything appear plain as it is." [57]

The adventures and misadventures enumerated here are all of a piece. Unity of purpose, not meditated but not less organic, informs the attempt to reconstitute prosody (in England, also on the Continent), to realize a universal character, to make a new orthography and new phonetics, to rid the language of aureate diction, to irradiate the "palpable darkness" where the strong-lines poet lives,

> Curling with metaphors a plain intention,
> Decking the sense as if it were to sell.

The common denominator or one informing purpose is a rage for order. Bentham enunciates it in a sentence. He is divulging his plan for a model prison or Panopticon. As fear and hatred are crescent in him, he demands "a method of becoming master of everything which might happen to . . . men, to dispose of everything around them so as to produce on them the desired impression, to make certain of their actions, of their connections, and of all the circumstances of their lives, so that nothing could escape." [58] The world is a prison with many wards and confines over which surveillance is total.

The view from the ideal prison is a partial view. What we see—I should say, what we hypostasize or run up between the real

---

57. *Booke at Large*, Blv; Sir Thomas Wilson, *Arte of Rhetorique*, 1553; Hobbes, *Leviathan*, end of Ch. XLVI; *Answer to Davenant* (on *Gondibert*), 1650.

58. *Panopticon*, 1791.

world and ourselves—is a homogeneous plain. Reality, so ordered, holds no surprises. The lights that wink in the firmament compel attention only as they function "to distinguish and preserve the numbers of time" (*Timaeus*). So we are reduced to the poverty of living in a nonphysical world. This world is the exhalation of desire, partly heroic, partly perverse. It is the "Fruit of our boughs, whence heaven maketh rods (Fulke Greville). Nimrod, the type of the great aspirer, is whipped but by his own devising.

The building of the Tower of Babel is analogous to the system-making of the Renaissance. The end in view is the liberation of man, clearing the shades of the prison house. Boehme says—for he is a notable systematizer—"look in what a dungeon we are lying, in what lodging we are, for we have been captured by the spirit of the outward world." So far, I think we give our assent. Then follows the equivocal codicil: the outward world "rules in our marrow and bones, in our flesh and blood, it has made our flesh earthly, and now death has us." The dominion of death is supposedly accomplished as the divine substance takes a body: as the Word is made flesh. Our mundane existence is only a dream, from which we emerge as we put off our clayey habiliments. This counsel frees us from mortality as it works our extinction. Mortality is what we have.

CHAPTER SEVEN

City of God,
How Broad, How Far

THE abrading of matter until at last the light shines through is the corrosive work of the sorcerer, the mystic, and the divinatory man. The audacious spirit which informs the work and ventures to pronounce for the whole of creation ought not to be missed. It transfigures the great lawgivers, even Descartes, who disdains "everything that is only probable as almost false." The polemical writers of the sixteenth and seventeenth centuries, whose attack on the theatre and secular verse is my subject in the *War Against Poetry*, are dedicated like their master Plato to building the city of God on earth. We are their descendants and the city we inhabit is their myopic legacy to us. They know what they know. Rationalism, the dominant psychology of "the Age of Gold," partakes of self-hatred, at the same time of a disinterested ardor for truth. In this context the philosophical revolutionaries belong—Fourier, Robert Owen, Étienne Cabet—as they are bent on redoing the world. "We must establish a kingdom of God," says Kropotkin. Like Comenius or Bruno, he longs "to take all mankind to his bosom and keep it warm." The passion is suffocating and the kingdom aseptic, but the aspiring man deserves better than he has got. One thinks of Einstein, alone on the sand dunes in Belgium in the Hitler spring, his house ransacked and padlocked against him, his friends, even Planck, in effect fallen off: and still searching doggedly for the clue to the unified field theory which forever eludes him.

In Canto XII of the *Inferno,* Dante records a curious and felicitous inversion of the story of Babel. At the Harrowing of Hell, the fetid valley is driven by an earthquake. "The universe felt love, and some believe that by love the world has been turned into chaos." This belief is fathered on Empedocles, who teaches that the material order of the world depends on the discord of its constituent parts. The Middle Ages find the dependency congenial. The world is a confused but amicable mixture, says the English Augustinian Alexander Neckham (1157–1217), "a certain concordant discord of the elements." When these diverse elements are brought into a harmony or unified field, as by the eleemosynary men on whose track I have been following, the world's variety disappears and chaos comes again. So the circle, "a shape of spare appeal," which resolves the infinite variety of analogous forms, makes a violent order. Now we must go backward,

> filling by one and one
> Circles with hickory spokes and rich soft shields
> Of petalled dayseyes, with herehastening steel
> Volleys of daylight.
>
> (Richard Wilbur)

Living order is tossing circles skyward, to be replaced by actual wings.

In a paper on Relativity Theory, Max Born sees the likeness to a great work of art. "But its connections with experience were slender." The aborting of the connection by the classical scientist and linguistic reformer makes mischief for the future. The divinatory man, closing his eyes against "the outward world," engineers our captivity to a world of exiguous forms. As we languish there, in the enclosed garden of his hectic imagining, we die of inanition. I suppose the violence and nausea of this second half of the twentieth century—expressed, for example, in the "counter culture"—to attest our desperate effort to break free. The effort seems more desperate than successful. No apparent alternatives commend themselves to us. Who is going to resuscitate the dark age before the flood? Dante and Shakespeare never nourished the million, now they hardly nourish the few (who are not elect, only lucky). Anyway, it has always been wrongheaded to look to them for Truth. The artist is a hierophant only in his own time, after that we consult him for our pleasure. Nostalgic professors like Matthew Arnold summon up remembrance of what is indubitably past. Art is not religion, not even a secular religion, and the Middle Ages, when for a while the two acknowledged a mutual consent, are dead as mutton.

The Enlightenment or modern age, our common matrix, is already five hundred years old. So far as most of us know, it is the definition of history. Not surprisingly, therefore, contemporary disaffection, as it perceives no way of ameliorating our condition by appealing to a different historical order, turns its back on history. "Wherever man shudders before the menace of his own work and longs to flee from the radically demanding historical hour, there he finds himself near to the apocalyptic vision" (Martin Buber).[1] Recorded history, as opposed to the round of daily pieties, is an abattoir, so it is tempting to hypothesize another and preexistent culture—really it is a-historical—a more nutritive or natural culture in which we do not write over our lintel: Cogito, ergo sum, but: I have breasts, therefore I am.

History means sequence, though not necessarily propter hoc, the referring of every event to its source in anterior time. The contemporary soothsayer, as he wants to snap this referential chain, sponsors a fictive psychology and cosmology which, if not wholly fictive, is certainly partial and rooted at least as much in denial as acceptance. "Women's Liberation" will inevitably seem reactionary to him, like racial equality to the black militant in the grain, because it is evolutionary and looks to a pragmatic end. This end is compassed by the conscious activity of the intellect. Hence it is vilified. More seductive than intellectual address is the cult of the unselfconscious woman who cannot think but dwells in the blood and who differs from the ignorant female of unhallowed convention only because Anaïs Nin insists on the difference. In the ebbtide of the Age of Faith, who needs another ipse dixit? The domination of the Stone-Ecstatic-Vaginal-Earth Mother, created in the first place

1. *Pointing the Way*, p. 203.

by Nietzsche and his disciples out of their own inadequacy, seems hardly preferable to Freud's patriarchal father-master of the primal horde. St. Paul says: The man is the head of the woman. Now his provincial formula is reversed. Instead of this monstrous bifurcation, why not give us the yoke and white of the one shell?

The way to a viable future lies neither in returning to the long past nor in repudiating the modern age which has displaced it. Not a provident but a foolish man repudiates the stuff he is made of. I think we echo Blake's prayer that God keep us "from single vision and Newton's sleep," but not the invoking of the tigers of wrath as by Josephus and Gregory of Tours or the gurus of the adversary culture. Their worship is given to a God afar off, made in the likeness of frustration, one greater Man who is slivered and disbranched; ours in hope to a God at hand (Jeremiah 23:23), made in the plenary likeness of ourselves. Dante, who pits the truth of Heaven against "the present life of wretched mortals," when he takes us to Heaven finds that the Light Eternal is painted with our image. The Old Testament prophet Daniel presents the conventional-horrid apocalyptic vision. He craves a future beyond history when the Ancient of Days will sweep away all that detritus which is our vexed and good life, "like the chaff of the summer threshing-floors" (2:35). Dante, employing the same figure, sees "this little threshing-floor" as blotted with sadness and participating concurrently in the joy which breathes from the womb, the dwelling-place of our desire.[2] Either/or is not in it.

The classical scientist and philosophical grammarian are often the butt of this discourse. Nonetheless they point the way as they accommodate their opposite, the vates or seer, who is inextricably part of themselves. King Conchobar, in the old Celtic story, lives for seven years with a ball in his head, made of the dried brain of an enemy. And when he dislodges the ball in his fury, he dies. He does not know or estimate his lucky possession. Understanding is crucial. Ceremony, sanctified by grace or fiat, insures that as the communicant partakes of the body and blood of Christ (or Dionysus), he is changed. The fact of the metamorphosis is, however, not

2. *Paradiso* XXVIII, XXXIII, XXVII, XXIII.

enough. The introjecting must be conscious. It is not conscious in the Enlightenment. Sprat and the others do not really know what they are doing nor why. So the liberal progressivism of the modern age, as it is ingenuous, fails to chain the demons of the Ucs. In the persons of Hitler and his accomplices, they keep breaking free to thumb their noses at the rest of us who suppose complacently that God's in His Heaven and the Devil perdurably elsewhere. I think the demons will always resume their hateful freedom, that chaos will always recur and history be no other than a charnel house—unless we confront them, not deny or repress them, in the conscious state. The condition of health is not an exalting of the dionysiac gods but an acknowledging of their existence. We are not fulfilled as we cast out once and for all the old serpent of the uroboros, or the old Adam. Here, the conventional Christian wisdom needs modifying. "Two kings encamp them still in man as well as herbs"—the saying of Friar Laurence in *Romeo and Juliet*—and though the hegemony of the baleful king is certainly to be disallowed, his station within us as an inevitable part of our totality is as certainly to be affirmed. He is the perennial insurgent against whom we must be perennially on our guard. At the same time he is the dark other, or brother even, as Jacob, whose crooked power sustains us as we understand it, is the brother of that credulous Esau.

In concluding my account of the making of the modern world, I want to go back into the humus of the beginning and see what is retrievable. Our enfranchisement requires that we cast a cold eye on the psychology of the Enlightenment—never an age so perversely denoted—at the same time that we seek to locate in it and take sustenance from the hidden source of its dynamism. The wellspring or source—following the metaphor—lies underground. Cusa and Einstein, Freud not less than Jung, who live in history as light bringers or apostles of reason, live for us primarily as charismatic men. In terms of their kind, they belong with the greater mystics like Meister Eckhart and St. Bernard of Clairvaux. Skepticism in the teeth of the reasonable expectation links them together, also its obverse, the creativity that partakes of intuition. Scholarship, which St. Francis has no desire to see developed in his Order, does not guarantee possession of the truth; neither, step by step, does the exercise of our rational faculty. "Non diffinio," says Richard Rufus of Cornwall, the leader of the Oxford Franciscans. His passionate distaste for splitting hairs associates him surprisingly with that "Lord Bacon" whom Shelley characterizes—I think rightly—as a poet. The Enlightenment discredits the mode of perceiving which is poetic or intuitive, ecumenical, as when one takes all nature for his province. Now the discredited mode returns in the inclusivism of contemporary science. Quoting Erwin Schrödinger: "you—and all other conscious beings as such—are all in all. Hence this life of yours which you are living is not merely a piece of the entire existence, but is in a certain sense the *whole;* only this whole is not so constituted that it can be surveyed in one single glance." [3]

The proviso implies an end to the imperialistic and cursory kind of seeing which describes the modern age. The biophysicist is saying: *tutto in tutto.* He recalls Comenius or Ramón Lull. In his recension, however, the individual is not annihilated in the whole. As the devoted eye which rationality does not countenance contemplates all human beings, it discovers their diversity. Dante peoples the heavens with a multitude of angels, "each distinct in brightness and in function" (*Paradiso* XXXI). They show forth the Eternal Goodness, a broken mirror which remains one in itself but refracts the light variously as the shivered pieces of the mirror determine (XXIX). "We are all yours, mi signore!" Henry Adams is paraphrasing St. Francis in the "Canticle of the Sun." "We are all varying forms of the same ultimate energy; shifting symbols of the same absolute unity; but our only unity, beneath you, is nature, not law!" [4] The nature invoked by the mystic, if not discrete is particolored, adamantly resisting classification. Only in death, the consummation to which the Schoolman and the new philosopher are appealing, is the multiplicity of forms resolved.

Scholasticism and new philosophy are polar opposites. This is the primary reading of their relationship. Looking at my material

3. *My View of the World,* pp. 21–22.

4. *Mont-Saint Michel and Chartres,* end of Ch. xv.

from a different point of view, it seems equally legitimate to emphasize the way in which they come together. Alexander of Hales (d. 1245), the Irrefragible Doctor who turns the Franciscan Order from its original bias, anticipates T. H. Huxley, who would have affected to despise him. The religious skeptics like St. Francis, the great divinators like Bacon are the heralds of contemporary science. I know all this will raise eyebrows, as in part it makes against what I have been asserting previously of the scientist and mystic. I answer, like Macbeth, that "Two truths are told." The power of these protean men and women—ours, as we grapple with them successfully—is first and obviously a rational power, but also and in last things a numinous power and derives from the spectral kingdom where the sorcerer still preserves a tenuous but enduring vitality. He is not our hope nor does he incarnate, unless to an astigmatic reading, "the submerged magic of the earth" (Roszak).[5] He is the enemy with whom we take truce so that we may pick from his muttered counsels the scintilla of truth. For he has something to offer.

Mostly what he offers is self-laceration—St. Francis strewing ashes on his food—vulgar mumbo-jumbo, not coping but passivity. Guilt, as he construes it, goes by association, good fortune also. "A harlot is not only impudent in herself" but infectious, "so that if a man do often behold himself in her glass or put on her garments, it will make him impudent and lecherous as she is." Della Porta in these observations is indifferent to social disease. As he fixes his mind on metaphysical correspondences, he does not help us much. Neither does Agrippa in relating each member of the body to "some sign, some star, some intelligence, some divine name." Seize the left thigh with your left hand and you have uttered, not symbolized, the number 60,000. This far transcends the arbitrary connections worked up in the hieratic language of Egypt. The magus supposes the connections to be real. The supposition is tenable only as he abjures honest commerce with reality.

There is a world out there but the adherence to Neoplatonism, variously filtered, insures that nobody sees it. Cohn in his

5. *The Making of a Counter Culture*, p. 268.

account of the millenarians of the waning Middle Ages stresses their amoralism and megalomania. Reason fusts in them. They need no priest or adept to mediate their salvation. They abhor the sexual life or indulge it orgiastically. In either case, they are announcing their contempt for the body. Flagellation dramatizes this contempt. Infants are not baptized with water but scourged until they bleed. So enfranchisement does not consist in a romantic-modern evoking of the dark chthonic gods. The pronouncements of *Love's Body* are not sibylline but sentimental. They do not effect our reconciliation with Nature but subdue us to that baleful nature, unlicked hence amorphous, which Edmund the Bastard apostrophizes in *King Lear*. Donne says in a sermon: "Knowledge cannot save us, but we cannot be saved without knowledge." [6] There is no knowledge here, or not the knowledge of Apollo, the canonical wisdom to which we rightfully defer. Before Apollo there was, however, the Python.

Apollo is recognized as he vanquishes the Python, Mary as she bruises the serpent with her heel. The opposition is absolute, so perhaps a falsifying of the truth. Plato in the *Symposium* thinks we once presented a more ample figure until a jealous god cut us in two, "as men cut sorb-apples in two when they are preparing them for pickling, or as they cut eggs in two with a hair." Now each of us is only "the half of a human being . . . each is forever seeking his missing half." The similitude is inexact as the two halves appear the same. They are not the same but they make a concurrence. Valéry suggests it:

> Mais rendre la lumière
> Suppose d'ombre une morne moitié.

I take this to mean that the single vision bequeathed us by the new philosophers is purblind. Jove in the clouds had his inhuman birth. No earthly mother suckled him. We are more nearly catholic as we are impure, an amalgam of the bread and wine, and are saved as we smell of mortality.

6. *Fifty Sermons*, 36, fol. 325 (Christmas Day, 1621).

The Griffin who appears in *Purgatorio* XXXI—a type of Christ in his earthly life—is the twice-begotten animal, that "beast which is one sole person in two natures." Our erected flesh is not dross to him but alloy. Like the Centaur he is ferine, and like him the embodiment of good. The Centaur in Bruno's vision—"this man that is planted in a beast . . . this beast that is engrafted on a man"— maintains his place among the heavenly constellations so that the whole may be complete. He is there not as he extirpates but as he enlarges the beast that lives within him. His animality declares his greatness, like the horn which distinguishes the Grand Turk or the Doge of Venice. Bruno, who inquires why Moses is preeminent in learning, finds the answer in his possession of that "beautiful member nature has conceded to beasts." He could not have descended from Mount Sinai with the Decalogue "in the form of a mere man." What does it mean unless it means propriety, the "great pair of horns that branched out from his forehead?" [7] St. Jerome, misreading Scripture, authorizes the horns. Try, however, to imagine Michelangelo's Moses without them. The misreading is inspired and in the direction of truth, like the famous crux from Habakkuk in the translation of the Seventy: "And thou shalt be recognized in the midst of two animals" (3:2). The man-wolf does not exist, nor the man-bull nor man-pig. But these anomalous creatures, who live in the popular culture of the Middle Ages, emblematize the dual nature by which we also, like the man-god, are recognized.

A Biblical exegete of the early centuries likens the Word made flesh to Antaeus, the Son of Earth. As Christ in his combat with Sin, the Father of Death, is wrestled to earth, he feels his strength return.[8] The animality which succors him and which the earth is meant to figure is not the complement but the condition of divinity. I think that is Dante's point in choosing to honor the old tradition which makes Chiron, the wisest of the Centaurs, the tutor of Achilles, and not only of Achilles. The most distinguished heroes of Greek antiquity go to school to this ambiguous creature. In Bruno's

7. Third Dialog of *Lo Spaccio.*

8. Following Gallic sermons in Latin ascribed to Eusebius (died c. 359), Bishop of Emesa.

theogony—it is also a bestiary—the Centaur is a priest "made up of two natures" and sacrificing the animal to which he is tied. His sacerdotal office is defined as he is himself "the sacrifice and the sacrificer." It is not that he is putting off the old man or losing his life to find it. In one person he partakes of two lives. Their fusion is the subtle knot that makes us man.

The serpent by convention represents the carnal principle, but not exclusively. He is the underground water fertilizing the womb. He is also that celestial water, the Golden Rain of Danaë or emanation of the Holy Ghost, entering into the feminine soul as *nous* or spirit. Fecundity contains and requires its opposite. The serpent must destroy himself, like the savage penitents of the Free Brethren, to reinvigorate the world with his blood. I do not know that we welcome the imperative, but there it is. Sometimes in Renaissance art, the winged Cupids who accompany the Goddess of Love are equipped with hideous claws. They are proclaiming the dual role of the Goddess, who is both siren and harpy and who carries in her hands life and death. Erich Neumann, in his massive analysis of the archetype of the Great Mother, illustrates from a fifteenth-century tray painting of "The Triumph of Venus." The triumph is mixed, neither good nor bad but good and bad together. Apollo in his beginnings is not wholly Apollonian. The sanctuary on the island of Delos where the god of light and reason is born makes room for grinning faces with protruding tongues. Their kinship is more with darkness than light. Dionysus, the immemorial adversary, still rides the leopard in the House of the Masks. These unlikely pairings do not disvalue rationality. They suggest that rationality is not all in all sufficient. Better than the familiar dichotomy of reason and will or Apollo and Dionysus is Yeats's reformulation: "Within ourselves Reason and Will, who are the man and woman, hold out towards a hidden altar a laughing or crying child."

In the early years of the fourteenth century, the meditations of Henry Suso are broken in upon by a mysterious being. "Whence have you come?" asks the mystic. "I come from nowhere." "What are you?" "I am not." "What do you wish?" "I do not wish." "What is your name?" "I am called Nameless Wildness." The insight with which the apparition is dowered conducts to untrammeled freedom where "a man lives according to all his caprices without distinguishing between God and himself, and without looking before or after." The vision resembles that utopian commonwealth enjoined by the rebel Cade, in which the pissing conduit runs nothing but claret wine. As he calls for the annulling of demarcation and propriety, this apparition is wild. But the entail of what he says has its hopeful side. The Brethren of the Free Spirit, who do not wish, define the perfect man as the motionless Cause. No doubt they are quietistic. A heretical Polish catechism of the 1560s merges the perfect in the abject personality. "If his master commands him to go to war or to pay taxes, and eventually even makes him a slave, a Christian must suffer and pray to God for his master." [9] Partly, the exalting of the motionless Cause strips from us our autonomy. And partly, as it ridicules the expiation of sin, rejects the doctrine of Purgatory: works, writ large, declines to look before or after, it asserts our autonomy.

Labor, the modern narcotic, has perturbed the centuries, bound us on the wheel, led the world "into a ferrous, muddy, and argillaceous age," iron in its aspect, otherwise insubstantial because molded of clay. So leisure, which is not comprehended in supineness, enters its claim to a hearing, also the body, which you do not have to call a tabernacle if you decline to call it a sink. We are not what we are ashamed of. As in our simplicity we hearken after the flesh, there is no occasion of shame. "S'ei piace, ei lice." If it pleases, it is permitted to you. Bruno and Tasso, whom I am conflating, make their peace involuntarily with the repressive spirit of the Counterreform. Leisure and pleasure are interdicted. But the extravagant psychology of the mystics and millenarians, whose extravagance is indubitable, is laid up for the future. St. Paul is always rising to their lips: "To the pure all things are pure." Antinomianism is the perversion of this saying, so not wholly devoid of pith. Maybe we want to look at it again.

You can argue that the Copernican theory makes no difference to our daily intercourse or the aspirations which inform it. Donne

9. Kot, *Socinianism*, p. 17.

takes this line, in the satiric romance called *Ignatius His Conclave*, when he asks rhetorically if the intuiting of a heliocentric universe has "brought men to that confidence that they build new towers or threaten God again." In fact the answer is affirmative. Men in the modern age do not live "just as they did before" but not because the geocentric universe is dead, rather because the new universe adumbrated in the sixteenth century postulates the absolute authority of law and so threatens the Old One or whimsical Creator, who is wont to cut across Creation as He wills. Subsequently, the propositions of classical physics, the moat defensive to the modern world, are challenged or filled in. The army of unalterable law is routed and the individual man resumes his lonely station on the plain of Shinar. In the event, the Old One has confounded us. The bleak jocosity of the latter-day Antinomian who, like Polonius, is true to himself, dramatizes one possible reaction. Another reaction is, however, possible. We can accept our indeterminate condition, saying laconically: I am what I am.

To belabor the irenic philosophers is neither difficult nor amiss. They tolerate everything, believing nothing themselves. But the pale fire of Erasmus, Glanvill, Montaigne, if it means Laodiceanism, is also the condition of that pluralistic society which entertains different modes of behavior and belief as it asserts the purity, anyway the integrity, of the individual man. The Unitarians, or their forebears in the seventeenth century, exhort us to love each other, irrespective of the opposing creeds by which we hope to be saved. "Dogmas do not constitute the essence of Christianity, but devout living; no man is in measure to fathom the nature of God, thus we should allow even those faiths which may seem mistaken to some." As each of us "has a right to his own individual evaluation," the well-ordered society will not abrogate our right but defend it.[10] In this plea for the coexistence of opposites, which is not the same thing as the old *coincidentia oppositorum*, the Pauline dictum takes on another meaning. Perhaps a corner of the original meaning is disclosed. Our rationalist masters like to reconcile opposites. But Jung in *Aion* argues for "a *complexio opposi-*

---

10. Tract of 1628 in *Socinianism*, p. xxv.

torum precisely because there can be no reality without polarity." Always, Christ hangs on the Cross between the good and evil thief.

The lay mendicants called Beghards who propagate the Brotherhood of the Free Spirit emphasize the pantheism of Plotinus. The Brethren assure us that "Every created thing is divine." As what absorbs them is the impalpable core, not the concrete emanation, they are the distressing harbingers of new philosophy. But their sense of a divinity in things, like the quality of mercy, refreshes the earth. This sense, which Neoplatonism enforces even as it prepares the extinction of the physical world, also survives—not in the public library, the repository of the official point of view, but in the library of Babel where the outlandish formulations of the astrologer, the alchemist, and the devotee of the Cabala are gathered. Michael Servetus, the heretic and martyr, professes Neoplatonism and proceeds to invert it, like Marx inverting Hegel. Servetus thinks the Word is nothing until it puts on flesh. But the flesh is inert until leavened by the Word, when Christ's Spirit "confers being upon matter." Singleminded men, like the Monophysites in the old ascetic time or the Calvinists whipping out the offending Adam, "talk of humanity as if it were devoid of spirit and . . . think of flesh after the flesh." Servetus proposes one capacious vessel. Sensible matter becomes, not defect and negation, but the source of all being. Everything you can show him is the substance of God. "There is in our spirit a certain latent working energy . . . a latent divinity and it bloweth where it listeth and I hear its voice and I know not whence it comes nor whither it goes." For Clerk Maxwell, three centuries later, all atoms are of the same nature all through. He does not say the nature is godlike. The sap has gone out of the metaphor.

To assert that we and all minute particulars are "born of the spirit of God" infuriates the pneumatic man, who acknowledges only the animate One and who is the Neoplatonist on his negating side. "What, wretch!" says Calvin. "If one stamps the floor would one say that one stamped on your God? Does not such an absurdity shame you?" But Servetus believes unashamedly that the bench on which he is sitting or anything his interrogator points to is part and parcel of deific essence. "And when again it was objected, 'The

devil then will be substantially God?' he broke out laughing and
said, 'Can you doubt it?' " [11] Calvin in his triumphant clarity loses
as much as he gains. He is not provident enough nor sufficiently
pious. I should venture the same comment of classical science, as it
burns the books which divulge its paternity or pronounces them il-
legible. The children of Israel, pillaging the Egyptians, are more
astute.

The Neoplatonic *nous* or world spirit is disembodied, so bane-
ful, but argues a living force pervasive in the cosmos. The mathematical mode by which Plato proceeds in the *Timaeus* blanches the
cosmos. But concurrently Plato decides that all matter is alive. The
animistic idea—hylozoism—carries on a subterranean existence
throughout the Middle Ages. For Hermes Trismegistus and the
keepers of the flame, all things are God and the world a living
animal "and nothing in the world is mortal. Since every single part,
such as it is, is always living and is in a world which is always one
. . . there is no place in the world for death." [12] Schrödinger win-
nows the chaff or superfluity of nonsense from the wheat. "Eternally and always there is only *now*, one and the same now; the
present is the only thing that has no end." In the Tower at Bol-
lingen, Jung feels himself inhabiting all time simultaneously. "It is
as if a silent, greater family, stretching down the centuries, were
peopling the house." Yeats's Tower is like this: so, less grandly, is
the house I inhabit as it credits the past and honors the present.
"There I live in my second personality and see life in the round, as
something forever coming into being and passing on." I take Robert Bly to be glossing Jung's *Memories* as when he makes out a consciousness under the mind's feet, civilizations dead and gone under
the footsole.

> It is a willow that knows of water under the earth,
> I am a father who dips as he passes over underground rivers.

In the thirteenth century, the Church on its official side condemns the doctrine of eternal creation, as expounded by the Arab

11. Following, here and hereafter, Bainton's *Servetus*.

12. Ficino's translation of dialog between Mercury (Hermes) and Asclepius.

philosopher Averroës who preserves the teachings of Aristotle and transmits them to the Christian Middle Ages. But logic, the finicking kind which enchants the medieval intelligence, appears to sanction this doctrine. So it persists. You cannot conceive God as a timeless and necessary cause without supposing, together with Him, the existence of some of His effects. How else would He cause? Created beings have always existed. They themselves enjoy only finite duration, they are born and die in time. But the species is forever, and the repertory of ideas by which it lives. "Have you ever asked yourself where the old gods go, the gods whom the world has forgotten?" Pavese puts the question in his *Dialogues with Leucò*. Jung addresses it implicitly. The passions and shibboleths of all previous time sink deep, like stones in the ground—but after all not like stones, for they live, though quiescent, in the *Anima Mundi,* waiting the auspicious moment. Jove, as the expulsion of the triumphant beast prepares, is thinking fearfully of such a moment, for the term of 36,000 years is upon him, "at which time," says Bruno, "the revolution of the year of the world threatens that another Caelus will come to take back his dominion." Maybe the threat is empty. The idea of the Renaissance suggests otherwise.

In dead winter of 1953, a team of archaeologists digging near the village of Châtillon-sur-Seine bring up to the light a gigantic bronze vase chased with figures of astonishing power. This, the so-called "Trésor de Vix," offers mute testimony to a Burgundian civilization of high artistic culture that flourished and decayed five centuries before the beginning of the Christian era and the Roman colonizing of Gaul, a civilization contemporaneous with Tarquin the Proud, and Themistocles, and Darius. A monstrous face, whose staring eyes are as innocent as the tiger's, adorns the anse or handle, the first segment of the vase to emerge from the frozen earth. This face suggests the fragility of the Beatitudes, paradoxically the permanent chance of their renewal. Hermes is vindicated. Nothing wholly dies. Once more the image of the double helix confronts us. The Augustinian dualism of time and eternity— or say, the fatal hypothesizing of the two cities—gives way to a universal pageant which presents unlimited continuity. If I know anything about Dante, I know that his vision is seamless. The Church Militant in Paradise is not a transforming but only the apogee of the Holy Roman Empire, which does not transform but continues the Rome of the Caesars. There is only one city and it is endlessly accommodating.

In the Middle Ages, the monastic community or better habitation is set against the world. The edification of the monks at Lindisfarne preoccupies the medieval ecclesiastic like Alcuin of York, the coadjutor of Charlemagne. He wants the Word of God to be read when the monks are at meals, and only the Word. Listen to the lector, not the harpist. "Your house is small, there is not room for them both." On the other hand, Beatrice, the truth of God, bids us behold how vast is the assembly of the white robes or dwellers in the celestial sphere. "See our city, how great is its circuit! See our seats so filled that few souls are now wanting there!" (*Paradiso* xxx) These souls have found out salvation by differing routes. At the summit they discover themselves "united with all those who, from every direction, have made the same ascent." I am quoting Teilhard de Chardin, whose vision of a universe fraught with infinite potentiality, an intensely personal universe "neither cold nor closed," is like that of Dante and Aquinas. "Everything that rises must converge." [13] But the convergence envisaged here is not that of the pansophist or Leveller who wishes to turn the world into a plain. It is the meeting of contrarieties, where the concave rests on the convex.

Though "there is one simple Divinity found in all things," she appears in various guises. So, Bruno thinks, "we must diversely ascend to her." His incessant curiosity follows. The divinity or truth he finds in Hermeticism and the Pythagoreans abides our question. The ecumenical habit remains. Kepler's praise of Bruno is just right. He is "the defender of infinity." Another way to put this is to disavow—like Louis de Broglie, after Duhem—the sanguine belief of new philosophy in the proof-positive test or *experimentum crucis* which declares the one reading of things. Eighteenth-century excavations beneath the choir of Notre Dame disinter the great Gallic

13. Foreword to *Construire;* and conclusion, pp. 111–12.

god of Nature, an uncouth apparition bringing in its revenges on the éclaircissement. In the Roman basilica of San Clemente, the paleo-Christian shrine has for its complement a temple to Mithras, whose slaying of the bull is the origin of life but also the origin of evil. It is not true that there is only one god, and his name one.

From the intuiting of a continuum or comprehensive city comes the permanent power in the art and the occulted thinking and feeling of the medieval Church. This intuiting baffles the strictures of Bishop Tempier and the rationalizing theologians of the thirteenth century, it survives until the advent of the modern age. The representations of fire and water, the clouds and the stars, the parts of the body, animals and plants which the medieval herald interprets do not function as adornment. It seems not even enough to say that they betoken. The squirrel is himself, he is also foresight, as the pelican is devotion, and the halcyon nesting on the waters is tranquility. In the columbine, we recognize our hope. It flowers in the spring, so augurs the coming of summer and the autumnal harvest. Between the physical world and the ethical world, the barriers go down. All things make a nexus. The dancer with female breasts on the twenty-first card of the Major Arcana in the Tarot Pack is draped with a veil which obscures the male genitals. That is what the neophyte is told. So, this dancer is androgynous. It presents the World, and the merging of the selfconscious and subconscious personalities, and the blending of these antinomies-by-convention with the cosmic Consciousness. Uncircumscribed itself, it circumscribes all (*Paradiso* xiv). Except for the environing presence of God, we look in vain for fixed environs.

In this expanding city, or universe, "cosmic" by no means argues "abstract." The world exists in time, which has its roots in the Crystalline sphere and exfoliates in the movements of the planets. The primal sphere (Primum Mobile) branches like a tree, and is the swiftest of the spheres, unlike a torpid stream in Tuscany. Fourteenth-century frescoes in the Campo Santo at Pisa depict the Creator grasping with His hands the concentric circles which carry the planets, "and the other stars." He is not so much wielding as interfusing the world. How different from the titanic figure, superb in his remoteness, to whom Hobbes on the title page of *Leviathan* offers allegiance. Dante's God in His heart so loves the work He has fashioned that His eye never leaves it. Mostly, Dante is unwilling to delineate God. I think he is not so much humble as artistically cautious. Such hints as we get from him—more, from his medieval contemporaries—work to present the image of a feudal lord, whose sustaining arms are sinewy and real. From our sacrificial altars, the crooked smoke climbs to His nostrils. To this personal god, the apotheosis of our best and brightest, we look for a pattern of behavior. The pattern is indispensable, but not for our salvation. In such a spacious mirror we must see ourselves. On one side, that is what anthropomorphism means.

The medieval cosmos seems literally a *mundanum corpus* as inviolate particulars ally with each other. On the doors of the church of St. Lazare in Avallon, the expected hagiography is missing. In its place are the labors of the months, vine leaves, lilies and roses, the inevitable acanthus, the zodiacal constellations. The indigenous character of each of these reliefs is apparent. But they do not exist in isolation, nor are they profane to the ecumenical psychology. A single power, coursing through them, binds them together. This unifying power resembles, I suppose it begets the quickening element hypothesized by classical science—and differs from it profoundly. The official point of view, first bruited in the Renaissance, insists on material homogeneity, the unity of the *fasces* where the component parts are the same, but dismisses further connections—as between the four seasons and the four ages of man, or among the bodily humors, the four elements, and the cardinal points of the compass—as mysticism or teleology. St. Isidore in his *De Rerum Natura* has no warrant in nature for supposing that four zones surround the earth, engendering four winds, which in turn impress their character on four bodily organs. His exploded doctrine, like the fishy ideas of Della Porta and Agrippa, depends, however, on the oblique perceiving of an active communion between man and the world.

Man, as he participates in this communion or "surround"—the argot of holography—is neither magnified nor diminished. More simply, he is realized. Above his head are the seven planets, because "the head of the microcosm is round like the heavenly spheres. In it are two eyes as the two luminaries shine in the heavens and there are seven orifices [which] adorn it like the seven heavens of harmony." [14] In the Renaissance, before the new learning becomes overmastering, parallels are educed everywhere between the macrocosm and the little kingdom of man. See Falstaff's disquisition on the virtues of good sherris sack. "As for us," says Gilbert in his treatise on the magnet, "we deem the whole world animate." Man the microcosm straddles the universe, as on the title page of Dr. Fludd's *De supernaturali*. The relation is not imperial but one of giving and taking. In this relation, the cohesive element is love. We do not dance mechanically to the music of an invisible piper. We make the music ourselves, in concert with the whole of Creation. The adverbial phrase suggests that personality, though critical, is also submerged, but not submerged as for Einstein. Collaboration, interinanimating—Donne's word—are of the essence. I think that is what the mystic means—for example, Hildegard of Bingen—in declining to distinguish between physics and philosophy, the material and the moral world, internal and external. She cannot tell the dancer from the dance.

The burning lights that envelop Dante the pilgrim in the sphere of the Sun are like ladies not yet freed from the dance. Dante's universe at the zenith is a sacred Saturnalia where the angels make sport and joy is the whip to the top. The "geographical globe game" imagined by Nicholas of Cusa "is played, not childishly, but as the Holy Wisdom played the game for God at the beginning of the world." In this earnest game or play of love, every kind of activity participates—"fasting and vigils and all good works"—and all "are turned into pleasure" (Hugh of St. Victor). For the Logos, though strenuously active, is not dour. The Franciscans, who are charged with disseminating the Word, are sworn as wandering minstrels, "the jongleurs of God." The world they celebrate is heterogeneous and makes a composition, not monophonic but analogous to part song, as it manifests the bent of the Creator. He plays His lute on high, says St. Gregory Nazianzen,

14. The 12th century abbess and mystic Herrade de Landsberg, glossing illustrations in the *Hortus Deliciarum*.

"making, moving, and preserving all created things." These various
things which people and define our middle earth are memorialized
by Cuthbert, the monk of Whitby, who—in the affecting story
recounted by the Venerable Bede—is instructed by the Creator to
"sing me Creation." [15]

The Creator is recognized by singing and dancing. As Dante
imagines Him, He tightens and relaxes with His right hand the
string of the lyre to whose music we move. So, He impels us. At
the same time, He is in our debt. The nature of man lends to the
planetary radiations their peculiar effects just as, Kepler thinks,
"the sense of hearing, endowed with the faculty of discerning
chords, lends to music such power that it incites him who hears it
to dance." The vision with which *Purgatorio* xv commences—that
of the ecliptic playing through the year, always in the manner of a
child—is still vivid four centuries later to the vagrant intelligence,
as personated by Robert Fludd. God, "the player of the string . . .
at the center of the whole," tunes the world as a musical instrument. His playing and our attending "creates the consonant effects of life in the microcosm." [16] Dante we say is superstitious but
lived a long time ago. Dr. Fludd is a modern man, therefore crazy.
But the music he hears, as it is consonant, a polyphonic music in
which different tones are blent, is the true music of the spheres.

The idea of polyphony, the coexisting of dissimilar voices,
more generally the reticulating of dissimilar parts, suggests what is
retrievable in alchemy, astrology, the doctrine of signatures. I
know of nothing that must persuade one to accept for true the cur-
rently fashionable imputing of power to sidereal influence or the
labors of Dr. Subtle and Dr. Dee. But consider the purport in this
doggerel couplet by the seventeenth-century German mystic,
Angelus Silesius:

> Turn inward for your voyage! For all your arts
> You will not find the Stone in foreign parts.

15. Bede, *History of the English Church and People*, Bk. iv, Ch. 24; Gregory, "The Second
Theological Oration," p. 290 in *Nicene and Post-Nicene Fathers*, 2nd series, Vol. vii; Hugh of
St. Victor, *De Arrha Anima;* Cusa, *De ludo globi,* c. 1463.

16. Fludd presents God as the "pulsator Monochordii" in *Utriusque mundi . . . historia,*
1618, ii, 274–75; Kepler, *Mysterium Cosmographicum; Paradiso* xv.

If the wisdom of the magi is not enabling in material ways, it is nonetheless enabling. That is the conclusion to which my reading in this arcane material draws. The alchemist likens the developing of metals to that of the infant in the mother's womb or to the emerging of the chicken from the egg by the natural incubation of the hen.[17] The analogy is eccentric—and makes the world apprehensible. We want to construe it in terms of those "natural perspectives" of which Shakespeare writes, unfocussed pictures

>   which rightly gazed upon
> Show nothing but confusion, eyed awry
> Distinguish form.

It seems to me we forfeit a cantle of the truth when we say that the magus, proposing his uncanny connections, is living in the darkness of a pre-scientific age, so doing the poor best he can. His reading of the phenomenal world still talks to us, as we are willing to listen.

The herbal literature of the sixteenth century makes the point. The herbalist observes that ivy hurts all trees and growing things, but the grape vine worst. So ivy is good for drunkenness. As a wild bull grows tame when tied to a fig tree, it follows that beef will cook faster if to the boiling water you add the stalks of the fig. The empirical intelligence will decline to take these recipes on trust: also, as it is honest, to dismiss out of hand the psychology that begets them. The root impulse in this psychology is to humanize the world—not a contemptible impulse and not without consequence for living a life. Certainly the impulse is mysterious to Calvin, else he could not say—justifying his condemnation of Servetus—"I had never entertained any personal rancor against him." For Calvin, there are no personal considerations. The analogical habit makes everything personal, and relates to the single vision of the new philosophers as the Python relates to Apollo.

To represent the conjunction of elements, chemistry levies on symbology. This is one way of addressing the problem and is a function, not of truth, but psychological bias. "All science aims to

17. "The Only True Way," in Waite, Hermetic Museum, I, vi, 160.

replace experience with the shortest possible intellectual operations." Ernst Mach is speaking here for the classical scientist,
whom one sees as folding back a piece of paper to achieve, as often
in the art of the fifteenth century, the perfectly symmetrical thing.
There remains, however, the intolerable crease in the middle, the
thing which has no verso or recto. Whitehead says—he is approving the artist who joys in the apprehension of things—"the simple
and immediate facts are the topics of interest, and these reappear
in the thought of science as the 'irreducible stubborn facts.' " [18]
Whitehead is speaking for contemporary science, also—as we apply
his saying—for the doyens of metaphor. Resort to the analogical
method witnesses to a psychology that has come to terms with the
irreducible fact.

> Le paradis n'est pas artificiel
> but is jagged.

This psychology—Pound bespeaks it in the *Cantos*—does not manipulate but honors the world, which is quick, so frustrates classification.

In the *mundanum corpus*, metals marry and die and are endlessly reborn. An English alchemist of the fifteenth century represents conjunction as the copulation of dissevered entities or beings.
Man, whom sulphur figures or in whom sulphur is figured, impreg-
nates the woman, who is mercury. The fiery King, seized with
great love towards the Queen, takes his fill of delight in embracing
her, "until they both vanish and coalesce into one body." [19] The
resulting amalgam is purer—it possesses more integrity—than its
constituents. In the interfusing of parts, personality is aggrandized,
exalted even, as in Donne's "Ecstasy":

> A single violet transplant,
>   The strength, the color, and the size,
> All which before was poor, and scant,
>   Redoubles still, and multiplies.

18. *Science and the Modern World*, p. 23.

19. *Hermetic Museum*, I, 336.

Analogy illuminates the nature of "that abler soul" which mingles "this and that" to create a new and indivisible concoction.

We move from the flower to the mixed soul, thence to the celestial orbs. The planets in their "aspects" are friendly or malign, they are also contagious. One angle presents *inimicitia*, another makes this hostility good. If you are born under Cancer, you are likely to be ruthless, using your pincers, given to trading overseas, florid and carapaceous, changeable, as the crab scuttles sideways, venereal, as it is sacred to the goddess who rises out of the foam. From the zodiacal "house" which reigns on your natal day, supernal power comments in secret on your spirit—Ficino says, venturing an analogy, "as music does openly." [20] In fact, the stars do not comment on our mundane business. But the man who thinks they do is acknowledging that he is not himself alone. He is the better man. "My medieval knees lack health until they bend." The superstitious Gloucester in *King Lear*, who inhabits and acknowledges a context, is better, he is also more sagacious than Edmund, his emancipated son, who lives in a vacuum and is responsive to no imperative but the promptings of an isolated ego.

The new philosopher is not looking for resemblance but perfect equivalence. Optics, as he conceives it, is a scientific enterprise which purports to describe once and for all. To the medieval theologian, optics is the most useful of the mathematical sciences, but that is only as he sees its illustrative possibilities. The direct or perpendicular impinging of light resembles the infusing of grace, since good men do not reflect grace from themselves nor refract it from the straight course which extends along the road of perfection. On the other hand, men lapsed in mortal sin reflect the grace of God, repelling it from them. So we learn about the world, a congeries of matter and spirit, but only metaphorically. The solipsist thinks this is the extent and definition of learning. It is not required that we agree with him, in justifying the analogical way. If it is tautologous, it is also inclusive. Everything becomes everything. The astrologer, Like Elias Ashmole in his

20. *De vita coelitus*, 1489, cap. xviii, L4r.

seventeenth-century farrago of science and nonsense, abolishes distinction. "By the Vegetable [Stone] may be perfectly known the nature of man, beasts, fowls, fishes, together with all kinds of trees, plants, flowers." [21] There is no other. "You and I," says Hermes, "are not parts but the whole." I take this point of view, however one may cavil at its particulars, to constitute the interesting virtue of the Hermetic or outmoded philosophy. Even as the authenticity of Hermes Trismegistus is being queried by Casaubon, Bruno and Campanella persist in their allegiance, and Athanasius Kircher long after the fraud has been exposed. They are clinging to the comprehensive vision.

The new philosopher appropriates the comprehensive vision and modifies it radically. He never really grasps the point of the Scholastic proposition: *Omnis determinatio est negatio*. Roger Bacon prefigures him in grounding the study of geography in mathematics. Determine latitudes and longitudes and the girth and shape of the globe and you have answered to the needs of this science. Bacon's contemporaries are censured as they "do not know one half of the globe which they inhabit." With respect to knowing, consult the plan of the city of Clermont in the Beauvais Tapestry (1530), a promiscuous mingling of plants and animals, men and women, the churches in which they worship, the houses where they live. This is real geography. It declines to exclude. The astrologer declines to demarcate. The horoscope he is casting encompasses not less than the entire universe at the moment of one man's nativity. The microcosm and the macrocosm run together. If you want the truth, he will tell you:

> A pitcher full of water is set down
> on the water—
> now it has water inside and water
> outside.

Best not to distinguish between them. Something like this gnomic saying, from the fifteenth-century mystic and poet Kabir, is in the

21. Prolegomena, *Theatrum Chemicum Brittanicum*, 1651.

mind of the Franciscan Richard Rufus, when he says: "I do not define."

If we are what includes us, we will sing the Creation, not seek to resolve it like the new philosophers, or to deny it like Bunyan's pilgrim and all those lugubrious Christians who negotiate a vale of tears. Our passage through life is not a linear progression but a gratifying "transit from one state to the other." No pleasure accrues if "bodies, matter, and entity" do not undergo constant "mutation, variety, and vicissitude." From this swapping back and forth or interpenetrating, Bruno derives the doctrine of the transmigration of souls. Mostly, the modern age has handed over this doctrine to the exophthalmic ones. That is a pity. For like the positing by the Gnostics of Thrones and Dominions in the air, it has its kernel of truth. Gnosticism supposes the intervening between God and ourselves of other powers—by convention, seven planets and demons—whose spheres must be passed, as in the *Paradiso* and the Book of Enoch, if we would escape from our dark mundane prison. The pejorative words we can dispense with; the idea of a progress, as in *The Magic Flute* which draws for its libretto on the ritual testing of Freemasonry, or the journeying through life, a house of many mansions, by the Fool in the Tarot Pack, is worth saving. "Nothing that is created, or born, is at rest"—quoting from a tract on the secret of the Stone [22]—but this "vicissitude" is our happiness. Bruno refuses to back off from the truth which other men— some of them great men—lament or gainsay. The playwright George Chapman, in the early years of the seventeenth century, is remembering Bruno when he admonishes the migrating soul to

> Join flames with Hercules. . .
> Make the vast continent crack with thy receipt,
> Spread to a world of fire, and the agèd sky
> Cheer with new sparks of old humanity.

We are not admonished, however, as by Plato and his epigones, to shuck our humanity, rather to enhance and make it new.

---

22. *Hermetic Museum*, I, vii, 167.

It is said of Plato's God—the same who cleft the apple and threw away the worser part—that he works continually by geometry. He is dramatizing the insipid doctrine of that fifth-century heresiarch for whom Christ is not human, only divine. The mysticism of Eckhart verges on the Eutychian heresy, it approximates the heresy which is new science, as it makes the deity ineffable. But the work of the mystic is not always or inevitably corrosive. To come to the life of Christ's divinity, says Walter Hilton in the fourteenth century, you must "follow Him along the way of His humanity." [23] The mystic lives for us, not so much in his ecstatic communion with God—we can hardly decide to emulate him there—as in his passionate devotion to the Word made flesh. Servetus says: "the divine has descended to the human in order that the human might ascend to the divine"; and St. Edmund Rich: "God became man to make man God." [24] The echo we want to catch is not of that insufferable Pelagius for whom man is already as puissant as God, but rather of Nestorius, the patriarch of Constantinople, who gives us a god in posse: Christ raising himself to divinity—by analogy, his followers as they pursue the Imitation of Christ—through the assiduous cultivating of virtue. The Son of Man is not born the Son of God. But the becoming which is his business and prerogative does not entail the degradation of divinity. It is the exhalation of humanity. Admit this reading, and we are able to retrieve the apparent crankiness of those latter-day mystics who defer the cleansing sacrament of baptism until we have tasted of the fruit of the Tree of Good and Evil. What do infants know or what heavens have opened before them?

God in the beginning is ignorant, like these infants. Though He possesses the heavens, He longs to possess the earth, to put on our muddy vesture and the vicissitude which human beings but not supernal beings inherit. The Word covets the flesh. The bestial incarnations of Jove—eagle, bull, and swan—reflect the pathos of the abstract and immutable *nous*. I think we agree with that heretical Sabellius whom Abelard condemned, in asserting that the Fa-

23. Hilton's "Christocentric" additions to his translation of James of Milan's *Stimulus Amoris*.

24. *The Mirror of Holy Church.*

ther is the same as the Son and suffered the Passion with Him. Wanting to suffer or participate, He is called Patripassians. But the Son of God is simultaneously the Son of Man, though the latter must learn divinity. This is the saving truth of Erigena, the ninth-century Neoplatonist, who makes the Creator one with His creatures, also—metaphorically—the issue of their loins. The life of every man and woman is the actualizing of God in human form. The legend of the Incarnation is spun about ourselves.

A medieval mosaic in the Roman church of Santa Maria in Trastevere depicts two prophets, each with a birdcage beside him. The scroll Isaiah is holding bears the familiar text: "Ecce virgo concipet et pariet filium"; Jeremiah's: "Christus dominus captus est in peccatis nostris." This means, say Emile Mâle, that Christ "imprisoning himself in the flesh so as to expiate our sins, was like a bird imprisoned in a cage." For the mystic, the "interinanimating" is the salient fact. "An amazing mystery it is that God can thus be conjoined with man and man with God" (Servetus). From this conjunction comes that infinitely poignant figure, the Son of Man who is made in our image and likeness and who is the possession of Christianity alone. He has no beauty that we should desire him. He is despised and rejected, and acquainted with grief. What the mystics have to teach us, the grace that still breathes in their orisons, is crystallized in these thirteenth-century verses:

> Now sinks the sun behind the wood apace:
> I sorrow, Mary, for thy lovely face.
> Now sinks the sun behind the Tree:
> I sorrow, Mary, for thy Son and thee.

The God of Eckhart is perhaps a silent and waste divinity; the God of the *Stimulus Amoris* or of the *Mirror of Holy Church* is not atemporal but substantially present and lives in the humbler types of history.

The permutations by which He is known, like the up and down of history, mimic the divine disorder. All ways are open to the Old One. So why does He choose to localize, which is to occlude? William Wotton, an eighteenth-century linguist evidently indifferent to the temper of his time, answers where Genesis is mute. Wotton, like his contemporaries, imagines before the ruin of the Tower of Babel a common language in which the Word is not yet occluded. Thereafter falls the shadow, the confusion of tongues laid "upon the workmen by the immediate Hand of God." The confusion is irreversible—here Wotton proclaims his eccentricity—and explicitly meditated. For this hardheaded clergyman there is no rationalizing of phenomena—no predicating of a linguistic diaspora, as by "philosophical" persons like Bishop Sprat who explain scientifically "things supernatural and causeless." We are to accept the old-fashioned account of "a miraculous formation of languages" whose diversity shall endure "as long as this earth." The account, as we are modern, therefore hopeful, is disconcerting. Einstein says to Weyl: "Who knows, perhaps He is a little malicious." But Wotton does not think so. The localizing or enshadowing of the word, its transubstantiation, is good. The judgment of the Old One on the men of Shinar is not malicious but "inflicted in mercy." [25] Babel is the fortunate fall. The Old One is wiser, beneficent even, in decreeing that the world not be turned into a plain. The old grey stone, the old windbroken tree have also to be brought to bear in the making of a total configuration.

A modern historian of science and technology brings to mind the new philosophers of the seventeenth century in the picture he evokes of scientists the world over sounding in concert their "nonambiguous, operational, bugle call rhetoric," so making good that cacophony which Wotton assigns to the Finger of God. Their homogeneous city, or Babylon before the fall, is open to the rest of us, as we are lucky. Only a Luddite, the historian thinks, would call our luck in question. The broken mirror which is language seems to him so many shards distorting the light. Or it is a shadow thrown by the genuine article. I think this shadow is our substance and all we are likely to have. The necessary provinciality of language—necessary, as the wine must still smell of the cask—occasions the despair of the hunters after equivalence. They have rea-

25. A *Discourse concerning the Confusion of Languages at Babel*, 1730, pp. 29, 36, 45, 50; Clark, *Einstein*, p. 613.

son to despair. "How then could they have admitted that the invisible and separate Nature can be explained by divisible words?" St. Gregory Nazianzen, in his Fourth Theological Oration, seems to take their part. No speech exhaustively contains the Being of God, or Truth. Nevertheless, this early Father continues, "we sketch Him by His Attributes, and so obtain a certain faint and feeble and partial idea concerning Him." Our mortal chain does not permit us to discover the whole. So our best exegete is he who has conceived, more than another, "the Likeness or adumbration of the Truth." [26] The Theologian finds the pursuit of likenesses engrossing. It quickens his wits. Also, it tells on our pulses. As he follows up his feeble or partial presentiments and seeks to delineate them as exactly as may be, he insures that we continue to read him and to approve his tentative conclusions, emanating as they do from a gravid or provincial style which is always throwing back to particulars. This radically different version of the divinatory man lives as he makes the Word flesh.

The power of language is contingent, paradoxically, on the chain which enfetters it. But not to appeal to the bright side, as when one discerns a silver lining. Shakespeare's character tells us, in *Measure for Measure*, that "best men are molded out of faults." Though the word delimits, because it delimits, it actualizes or embodies. "What is there that consists but by the word?" [27] The parochial family which is language stretches back to a long past, extends in hope to an indefinite future. The future is guaranteed as the initiates share, against the stranger, in the possession of occulted meanings, nuances, connotations, which are never perfectly translatable and are not supposed to be. When the hermetic community is appreciated for the singular thing it is, then it begins to speak to the world outside the walls. Poetry creates the modern tongues and flourishes in turn as their integrity is honored. The true pansophical language is indigenous. *Universalia post rem.* If it is opaque, only as it is opaque, the light shines through.

The indeclinable language to which the monistic temperament aspires does not signalize nor engender that "Pentecostal condition

---

26. *Nicene Fathers*, VII, 316.   27. The same, p. 317.

of universal understanding and unity" which the eupeptic man invokes today or his spiritual forebears in the first flush of the Enlightenment, an all-inclusive and uniquely comprehensible language whispering out notions of the deity.[28] Rightly perceived, the language of Adam is the bellowing of the imprisoned Nimrod who sets the word against the word, or that choughs' language—Shakespeare's essay in the making of the real character—which undoes the villainous Parolles. "I shall lose my life for want of language," says the villain, and he is right. In this context, emancipation means anarchy. We float upon a wild and violent sea, "each way and move." Dante's emancipated child, when his tongue is free and his speech is perfected, devours any food through any mouth and longs for the death of the mother or the order which reared him.[29] The differentiating of tongues, the halving of the sorb-apple, does not make for the dissolution of society, where society is a living organism, but for its coherence. In differences, identity resides. The miming of Babel, as by the men of Oc and Oeil, ratifies the wisdom of the Old One.

The parochial habitation to which He has committed us is linguistic, also temporal and spatial. From this habitation, we shall never emerge. No archer hangs his quiver over the raving tide: no apocalypse beckons. The dying Virgil, whom Broch presents as lamenting our perpetual imprisonment, must be left to wring his hands. It is a halting and provisional language we speak here, pestered by equivocation, "the language of an alien people whose guest one was, a language that one was barely able to understand." This is more and worse than Augustine in the *City of God* on the different tongues that divide man and man. There is, however, no help for our alienation nor for the incertitude in which we live. We are imperfect—concupiscent man—so we see as in a glass darkly. But the deformity which describes us, the dying animal to which we are fastened, is lucky. "There is no deformity But saves us from a dream." Yeats is saying: only what is incarnate, the minute particulars of mankind, can silence the mind and insure against demonic

28. Marshall McLuhan, *Understanding Media*, p. 80.

29. *Paradiso* XXVII; *Macbeth* IV.ii.21–22; *All's Well That Ends Well* IV.i.3; *Inferno* XXXI.

possession. All dreams end in a beautiful body. You can call this our failure or more simply our condition.

At the Fifth Solvay Congress in 1927, discussion of the Uncertainty Principle is submerged in a babel of tongues. But Ehrenfest, "the conscience of physics," does not lose his sense of humor. Oblivious of the uproar, moralizing it rather, he writes on the blackboard: "The Lord did there confound the language of the earth." In this redacting of the story of Pentecost, He is divulging His secret preference for the idiolect or indigenous thing. Against these mutable incarnations, man in the modern age has dreamed his dream of the incorruptible One. Now the wicks go yellow in another dawn.

WORKS CONSULTED

This bibliography assembles, by and large, only work bearing directly on the text, and does not purport to list every book and article bearing on the subject. It excludes well-known authors, like Shakespeare and Jonson, unless reference is to page or signature number in a particular edition. I have annotated entries, where clarification seemed desirable. And I have appended STC numbers (for books printed between 1475 and 1640) and Wing numbers (between 1641 and 1700), where available.

Adams, Thomas. *The Gallants Burden, A Sermon preached at Paules Crosse.* London, 1612.

Agrippa, Henry Cornelius. *Of the Vanitie and Uncertaintie of Artes and Sciences.* Tr. Ja.[mes] San.[ford]. London, 1569. STC 204.

—— *Three Books of Occult Philosophy.* Tr. J. F. London, 1651.

Alciati. *Andreae Alciati Emblematum Libellus.* Paris, 1536.

Allen, Don Cameron. *Doubt's Boundless Sea: Skepticism and Faith in the Renaissance.* Baltimore, 1964.

—— *The Legend of Noah: Renaissance Rationalism in Art, Science, and Letters.* Urbana, Illinois, 1963.

—— *The Star-Crossed Renaissance: The Quarrel about Astrology and Its Influence in England.* Durham, North Carolina, 1941.

Ames, William. *Conscience with the Power and Cases Thereof.* Tr. (from Latin). London, 1639, ?1643. STC 552.

—— *A Fresh Suit Against Human Ceremonies.* [Rotterdam?], 1633. STC 555.

—— *The Marrow of Sacred Divinity.* London, 1642. STC 558.

Ammann, P. J. "The Musical Theory and Philosophy of Robert Fludd." *Journal of the Warburg and Courtauld Institutes*, 30 (London, 1967), 198–227.

Ancelet-Hustache, Jeanne. *Master Eckhart and the Rhineland Mystics.* London and New York, 1957.

Ante-Nicene, Nicene, and Post-Nicene Fathers of the Christian Church. Ed. Alexander Roberts, James Donaldson, A. C. Coxe, Philip Schaff, et al. 38 vols. Grand Rapids, Michigan, 1956.

Anton, Robert. *Vices Anotimie, Scourged and Corrected.* London, 1617. STC 687.

Arber, Edward. See *Stationers' Register.*

Arnauld, Antoine, and Claude Lancelot. *Grammaire générale et raisonnée* ["Port-Royal Grammar"]. Paris, 1660. Tr. ?Thomas Nugent as *A General and Rational Grammar.* London, 1753; rpt. Menston, England, 1968.

Ashmole, Elias. *Theatrum Chemicum Britannicum Containing Several Poetical Pieces of Our Famous English Philosophers* [and poets] Who Have Written the Hermetic Mysteries in Their Own Ancient Language. London, 1651.

Aubrey, John. *Miscellanies upon Various Subjects* [for number symbolism], London, 1890.

Auge-Chiquet, Mathieu. *La Vie, les idées et l'œuvre de Baïf.* Paris, n.d. (?1909).

Bacon, Francis. *The Works.* Ed. James Spedding, R. L. Ellis, D. D. Heath. 14 vols. London, 1859; rpt. Stuttgart, 1963.

Baïf, Jean-Antoine de. *Etrenes de Poezie Fransoeze an Verse Mezures.* Paris, 1574.

—— *Psaultier . . . contres les Psalmes des Haeretiques* (1569). Ed. Ernst Joh. Groth. Heilbronn, 1888.

Bainton, Ronald H. *Hunted Heretic: The Life and Death of Michael Servetus, 1511–1553.* Boston, 1953.

Baldwin, Charles Sears. *Renaissance Literary Theory and Practice.* New York, 1939.

Barfield, Owen. *History in English Words* (1953). Grand Rapids, Michigan, 1967.

Barkan, Leonard. *Nature's Work of Art The Human Body as Image of the World.* New Haven and London, 1975.

Barras, Moses. *The Stage Controversy in France from Corneille to Rousseau.* New York, 1933.

Beauzée, Nicholas. *Grammaire générale.* 2 vols. Paris, 1767.

Becher, J. J. *Character, pro Notitia Linguarum Universali.* Frankfurt, 1661.

Beck, Cave. *The Universal Character.* London, 1657. Wing 1647.

Benedict. *The Rule of St. Benedict.* Tr. Cardinal Gasquet. New York, 1966.

Bentham, Jeremy. "On Universal Grammar," pp. 185–91; "Fragments on Universal Grammar," pp. 339–57. In *Works,* Vol. VIII. Ed. John Bowring. Edinburgh, 1853.

Birch, Thomas. *The History of the Royal Society of London.* 4 vols. London, 1756. [Continues and supplements Sprat's account, pub. 1667.]

—— *The Life of the Honourable Robert Boyle.* London, 1744. [Includes letters to Hartlib on universal language.]

Blau, J. L. *The Christian Interpretation of the Cabala in the Renaissance.* New York, 1944.

Bloomfield, Leonard. *Language.* New York, 1933.

—— "Linguistic Aspects of Science." *International Encyclopedia of Unified Science,* Vol. I, No. 4. Chicago, 1939.

Boas, George. *Rationalism in Greek Philosophy*. Baltimore, 1961.

Boehme, Jacob. *Six Theosophic Points and Other Writings*. Introd. N. Berdyaev. Ann Arbor, Michigan, 1958.

Boetii Opera. Venice, 1497. [Includes Victorinus Afer's tr. of Porphyry.]

Bolton, Edmund. *Hypercritica*. [c. 1617; for attack on archaic language]. Included in N. *Triveti Annalium continuatio*. Oxford, 1722.

Bongo, Pietro. *Numerorum Mysteria*. Bergomi, 1591.

Born, Max. *Einstein's Theory of Relativity*. Tr. H. L. Brose. London, 1924.

—— "Physics and Metaphysics." *The Scientific Monthly*, 82 (May 1956), 229–35.

Bowen, Catherine Drinker. *Francis Bacon: The Temper of a Man*. Boston, 1963.

—— *The Lion and the Throne: The Life and Times of Sir Edward Coke (1552–1634)*. Boston, 1956.

Bridgman, Percy W. *The Logic of Modern Physics*. New York, 1927.

Bright, Timothy. *Characterie, An Arte of shorte, swifte, and secrete writing by Character*. London, 1588. STC 3743.

Brown, Peter. *Augustine of Hippo*. London, 1967.

Bruno, Giordano. *The Expulsion of the Triumphant Beast (Spaccio della bestia trionfante)*. Tr. Arthur D. Imerti. New Brunswick, New Jersey, 1964.

Buber, Martin. *Pointing the Way*. Tr. and ed. Maurice Friedman. London, 1957.

Buchan, John. *Oliver Cromwell* (1934). London, 1957.

Bullokar, William. *Aesops Fables in tru Ortography with Grammar-notes . . . [and] sentences of the wys Cato*. London, 1585.

—— *Bullokars Booke at large, for the Amendment of Orthographie for English speech*. London, 1580. STC 4086.

—— *The English Pronunciation at Shakespeare's Time as Taught by William Bullokar*. R. E. Zachrisson. Uppsala and Leipzig, 1927.

Burckardt, Sigurd. *Shakespearean Meanings*. Princeton, 1968.

Burnet, Gilbert. *The Life of William Bedell*. London, 1685. Wing 5830.

Butler, Charles. *The English Grammar*. Oxford, 1633. STC 4190.

Butterfield, Herbert. *The Origins of Modern Science, 1300–1800*. New York, 1951.

Caesarius of Heisterbach. *The Dialogue of Miracles*. Vol. I. Tr. H. Scott and C. Bland. London, 1929.

Cajori, Florian. *A History of Mathematical Notations*. 2 vols. London, 1928–29.

—— *A History of Mathematics*. New York, 1894.

Camden, William. *Remains*. London, 1614. STC 4522.

Campanella, Tommaso. *Atheismus Triumphatus, Seu Reductio ad Religionem Per Scientiarum Veritates*. Rome, 1631.

Campenhausen, Hans von. *The Fathers of the Latin Church*. Tr. Manfred Hoffman. London, 1964.

Capelli, Adriano. *Dizionario di Abbreviature Latine ed Italiane*. Milan, 1949.

Cardano, Girolamo. *The Book of My Life* (*De Vita Propria Liber*, 1575, first pub. 1643). Tr. Jean Stoner. New York, 1930; London, 1931.

—— *Cardanus Comforte.* Tr. Thomas Bedingfield. London, 1573. STC 4607.

—— *Practica Arithmetica.* Mediolani, 1539.

—— *Cardano, the Gambling Scholar.* Oystein Ore, with trans. of *Liber de Ludo Alea* by S. H. Gould. Princeton, 1953.

Carré, Marie-Rose. "Pensée rationnelle et responsabilité morale: Le Traité de sagesse dans *La Logique* de Port-Royal." *PMLA*, 89 (October 1974), 1075–83.

Carruccio, Ettore. *Mathematics and Logic in History and in Contemporary Thought.* Tr. Isabel Quigly. Chicago, 1964.

Cassidy, Harold Gomes. *The Sciences and the Arts.* New York, 1962.

Cassiodorus Senator. *An Introduction to Divine and Human Readings,* Tr. and ed. Leslie Webber Jones. New York, 1946.

Cassirer, Ernst. *The Philosophy of Symbolic Forms.* 3 vols. New Haven, 1953.

—— *The Platonic Renaissance in England* (1932). Tr. James P. Pettegrove. London, 1953.

Cassirer, Ernst, P. O. Kristeller, and J. H. Randall, Jr., eds., *The Renaissance Philosophy of Man.* Chicago, 1948.

Castiglione, Baldassare. *The Courtier.* Tr. Thomas Hoby. London, 1561. STC 4778.

Cheke, Sir John. "Septem contrariis epistolis comprehensae." Pub. as *Joannis Cheki Angli De Pronunciatione Graecae.* Basle, 1555.

Chomsky, Noam. *Cartesian Linguistics.* New York and London, 1966.

—— "Explanatory Models in Linguistics." Pp. 528–50 in *Logic, Methodology and Philosophy of Science.* ed. E. Nagel, P. Suppes, and A. Tarski. Stanford, 1962.

—— *Syntactic Structures.* The Hague, 1957.

Church, Alonzo. "A Bibliography of Symbolic Logic" [covers 1661–1935]. *The Journal of Symbolic Logic,* 1 (December 1936), 121–216.

Clark, Donald Lemen. *Rhetoric and Poetry in the Renaissance* (1922). New York, 1963.

Clark, Ronald W. *Einstein The Life and Times.* New York and Cleveland, 1971.

Clement, Francis. *The Petie Schole with an English Orthographie.* London, 1587. STC 5400.

Clouse, Robert G. "John Napier and Apocalyptic Thought." *The Sixteenth Century Journal,* 5 (April 1974), 101–114.

Coffin, Charles M. *John Donne and the New Philosophy* (1937). New York, 1958.

Cohen, Jonathan. "On the Project of a Universal Character." *Mind,* 63 (January 1954), 49–63.

Cohn, Norman. *The Pursuit of the Millenium.* New York, 1961.

Colledge, Eric, ed. *The Mediaeval Mystics of England.* New York, 1961.

Collier, Jeremy. *A Defence of the Short View of the Profaneness and Immorality of the English Stage.* London, 1699. Wing 5248.

—— *A Short View of the Immorality and Profaneness of the English Stage.* London, 1698. Wing 5263.

Comenius, Jan Amos. *Continuatio admonitionis fraternae de temperando charitate zelo ad S. Maresium.* Amsterdam, 1669.

—— *Janua Linguarum Reserata. . . . The Gate of Languages Unlocked.* Tr. Thomas Horne. London, 1650. Wing 5514.

—— *Pansophiae Diatyposis.* Amsterdam, 1645. Tr. Jeremy Collier as *A Patterne of Universall Knowledge.* London, 1651. Wing 5527.

—— *The Way of Light.* Amsterdam, 1668. Modern trans. E. T. Campagnac. London, 1938.

Comenius in England [a compilation of contemporary documents]. Tr. Robert F. Young. London, 1932.

Coote, Edmund. *The English Schoole-Master.* London, 1596. STC 5711.

Cope, Jackson I. *Joseph Glanvill Anglican Apologist.* St. Louis, Missouri, 1956.

Court and Times of Charles the First, The. Ed. R. F. Williams. 2 vols. London, 1848.

Court of Venus, The. Ed. R. A. Fraser, Durham, North Carolina, 1955.

Couturat, Louis. *La Logique de Leibniz.* Paris, 1901.

—— *Opuscules et Fragments Inédits de Leibniz.* Paris, 1903.

Cowley, Abraham. *The Works.* London, 1656, 1668. Wing 6649.

Crashaw, William. *The Parable of Poyson. In Five Sermons.* London, 1618. STC 6024.

Craven, J. B. *Doctor Robert Fludd: Life and Writings.* Kirkwall, 1902.

Crosse, Henry. *Vertues Common-wealth.* London, 1603. STC 6070.

Culler, Jonathan. *Structuralist Poetics Structuralism, Linguistics and the Study of Literature.* Ithaca, New York, 1975.

Cunningham, J. V. " 'Essence and the 'Phoenix and Turtle.' " *ELH*, 19 (1952), 265–76.

Curtius, Ernst Robert. *European Literature and the Latin Middle Ages* (1948). Tr. W. R. Trask. New York, 1953.

Dalgarno, George. *Ars Signorum, vulgo Character Universalis et Lingua Philosophica.* London, 1661. Wing 128.

—— *Didascalocophus.* Oxford, 1680. Wing 129.

—— *Tables of Universal Character.* Oxford, 1657. Wing 130.

—— *Works.* Edinburgh, 1834.

Della Porta, Giovanni Baptista. *Magiae naturalis libri viginti.* Neapoli, 1589.

DeMott, Benjamin. "Comenius and the Real Character in England." *PMLA*, 70 (1955), 1068–81.

—— "Science versus Mnemonics: Notes on John Ray and on John Wilkins' *Essay.*" *Isis*, Vol. 48, Pt. 1, No. 151 (March 1957), 3–12.

—— "The Sources and Development of John Wilkins' Philosophical Language." *JEGP* 57 (January 1958), 1–13.

Descartes, René. *Lettres de Mr. Descartes.* 3 vols. Paris, 1657, 1659, 1667.
—— *The Philosophical Works.* Tr. E. S. Haldane and G. R. T. Ross. 2 vols. Cambridge, 1967.
Dewar, Mary. *Sir Thomas Smith.* London, 1964.
Digges, Leonard [and his son Thomas]. *A Prognostication.* London, 1576. STC 6864.
Dobson, E. J. *English Pronunciation 1500–1700.* 2 vols. Oxford, 1957.
Dod, John. *A Plaine and Familiar Exposition of the Ten Commandments.* London, 1604. STC 6968.
Donne, John. *Essays in Divinity.* Ed. Evelyn M. Simpson. Oxford, 1952.
—— *The Life and Letters.* Ed. Edmund Grosse, 1899. Rpt. 2 vols. Gloucester, Mass., 1959.
—— *The Sermons.* Ed. George R. Potter and Evelyn M. Simpson. 10 vols. Berkeley and Los Angeles, 1962.
Drachmann, A. G. *The Mechanical Technology of Greek and Roman Antiquity.* Copenhagen; Madison, Wisconsin; and London, 1963.
Drake, Stillman, and E. Drabkin. *Mechanics in Sixteenth-Century Italy.* Madison and Milwaukee, Wisconsin; and London, 1969.
Dreyer, J. L. E. *History of the Planetary Systems from Thales to Kepler.* Cambridge, 1906.
DuBellay, Joachim. *La Défense et Illustration de la Langue Française* (1549). Paris, n.d.
Duckett, Eleanor. *Death and Life in the Tenth Century.* Ann Arbor, Michigan, 1967.
—— *The Gateway to the Middle Ages: Monasticism.* Ann Arbor, Michigan, 1961.
Duhem, Pierre. *The Aim and Structure of Physical Theory* (1914). Tr. Philip P. Wiener. New York, 1962.

Eastman, Max. *The Literary Mind: Its Place in an Age of Science.* New York and London, 1932.
Edmundson, Henry. *Lingua Linguarum, The Naturall Language of Languages.* London, 1658 (first edition 1655). Wing 184.
Edwards, Jonathan. *The Nature of True Virtue* (1755). Ann Arbor, Michigan, 1960.
Eiseley, Loren. *Francis Bacon and the Modern Dilemma.* Lincoln, Nebraska, 1962.
—— *The Unexpected Universe.* New York, 1969.
Eliot, John. *Ortho-Epia Gallica.* London, 1593. STC 7574.
Euclid. *The Elements.* Tr. Sir Henry Billingsley. Preface by Dr. John Dee. London, 1570. STC 10560.
Eusebius. *The History of the Church from Christ to Constantine.* Tr. G. A. Williamson. New York, 1966.

Farrar, Frederic W. *History of Interpretation* (1886). Grand Rapids, Michigan, 1961.

Faulhaber, Johann. *Numerus Figuratus sive Arithmetica*. [Frankfurt], 1614.

Feder, Lillian. *Ancient Myth in Modern Poetry*. Princeton, 1971.

Ferguson, Robert. *The Interest of Reason in Religion*. [London, 1675.] Wing 740.

Ficino, Marsilio. *De vita coelitus comparanda*. Florence, 1489. [This third of the three books entitled *De Triplici Vita* concerns astrological influence.]

—— *Mercurii Trismegisti Liber de Potestate et Sapientia Dei. . . . Pimander Incipit*. Florence, 1471.

—— *The "Philebus" Commentary*. Ed. and tr. Michael J. B. Allen. Berkeley, Los Angeles, and London, 1975. [Treats the *prisci theologi* or ancient theologians, especially Hermes Trismegistus.]

Fletcher, Angus. *Allegory: The Theory of a Symbolic Mode*. Ithaca, New York, 1964.

Fludd, Robert. *De supernaturali, naturali, praenaturali et contra naturali microcosmi historia*. Oppenheim, 1619.

—— *Utriusque cosmi . . . historia*. Oppenheim, 1617. [In three parts, pub. 1617–19; Book III: *De musica mundana*, presents God as the *pulsator Monochordii*.]

Folkingham, William. *Brachigraphy, or the art of short writing*. London, 1620. STC 11122.

Fowler, Alastair. *Spenser and the Numbers of Time*. London, 1964.

—— *Triumphal Forms: Structural Patterns in Elizabethan Poetry*. Cambridge, 1970.

Fraser, Russell. *The Dark Ages and the Age of Gold*. Princeton, 1973.

—— *Shakespeare's Poetics*. London, 1962.

—— *The War against Poetry*. Princeton, 1970.

French, Peter J. *John Dee: The World of an Elizabethan Magus*. London, 1972.

Freud, Sigmund. *Collected Papers*. Tr. Joan Rivière. 5 vols. New York, 1959.

Friedrich, Carl J. *The Age of the Baroque 1610–1660*. New York, 1952.

Galileo, Galilei. *Dialogue Concerning the Two Chief World Systems*. Tr. Stillman Drake, foreword by Albert Einstein. Berkeley and Los Angeles, 1967.

Garside, Charles. *Zwingli and the Arts*. New Haven, 1966.

Geliot, Louvan. *Indice Armoriae*. Paris, 1635 (*Armorial Index*, London, 1650).

Gesner, Conrad. *The practise of the new and old phisicke, wherein is contained the most excellent Secrets of Phisicke and Philosophie*. London, 1599. STC 11799.

Gil, Alexander. *Logonomia Anglica*. London, 1619. STC 11873.

Gilson, Étienne. *Héloïse and Abelard*. Tr. L. K. Shook (1948). Ann Arbor, Michigan, 1960.

—— *Reason and Revelation in the Middle Ages*. New York, 1938.

Glanvill, Joseph. *A Blow at Modern Sadducism in Some Philosophical Considerations about Witchcraft*. London, 1668. Wing 799.

—— *Plus Ultra or The Progress and Advancement of Knowledge since the Days of Aristotle*. London, 1668. Wing 820.

—— *Saducismus Triumphatus: or, Full and Plain Evidence Concerning Witches and Apparitions.* London, 1681. Wing 822.

—— *The Vanity of Dogmatizing.* London, 1661. Wing 834.

Goodman, Nelson. *Languages of Art.* London, 1969.

Gray, Eden. *A Complete Guide to the Tarot.* New York, 1970.

Gregory of Tours. *History of the Franks.* Tr. Ernest Brehaut. New York, 1965.

Halévy, Elie. *The Growth of Philosophic Radicalism* (1901–04). Boston, 1955.

Hall, A. R. *The Scientific Revolution 1500–1800.* London, 1954.

Hall, John. *The Court of Virtue.* London, 1565 (ed. R. A. Fraser, London, 1961).

Hall, Joseph. *Works.* Ed. P. Wynter. 10 vols. Oxford, 1863.

Hall, Thomas. *Histrio-Mastix. A Whip for [John] Webster.* London, 1654.

—— *Vindiciae Literarum, The Schools Guarded.* London, 1654. Wing 441.

Harriott, Thomas. *Artis Analyticae Praxis.* London, 1631.

Harris, James. *Hermes.* London, 1765.

—— *Three Treatises.* London, 1741 (second edn., 1765).

Harris, Victor. "The Arts of Discourse in England, 1500–1700." *Philological Quarterly,* 37 (October 1958), 484–94.

Hart, John. *Orthographie,* 1569. In *John Hart's Works on English Orthography and Pronunciation, 1551, 1569, 1570.* Ed. B. Danielsson. 2 vols. Stockholm, 1955, 1963.

Havelock, Eric A. *Preface to Plato.* Oxford, 1963.

Heisenberg, Werner. *Physics and Philosophy.* New York, 1958.

Hill, Archibald, on Hopkins' "Windhover." In D. H. Stewart, "Linguistic Limits." *Idaho State Univ. Journal of Arts and Letters,* 3 (1968), 2–13.

Hill, Christopher. *The World Turned Upside Down: Radical Ideas During the English Revolution.* New York, 1972. [Ch. 14 develops the tie between magic and science, and the Puritan pneumatics and revolutionaries.]

Hobbes, Thomas. *Elements of Philosophy, The First Section concerning Body.* Tr. from Latin. London, 1656. Wing 2232.

—— *The English Works.* Ed. Sir William Molesworth. Vol. I. London, 1839; rpt. 1966.

—— *Leviathan.* London, 1651. Wing 2246.

Hobson, E. W. *John Napier and the Invention of Logarithms.* Cambridge, 1914.

Hollander, Robert. *Allegory in Dante's "Commedia."* Princeton, 1969.

—— "Babytalk in Dante's 'Commedia.' " *Mosaic,* 8, 73–84. [On the vernacular as redeeming the linguistic fall.]

Hooke, Robert. *Micrographia.* London, 1665. Wing 2620.

Hopper, Vincent F. *Medieval Number Symbolism.* New York, 1938.

Horapollo, The Hieroglyphics of. Tr. George Boas. New York, 1950.

Horne Tooke, John. *Diversions of Purley.* London, 1786.

Howell, James. *Epistolae Ho-Elianae.* London, 1650. Wing 3072.

—— *A New English Grammar.* London, 1662. Wing 3095.

Howell, Wilbur Samuel. *Logic and Rhetoric in England, 1500–1700*. Princeton, 1956.

Hugh of St. Victor. *The Didascalicon*. Tr. Jerome Taylor. New York, 1961.

Huizinga, J. *The Waning of the Middle Ages* (1924). New York, 1954.

Hume, David. *A Treatise of Human Nature*. London, 1738.

Hunter, G. K. *John Lyly: The Humanist as Courtier*. London, 1962.

Isidore of Seville, An Encyclopedist of the Dark Ages. Ed. and tr. Ernest Brehaut. New York, 1912. [Includes trans. of part of the *Etymologies*.]

Iverson, Erik. *The Myth of Egypt and Its Hieroglyphs*. Copenhagen, 1961.

Jacobus de Voragine. *The Golden Legend*. Tr. Granger Ryan and Helmut Ripperger. New York, 1969.

Jaeger, Werner. *Aristotle: Fundamentals of the History of His Development*. Tr. Richard Robinson. Oxford, 1934.

Jakobson, Roman, and Lawrence G. Jones. *Shakespeare's Verbal Art in "Th' Expence of Spirit."* The Hague and Paris, 1970.

Joffroy, René. *Le Trésor de Vix Histoire et portée d'une grande découverte*. Paris, 1967.

Jones, Richard Foster, and Others Writing in His Honor. *The Seventeenth Century: Studies in the History of English Thought and Literature from Bacon to Pope*. Palo Alto, California, and London, 1951.

Jung, Carl. *Collected Works*. Ed. Sir Herbert Read, Michael Fordham, Gerhard Adler. Princeton, 1968.

Kabir: Versions by Robert Bly. Northwood Narrows, New Hampshire, 1971.

Kepler, Johannes. *Kepler's Dream*. By John Lear, with the text and notes of *Somnium, Sive Astronomia Lunaris*. Tr. Patricia F. Kirkwood. Berkeley and Los Angeles, 1965.

Kinner, Cyprian. *A Continuation of Mr. John-Amos-Comenius School-Endeavours. Or a Summary Delineation . . . concerning Education*. Tr. Samuel Hartlib, London [1648].

Kircher, Athanasius. *Arithmologia sive De abditis Numerorum mysteriis*. Rome, 1665.

—— *Ars Magna Sciendi sive Combinatoria*. Amsterdam, 1669.

—— *Magnes, sive de arte magnetica*. Rome, 1641.

—— *Polygraphia*. Rome, 1663.

Klein, Martin J. *Paul Ehrenfest. Vol.* I. *The Making of a Theoretical Physicist*. Amsterdam, 1970.

Kneale, William C., and Martha Kneale. *The Development of Logic*. Oxford, 1962.

Knowlson, James. *Universal Language Schemes in England and France 1600–1800*. Toronto and Buffalo, 1975. [Comprehensive bibliography, including items not cited here; checklist of schemes of universal writing and language in the 17th and 18th centuries.]

Kocher, Paul. *Science and Religion in Elizabethan England.* San Marino, California, 1953.

Kot, Stanislas. *Socinianism in Poland* (1932). Tr. Earl Morse Wilbur. Boston, 1957.

Kuhn, Thomas S. *The Structure of Scientific Revolutions.* Chicago, 1970 (second enlarged edn.).

Lacroix, Paul. *Science and Literature in the Middle Ages and the Renaissance* (1878). New York, 1964.

Lake, Osmund. *A Probe Theologicall.* London, 1612. STC 15136.

Lamy, Bernard. *De l'art de parler.* Paris, 1676.

Laneham, Robert. *A Letter* [1575]. Ed. R. C. Alston. Menston, England, 1968. [This account of the Kenilworth entertainment elaborates a new phonetic system.]

Lea, Henry Charles. *The Inquisition of the Middle Ages* (1887–88). New York, 1961.

Lear, John. *See* Kepler.

Leibniz, Gottfried Wilhelm. *New Essays Concerning Human Understanding* (1696). Tr. A. G. Langley. La Salle, Illinois, 1949.

Leonard, Sterling A. *The Doctrine of Correctness in English Usage, 1700–1800.* New York, 1962.

Leonardo da Vinci. *Frammenti letterari e filosofici.* Ed. E. Solmis. Florence, 1904.

Lever, J. W. *The Elizabethan Love Sonnet.* London and New York (1956), 1974. [Appendix on numerology in Spenser; ch. 5 on interlacing rhyme, obtrusive alliteration.]

Levin, Samuel R. *Linguistic Structures in Poetry.* The Hague, 1962.

Lewis, Clarence I. *A Survey of Symbolic Logic.* Berkeley, 1918.

Lewis, Wyndham. *Time and Western Man.* (1927). Boston, 1957.

Lilly, William. *England's Prophetical Merlin, Foretelling to All Nations of Europe until 1663 the Actions Depending Upon the . . . Conjunction of Saturn and Jupiter, 1642/3.* London, 1644. Wing 2221.

Lindberg, D. C., ed. and tr. *John Pecham and the Science of Optics.* Madison, Wisconsin, 1970. [The medieval reading.]

Lodwick, Francis. *A Common Writing.* London, 1647. Wing 2814.

—— *An Essay towards an Universal Alphabet.* London, n.d.; second edn. 1686. Wing 2815.

Lull, Ramón. *Arte General para todas las sciencias.* Madrid, 1586.

—— *Philosophical and Chymical Experiments. . . .* [containing the] *true Composition of Both Elixirs and Universal Medicine . . .* [and] *the great Stone of the Philosophers.* Tr. W. W. and Robert Turner. London, 1657.

Lully, Raymund. See Arthur Edward Waite.

Lyons, Bridget Gellert. *Voices of Melancholy: Studies in Literary Treatments of Melancholy in Renaissance England.* London, 1971.

Macfarlane, Alan. *Witchcraft in Tudor and Stuart England.* London, 1970.

McLuhan, Marshall. *The Gutenberg Galaxy* (1962). New York, 1969.

—— *Understanding Media.* New York, 1964.

Mâle, Emile. *The Early Churches of Rome.* Tr. David Buxton. London, 1960.

—— *Religious Art in France of the Thirteenth Century,* 1913. Republished as *The Gothic Image.* New York, 1958.

Meadows, A. J. *The High Firmament: A Survey of Astronomy in English Literature.* Leicester, 1969.

Meigret, Louis. *Defenses de L. Meigret touchant son Orthographie Françoeze, contre les çensures ę calonies de Glaumalis du Vezelet ę de sę adherans.* Paris, 1550.

—— *Le Tretté de la Grammere Françoeze.* Paris, 1550.

Mendenhall, John Cooper. *Aureate Terms: A Study in the Literary Diction of the Fifteenth Century.* Lancaster, Pennsylvania, 1919.

Merrill, L. R. *The Life and Poems of Nicholas Grimald.* New Haven, 1925.

Mersenne, Marin. *Quaestiones Celeberrimae in Genesim.* Paris, 1623.

—— *Universae Geometriae.* Paris, 1644.

Mesnard, Pierre. "The Pedagogy of Johann Sturm (1507–1589) and Its Evangelical Inspiration." *Studies in the Renaissance,* 13 (1966), 200–19.

Metzner, Ralph. *Maps of Unconsciousness* [concerning Tarot, alchemy, astrology, etc.]. New York, 1971.

Mill, James. *Analysis of the Phenomena of the Human Mind.* London, 1829.

Milton, John. *Accedence Commenc't Grammar.* London, 1669. Wing 2088.

—— *The Reason of Church Government.* London, 1641. Wing 2175.

Moorman, John. *A History of the Franciscan Order from Its Origins to the Year 1517.* Oxford, 1968.

More, Henry. *An Antidote Against Atheism.* London, 1655. Wing 2640.

Morison, James Cotter. *The Service of Man: An Essay Towards the Religion of the Future.* London, 1887.

Morris, Christopher. *Political Thought in England: Tyndale to Hooker.* London, 1953.

Mulcaster, Richard. *The First Part of the Elementarie.* London, 1582. STC 18250.

Murray, Margaret. *The Witch-Cult in Western Europe.* Oxford, 1921.

Nagel, Ernest, and James R. Newman. *Gödel's Proof.* New York, 1958.

Napier, John. *Logarithmorum.* Edinburgh, 1614. STC 18349.

—— *A plaine discovery of the whole Revelation of St. John.* Edinburgh, 1593. STC 18354.

—— *See* Robert G. Clouse.

Needham, Joseph. *Science and Civilisation in China.* Vol. ii, Cambridge, 1956; Vol. v, 1973.

Nethercot, Arthur. *Abraham Cowley, the Muse's Hannibal.* London, 1931.

Neuman, Erich. *The Great Mother: An Analysis of the Archetype.* Tr. Ralph Manheim. New York, 1955.

—— *The Origins and History of Consciousness* (1949). Tr. R. F. C. Hull. Princeton, 1954.

Newton, Sir Isaac. *Mathematical Principles of Natural Philosophy.* Tr. Andrew Motte, 1729; revised Florian Cajori. Berkeley, 1947.

—— *Observations Upon the Prophecies of Daniel, and the Apocalypse of St. John* (1733). Introd. Sir William Whitla. London, 1922.

Nicholas of Cusa [Nicolaus Khrypffs]. *Of Learned Ignorance* (1440). Tr. G. Heron. London, 1954.

—— *Works.* 2 vols. Strasburg, c.1490.

Nicolson, Marjorie Hope. *The Breaking of the Circle.* Revised edn. New York, 1962.

Nin, Anaïs. *The Diary 1931–34.* Ed. Gunther Stulhmann. New York, 1966.

Nussbaum, Frederick L. *The Triumph of Science and Reason 1660–1685.* New York, 1953.

Ockham, William of, Collected Articles on. By Philotheus Bochner. Ed. E. M. Buytaert. St. Bonaventure, New York; Louvain; and Paderborn, Germany, 1958.

—— *Studies and Selections.* By Stephen Chak Tornay. LaSalle, Illinois, 1938.

Ogg, David. *Europe in the Seventeenth Century.* London, 1925.

Olney, James. *Metaphors of Self: The Meaning of Autobiography.* Princeton, 1972.

Ong, Walter J. *Ramus: Method, and the Decay of Dialogue.* Cambridge, Mass., 1958.

Origen, The Writings of. Tr. Frederick Crombie. Edinburgh, 1869.

Orthografik Reform. Palm Springs, California, 1971.

Oughtred, William. *Key of the Mathematicks.* London, 1694. Wing 583.

Owen, W. J. B. "The Structure of 'The Faerie Queene.' " *PMLA,* 68 (December 1953), 1079–1100.

Palissy, Bernard. *Discours admirables de la nature.* Paris, 1580. Tr. Aurèle La Rocque. Urbana, Illinois, 1957.

Palmer, Rupert E., Jr. *Thomas Whythorne's Speech.* Anglistica, 16, 1969.

Pauwels, Louis, and Jacques Bergier. *The Eternal Man.* Tr. Michael Heron. New York, 1973. [Part Two: "Reveries about the Great Language."]

Peacham, Henry the Younger. *The Compleat Gentleman* (1622). Ed. G. S. Gordon. Oxford, 1906.

Peers, E. Allison. *Handbook to the Life and Times of St. Teresa and St. John of the Cross.* London, 1954.

Perkins, William. *A Case of Conscience*. N.p., 1595. STC 19667.

—— *A Direction for the Government of the Tongue*. London, 1615. STC 19692.

Petrarch, Francesco. *De Remediis Utriusque Fortunae;* and its English recension: *A Dialogue between Reason and Adversity*. Ed. F. N. M. Diekstra. New York, 1968.

Petty, William. *The Advice . . . to Mr. Samuel Hartlib, For the Advancement of some particular Parts of Learning*. London, 1648. Wing 1914A.

Philo Judaeus. *The Works*. Tr. from Greek by C. D. Yonge. 4 vols. London, 1854–55.

Pico della Mirandola, Giovanni. *Disputationes Adversus Astrologiam Divinatricem, Libri, I–V*. Ed. and tr. (into Italian) Eugenio Garin. Florence, 1946.

—— *On the Dignity of Man*. Tr. C. G. Wallis. Indianapolis and New York, 1965.

Pirenne, Henri. *A History of Europe*. 2 vols. Garden City, New York, 1956.

Popkin, Richard H. *The History of Scepticism from Erasmus to Descartes*. New York, 1964.

Port-Royal Logic, The. Tr. Thomas S. Baynes. Edinburgh, 1854.

Pound, Ezra. *The Spirit of Romance* (1910). New York, 1952.

Priestley, Joseph. *A Course of Lectures on the Theory of Language, and Universal Grammar*. Warrington, England, 1762.

Prouty, Charles T. *George Gascoigne*. New York, 1942.

Puttenham, George. *The Arte of English Poesie*. London, 1589. STC 20519.

Quine, W. V. "Toward a Calculus of Concepts." *The Journal of Symbolic Logic*, 1 (1936), 2–25.

Rabanus Maurus. *De Universo* (c. 844). In J.-P. Migne, *Patrologiae Latinae*. Vol. III, tom. 5. Paris, 1864.

Ramus, Peter. *Commentariorum de Religione Christiana, Libri quatuor* [with life by Theophilus Banosius and dedication to Sidney]. Frankfurt, 1577.

—— *Dialectica in two books*. Tr. R. F. London, 1632.

Randall, John Herman, Jr. *The Career of Philosophy from the Middle Ages to the Enlightenment*. 2 vols. New York and London, 1962.

Raspe, Rudolf. *A Critical Essay on Oil Painting*. London, 1781.

Rawley, William. *The Life of Lord Bacon*. In *Novum Organum*. Ed. J. S. Brewer. London, 1856.

Ray, John. *Historia plantarum*. London, 1686. Wing 394.

Recorde, Robert. *The Pathway to Knowledg*. London, 1602. STG 20814.

—— *The Whetstone of Witte*. London, 1557. STC 20820.

Reisch, Gregorius. *Margarita Philosophica*. Freiburg, 1503.

Reuchlin, Johannes, *De arte cabalistica libri tres*, Hagenau, 1517.

—— *De verbo mirificio*. Basle, ?1494.

Robbins, Rossell Hope. *Enclyclopedia of Witchcraft and Demonology*. New York, 1959.

Robinson, Robert. *The Art of Pronunciation*. London, 1617. STC 21122.

Ronsard, Pierre de. *Œuvres complètes*. Vol. XIV, Paris, 1949.

Rose, Paul Lawrence. "Humanist Culture and Renaissance Mathematics: The Italian Libraries of the *Quattrocento*." *Studies in the Rennaissance*, 20 (1973), 47–105.

Rossi, Paolo. *Francis Bacon from Magic to Science.* Tr. Sacha Rabinovitch. London, 1968.

Roszak, Theodore. *The Making of a Counter Culture.* Garden City, New York, 1969.

Rous, Francis. *Oile of Scorpions.* London, 1623. STC 21344.

Rousseau, Jean-Jacques. *Discours sur l'origine et les fondemens de l'inegalité parmi les hommes.* Amsterdam, 1755.

Rubel, Veré L. *Poetic Diction in the English Renaissance.* New York, 1941.

Runciman, Steven. *The Fall of Constantinople 1453.* Cambridge, 1965.

Russell, Bertrand. *A Critical Exposition of the Philosophy of Leibniz.* Cambridge, 1900.

Sainte-Beuve, Charles Augustin. *Port-Royal.* Vol. IV. Paris, 1926.

Saintsbury, George. *Loci Critici.* Boston and London, 1903.

Santillana, Giorgio de. *The Age of Adventure.* New York, 1956.

—— *The Crime of Galileo.* Chicago, 1955.

—— *The Origins of Scientific Thought.* New York, 1961.

Sapir, Edward. *Language.* New York, 1921.

Saporta, Sol. "The Application of Linguistics to the Study of Poetic Language." Pp. 82–93 in *Style in Language*, ed. Thomas A. Sebeok. New York and London, 1960.

Sarton, George. *The Appreciation of Ancient and Medieval Science during the Renaissance, 1450–1600.* Philadelphia, 1955.

Sassure, F. de. *Cours de linguistique générale.* Second edn. Paris, 1949.

Schaff, Philip. *History of the Christian Church* (1910). 8 vols. Grand Rapids, Michigan, 1964.

Schlegel, Ursula. "Observations on Masaccio's Trinity Fresco in Santa Maria Novella." *Art Bulletin*, 45 (1963), 19–33.

Scholes, Percy A. "Music and Puritanism." Lausanne doctoral thesis, 1934. Pub. as *The Puritans and Music in England and New England.* London, 1934.

Schonland, Sir Basil. *The Atomists.* Oxford, 1968.

Schrödinger, Erwin. *My View of the World.* Tr. Cecily Hastings. Cambridge, 1964.

Scott, Nathan A., Jr. "History, Hope, and Literature." *Boundary 2*, Spring 1973, pp. 577–603.

—— " 'New Heav'ns, New Earth'—the Landscape of Contemporary Apocalypse." *Journal of Religion*, 53 (January 1973), 1–35.

Scott, Walter. *Hermetica* [trans. of *Corpus Hermeticum*]. 4 vols. Oxford, 1924–36.

Sebeok, Thomas A., ed. *Style in Language.* New York and London, 1960.

Seligmann, Kurt. *The Mirror of Magic.* New York, 1948.

Seznec, Jean. *The Survival of the Pagan Gods* (1940). Tr. Barbara F. Sessions. New York, 1953.

Shelton, Thomas. *Tachygraphy* [shorthand]. London, 1641. Wing 3072.

Shumaker, Wayne. *The Occult Sciences in the Renaissance.* Berkeley, Los Angeles, London, 1972. [Includes extensive Bibliographical Note.]

Sidney, Sir Philip. *The Prose Works.* Ed. Albert Feuillerat (1912). 4 vols. Cambridge, 1962.

Singer, Charles. *From Magic to Science.* New York, 1958.

Singleton, Charles S. *Journey to Beatrice.* Cambridge, Mass., 1958.

Small, Robert. *Account of the Astronomical Discoveries of Kepler* (1804). Madison, Wisconsin, 1963.

Smalley, Beryl. *The Study of the Bible in the Middle Ages.* Oxford, 1952.

Smith, G. Gregory, ed. *Elizabethan Critical Essays* (1904). 2 vols. Oxford, 1950.

Smith, John. *Select Discourses.* London, 1660. Wing 4117.

Smith, Thomas. *De Recta et Emendata Linguae Anglicae Scriptione Dialogus.* Paris, 1568. Ed. Otto Deibel, Halle, 1913.

—— *De Recta et Emendata Linguae Graecae Pronuntiatione*, 1542. Pub. Paris, 1568.

Somerset, Edward. *A Century of Names and Scantlings*, London, 1663. Wing 3532.

Southern, R. W. *The Making of the Middle Ages.* London, 1965.

Speidell, John. *New Logarithmes.* N.p., 1619. STC 23063.

Spinoza, Baruch. *Œuvres complètes.* Ed. Roland Caillois, Madeleine Frances, Robert Misrahi. Paris, 1954.

Spitz, Lewis W. *The Religious Renaissance of the German Humanists.* Cambridge, Mass., 1963.

Sprat. Thomas. *A discourse made by the Lord Bishop of Rochester to the clergy of his diocese . . . 1695.* London, 1696. Wing 5031.

—— *History of the Royal Society.* London, 1667. Wing 5032. Modern edn. by Jackson I. Cope and Harold Whitmore Jones. St. Louis, Missouri, 1958.

—— "An Account of the Life and Writings of Mr. Abraham Cowley." In *The Works of . . . Cowley.* London, 1668. Wing 6649.

Stationers' Register. A Transcript of the Registers of the Company of Stationers, 1554–1640 (ed. Edward Arber). 5 vols. London, 1875–1894.

Stein, Gertrude. *Lectures in America.* New York, 1935.

Stifel, Michael. *Arithmetica integra.* Nurmberg, 1544.

Strabo. *Geography.* Tr. (into French) Germaine Aujac. Paris, 1969.

Stubbe, Henry. *A Censure upon certain passages contained in the History of the Royal Society.* Oxford, 1670. Wing 6033.

Sturmius, Joannes. *Ludus Fortunae.* Louvain, 1633.

—— *Precatio Pro Pace, Per Versum Protheum & numeralem pro anno 1640.* ?Louvain, 1640.

Summe of Sacred Divinitie, The. (Pub. by John Downhame.) London, c. 1630.

Taylor, E. G. R. *The Mathematical Practitioners of Tudor & Stuart England.* Cambridge, 1954.

Taylor, Henry Osborn. *Philosophy and Science in the Sixteenth Century.* New York, 1962.

Teilhard de Chardin, Pierre. *Building the Earth.* New York, 1969.

—— *The Phenomenon of Man.* New York, 1961.

Thomas, Keith. *Religion and the Decline of Magic.* London, 1971.

Thorndike, Lynn. *A History of Magic and Experimental Science.* 2 vols. New York, 1929.

Trevor-Roper, H. R. "The European Witch-craze of the Sixteenth and Seventeenth Centuries." Pp. 90–192. in *Religion: The Reformation and Social Change.* London, 1967.

Trinkaus, Charles. *In Our Image and Likeness Humanity and Divinity in Italian Humanist Thought.* 2 vols. Chicago, 1970.

Troubetzkoy, N. S. *Psychologie de langage.* Paris, 1933.

Turnbull, George. *Hartlib, Dury and Comenius.* Liverpool, 1947.

Tuveson, Ernest Lee. *Millenium and Utopia: A Study in the Background of the Idea of Progress.* Berkeley and Los Angeles, 1949.

Tyndale, William. *An answere unto Sir Thomas Mores dialoge.* N.p., n.d. [1530]. STC 24437.

—— *Obedyence of a Chrysten man.* N.p., n.d. [?Marburg, ?1536]; Marlborow, 1528. STC 24446.

Urquhart, Thomas. *Logopandecteison.* London, 1653. Wing 137.

—— *The Trissotetras: or, A Most Exquisite Table for Resolving all manner of Triangles.* London, 1645 [?for 1644]. Wing 140.

Valéry, Paul. *The Art of Poetry.* New York, 1958.

Valla, Lorenzo. *De Elegantia Latinae linguae.* Rome, 1471.

Vasari, Giorgio. *Lives of the Artists.* Ed. Betty Burroughs. New York, 1946.

Vico, Giambattista. *The New Science.* Tr. (from third edn., 1744) T. G. Bergin and M. H. Fisch. Ithaca, New York, 1948.

Victor, Joseph M. "The Revival of Lullism at Paris, 1499–1516." *Renaissance Quarterly,* 28 (Winter 1975), 504–534.

Vieta, François. *In Artem Analyticem Isagoge.* Turonis, 1591.

—— *De Numerosa Potestatum.* Paris, 1600.

Vives, Juan Luis. *On Education (De Tradendis Disciplinis),* Tr. Foster Watson. Cambridge, 1913.

Vossius, Gerardus. *De artis poeticae natura ac constitutione liber.* Amsterdam, 1647.

Waite, Arthur Edward, ed. *The Hermetic Museum.* 2 vols. London, 1893.

—— *Raymund Lully.* London, 1922.

Walker, D. P. *The Ancient Theology.* Ithaca, New York, 1973.

—— *Spiritual and Demonic Magic from Ficino to Campanella.* London, 1958.

Ward, Seth. *Vindiciae Academiarum.* Oxford, 1654. Wing 832.

Wastel, Simon. *A true Christians daily delight.* London, 1623. STC 25103.

Webster, Charles. *The Great Instauration: Science, Medicine, and Reform 1626–1660.* London, 1975. [On the connection of new science and Puritan ideology.]

Webster, John. *Academiarum Examen.* London, 1653 [t.p. reads 1654]. Wing 1209.

Weinberg, Bernard. *A History of Literary Criticism in the Italian Renaissance.* 2 vols. Chicago, 1961.

White, Helen C. *English Devotional Literature* [Prose] *1600–1640.* Madison, Wisconsin, 1931.

White, Lynn, Jr. "The Flavor of Early Renaissance Technology." Pp. 36–57 in *Developments in the Early Renaissance,* ed. Bernard S. Levy. Albany, New York, 1972.

Whitehead, Alfred North. *Science and the Modern World* (1925). New York, 1948.

Whythorne, Thomas, The Autobiography of. Ed. James M. Osborn. Oxford, 1961.

Wilkins, John. *A Discourse concerning the Beauty of Providence.* London, 1649. Wing 2177.

—— *A Discovery of a World . . . in the Moone.* London, 1638. STC 25640.

—— *Ecclesiastes: or, A Discourse concerning the Gift of Preaching as it fals under the rules of Art.* London, 1646. Wing 2188.

—— *An Essay towards a Real Character and a Philosophical Language.* London, 1668. Wing 2196.

—— *Mathematical Magic.* London, 1648. Wing 2198.

—— *Mercury.* London, 1694. Wing 2203.

Willey, Basil. *The Seventeenth-Century Background* (1934). New York, n.d.

Willis, John. *The Art of Stenographie . . . or, Secret Writing.* London, 1602. STC 25744.

—— *Mnemonica; or, the Arte of Memory.* London, 1661 [first pub. 1618 in Latin: *Ars Reminiscendi;* 1621 in English]. STC 25748.

Wilson, Thomas. *The Arte of Rhetorique.* London, 1553. STC. 25799.

Wingate, Edmond. *Arithmetique Made easie.* London, 1630. STC 25849.

—— *Logarithmotechnia.* London, 1635. STC 25851.

—— *Maximes of Reason: or, The Reason of the Common Law of England.* London, 1658. Wing 3021.

Winny, James. *The Frame of Order* [scientific and philosophical treatises pub. in Shakespeare's lifetime]. London, 1957.

Wither, George. *Abuses Stript, and Whipt.* London, 1613. STC 25891.

Wittkower, Rudolf. "Hieroglyphics in the Early Renaissance." Pp. 58–97 in *Developments in the Early Renaissance,* ed. Bernard S. Levy. Albany, New York, 1972.

Wolf, Abraham. *A History of Science, Technology, and Philosophy in the Sixteenth and Seventeenth Centuries.* 2 vols. London, 1935.

Wolff, Christian. *Logic: or, Rational Thoughts on the Powers of the Human Understanding.* Tr. from German. London, 1770.

—— *Psychologia Empirica.* Frankfurt and Leipzig, 1732.

Wotton, William. *A Discourse concerning the Confusion of Languages at Babel.* London, 1730.

Yates, Frances A. *The Art of Memory.* London, 1966.

—— *The French Academies of the Sixteenth Century.* London, 1947.

—— *Giordano Bruno and the Hermetic Tradition.* London, 1964.

—— *Rosicrucian Enlightenment, The.* London and Boston, 1972. [On the growth of mechanical science as an outcome of the Renaissance magical tradition.]

Ziff, Paul. *Semantic Analysis.* Ithaca, New York, 1960.

INDEX

Books, persons, and places referred to in passing in the text are cited in this index only when reference is to a particular point.